KEY CONFLICTS OF CLASSICAL ANTIQUITY

This series is composed of introductory-level texts that provide an essential foundation for the study of important wars and conflicts of classical antiquity. Each volume provides a synopsis of the main events and key characters, the consequences of the conflict, and its reception over time. An important feature is a critical overview of the textual and archaeological sources for the conflict, which is designed to teach both historiography and the methods that historians use to reconstruct events of the past. Each volume includes an assortment of pedagogical devices that students and general readers can use to further their knowledge and inquiry of the topics.

THE CONQUESTS OF
ALEXANDER THE GREAT

WALDEMAR HECKEL
UNIVERSITY OF CALGARY

CAMBRIDGE
UNIVERSITY PRESS

CAMBRIDGE UNIVERSITY PRESS
Cambridge, New York, Melbourne, Madrid, Cape Town, Singapore, São Paulo, Delhi

Cambridge University Press
32 Avenue of the Americas, New York, NY 10013-2473, USA

www.cambridge.org
Information on this title: www.cambridge.org/9780521842471

First published 2008

Printed in the United States of America

A catalog record for this publication is available from the British Library.

Library of Congress Cataloging in Publication Data

Heckel, Waldemar, 1949–
The conquests of Alexander the Great / Waldemar Heckel.
    p.   cm. – (Key conflicts of classical antiquity)
Includes bibliographical references and index.
ISBN 978-0-521-84247-1 (hardback)
1. Alexander, the Great, 356-323 B.C.   2. Greece – History – Macedonian
Expansion, 359-323 B.C.   I. Title.   II. Series.
DF234.2.H37   2007
938′.07–dc22   2007025559

ISBN   978-0-521-84247-1 hardback

For Julia and Darren

CONTENTS

PREFACE ~ *ix*   CHRONOLOGICAL TABLE ~ *xv*

1. INTRODUCTION ◉ 1

2. HOW DO WE KNOW? SOURCES FOR ALEXANDER THE GREAT ◉ 5

3. THE MACEDONIAN BACKGROUND ◉ 13

4. THE PERSIAN ENEMY ◉ 31

5. CONQUEST OF THE ACHAEMENIDS ◉ 41

6. RESISTANCE ON TWO FRONTS ◉ 87

7. CONQUEST OF THE PUNJAB ◉ 112

8. THE OCEAN AND THE WEST ◉ 126

9. THE LONG ROAD FROM SUSA TO BABYLON ◉ 142

APPENDIX 1: ALEXANDER'S OFFICERS ~ 153
APPENDIX 2: NUMBERS OF TROOPS ~ 158 APPENDIX 3: THE ADMINISTRATION OF THE EMPIRE ~ 164

GLOSSARY ~ 167   ABBREVIATIONS ~ 171   NOTES ~ 173
BIBLIOGRAPHY ~ 191   INDEX ~ 205

PREFACE

❧ ❧ ❧

THE AIM OF THIS BOOK IS TO PROVIDE AN INTELLIGENT INTRODUC-
tion to the conquests of Alexander the Great (334–323 BC). This is not
a biography, and I have said little or nothing about Alexander's youth,
his sexual orientation, the breaking of Bucephalas, and the like. Nor
do I go into detail concerning the nature of Alexander's death. Some
aspects of Alexander's personality are discussed, since they pertain to
our understanding of his "divinity" and his "orientalism"; but even here
the emphasis will be on the political impact of Alexander's attitudes
and personal actions. In short, this book was never intended to be an
exhaustive treatment. Although the emphasis is on military and political (including administrative) aspects, the battle descriptions focus on
key developments rather than providing blow-by-blow accounts. More
attention is given to aims and impact, to political consequences of
military action, and especially to the use of propaganda for both motivation and justification. Conspiracies and mutinies are viewed within
the context of the campaign, as reactions to Alexander's policies and the
apparent changes in his personality, as symptoms of battle fatigue or
disenchantment with career progress. But, again, little space is devoted
to the intricacies of the plots or to cloak-and-dagger scenes.

While it is important to consider Alexander and his military achievement in the context of his times, one must also remember that the basic
goals of conquest and keys to military superiority (once allowances
have been made for technology) have not changed dramatically over
the millennia. Indeed, Field Marshal Montgomery thought that even
in the twentieth century the fundamental principles of war had not
changed since ancient times.[1] Those who persist in seeing Alexander
as a reincarnation of Achilles, as an irrational youth on a heroic quest
for fame and immortality, have been taken in by the myth-makers who
shaped the Alexander legend, and they run the risk, in my opinion,
of reducing one of the world's greatest military strategists to a childish

daydreamer and a spoiled brat under the spell of sycophants and his own delusions.[2] This is reflected not only in the trendy subtitles of many books that are published today but in the naïve approaches taken by those who sell Alexander as a cultural icon. Even children are courted with titles such as *Alexander: The Boy Soldier Who Conquered the World* (by Simon Adams, for ages 9–12) or *Kids Who Ruled: Alexander the Great* (author's name not given). Worst of all, too much biography and not enough history has put the cart before the horse. No longer do we judge Alexander by his actions, policies, and historical achievement. Rather, we interpret his actions and his motives on the basis of preconceived notions about his psychological makeup and his social and sexual orientations. Too many of those who write about Alexander today claim to know what Alexander "would have" or "would not have done." This is, in fact, a process that has been handed down for several generations. For example, C. L. Murison, in an article that actually attempts of vindicate the actions of Darius III, comments: "In general, we should remember that Alexander was an impulsive young man, whose dash and vigor frequently led him into trouble: the idea of him lurking amid narrow places like some suicidal Quintus Fabius Maximus, *is so unlike the character we are familiar with* [my emphasis], that we must reject it, unless it is proved to the hilt."[3] I am entirely in sympathy with G. L. Cawkwell, who remarks that "those who tend to think that Alexander the Great could make no mistakes and that his victories . . . followed as night follows day . . . should be left to their hero-worship."[4]

Instead of accepting the arguments of Alexander's own propagandists and later hagiographers, I have chosen to take a minimalist view, attempting to understand the role of propaganda without being duped by it. The man who arrogantly dismissed the suggestion of a night attack with the words, "I shall not steal victory," had no compunctions about cheating when he cut through the Gordian knot with his sword; nor did he lose sleep over the fact that he had broken his word to the Indian mercenaries, whom he slaughtered after promising them free passage; perhaps, despite official claims to the contrary, he had been intimate with Darius' wife, a helpless captive. Hence, I make no apology for repeating my view on Alexander at the Hyphasis – which some have rejected as heretical – because it is, to my mind, what the evidence suggests rather than the theory that confirms a subjective preconception of the king. In the opinion of Professor E. A. Fredricksmeyer: "Alexander was *in truth* [my italics] so much a product of the ancient cult of the hero, which placed martial honor and personal glory above all ethical considerations, . . . that the notion of him as the deceiver who contrived to be defeated by his own men at the Hyphasis is not easy to countenance. What of his pride?"[5] If the aim of introducing *proskynesis* was, as a majority of scholars contend, an attempt to recognize Alexander's divinity, would not the rejection of this experiment have been an even greater blow to his pride? Such assumptions about Alexander's psychology are best avoided.

On the other hand, I have no desire to join the ranks of those whom novelist Mary Renault accuses of "blackwashing" Alexander (Renault 1974: 413) or to see Alexander as a precursor of Hitler and Stalin, men with an unrivalled talent for devising evil but, to some extent at least, also creatures of modern mythology. Indeed, these "blackwashers" are little more than biographers, who, as one writer noted, "divert attention from the work of a man to his petty or perhaps vicious habits . . . or direct interest from the best and lasting accomplishments of their subject to the utterly unimportant private matters of which he was ashamed."[6]

My aim is not to retell in full the story of Alexander's conquests. This has been done so many times that it seems pointless to repeat the exercise. Instead, I have tried to highlight major themes and, in places, to challenge accepted interpretations. When I do so, I have chosen to avoid the cumbersome priamel of scholarship – "some say this, others say that, but I say . . ." – in the belief that it should be obvious that what I present is my own interpretation (or most often one of those interpretations of other scholars that I accept) and should be treated as such by the reader. I have also referred in my notes and bibliography to a range of literature, including several popular titles that are readily accessible and thought-provoking. In a few places, I have referred to popular works that are likely to mislead the student, with the aim of preempting erroneous notions (e.g., the persistent view of Darius as a coward) or of illustrating how a superficial reading of the ancient evidence, with little regard for bias or practicalities, can lead to unlikely conclusions.

Those who study medieval, premodern, and even modern history regularly adduce parallels from antiquity. Not surprisingly, since the "Classics," for a long time, formed the basis of humanistic education. Some may consider it preposterous to attempt to understand the past in terms of later events. My own experience, particularly from lecturing on Alexander, suggests that students are more often helped than confused by such an approach. The use of analogies from other periods of history is not meant to imply the existence of exact parallels[7] – and certainly I make no claims to expertise in other areas – but rather to show that similar situations and problems often call for similar solutions.[8] I would draw attention to the observations of William H. Prescott, made in 1847, on the military training and official recognition of the Inca prince: "The reader will be less surprised by the resemblance which this ceremonial bears to the inauguration of a Christian knight in the feudal ages, if he reflects that a similar analogy may be traced in the institutions of other people more or less civilized; and that it is natural that nations, occupied with the one great business of war, should mark the period, when the preparatory education for it was ended, by similar characteristic ceremonies."[9] Many aristocratic and conquest societies are, to my mind, remarkably similar in their basic aims and organization. There is an emphasis on military action and honor, deeds and rewards, and the intertwining relationships of land, social status, military leadership, and patronage – or, to view it in another way, of king, companions, soldiers, and serfs. Hence, the persistent view of Alexander as the instigator, manipulator, and practitioner of all things, exercising power rather than restrained by it, strikes me as naïve and untrue. If he imposed his will, it was in most cases upon the willing, or on those whom defeat had rendered incapable of further resistance. All else was, ultimately, a matter of one form of negotiation or another.

I wish to thank Beatrice Rehl of Cambridge University Press not only for suggesting this book to me but for encouraging me to complete it. Thanks are due also to Peter Katsirubas, who oversaw the production of the volume, to William Stoddard, for his careful editing, and to James

Dunn, for producing the maps. The battle plans are my own, created with MS PowerPoint by someone unskilled in the art. Hence, they will not be as aesthetically pleasing as those done by professionals. I would particularly thank my informal military history group (our little "Army of Darkness," dedicated to *Risk*, wine and whisky): Chris Collom, Chris Jesse, Ryan Jones, Alison Mercer, Jordan Schultz, Carolyn Willekes, and Graham Wrightson. Finally, I have dedicated this book to my children, in the hope that one of them may, one day, actually sit down and read it.

CHRONOLOGICAL TABLE

EVENTS

776 BC	The first Olympic Games
750–550	Age of colonization
7th/6th cent.	Age of tyrants
594	Archonship of Solon
547–540	Ionia conquered by Cyrus the Great of Persia
513	Darius I conquers Thrace
510	Expulsion of Hippias, tyrant of Athens
508/7	Cleisthenes' democratic reforms
499–493	The Ionian Revolt
490	Battle of Marathon
480–479	Xerxes' invasion of Greece
479–431	The "Fifty Years": Delian League becomes Athenian Empire
449?	Peace of Callias
431–404	Peloponnesian War
401/0	Battle of Cunaxa; retreat of the Ten Thousand
404–371	Spartan supremacy in Greece
371	Battle of Leuctra
371–350s	Theban supremacy
362	Battle of Mantinea
359–336	Reign of Philip II
346	Peace of Philocrates
338	Battle of Chaeronea
337	First meeting of the League of Corinth
	Philip II marries his seventh wife, Cleopatra

336	Assassination of Philip; accession of Alexander III ("the Great")
335	Alexander's Thracian, Triballian, and Illyrian campaigns; destruction of Thebes
334	Beginning of the expedition against Persia
spring 334	Alexander leaves Macedonia and travels via Amphipolis to the Hellespont, which he crosses unopposed
334	Persian satraps meet to discuss strategy at Zeleia; the Battle of the Granicus River
334	Surrender of Sardis by Mithrenes
334	Sieges of Miletus and Halicarnassus
334/3	Alexander rounds Mt Climax, where the sea appears to perform *proskynesis*, withdrawing before the future King of Asia
	Arrest of Alexander the Lyncestian
333	The army reunited at Gordium; Alexander cuts the Gordian knot and claims to have fulfilled the prophecy, which promised him lordship of Asia
	Alexander in Cilicia; illness at the Cydnus River; (November); battle of Issus; defeat of Darius III and capture of his family
333/2	Capture of Darius' treasures at Damascus; surrender of the Phoenician cities, except Tyre
332	Siege of Tyre (January–August); defection of the Cypriote and Phoenician contingents of the Persian fleet; fall of Tyre; capture of Gaza
332/1	Alexander in Egypt: visit to the oracle of Amun at Siwah; foundation of Alexandria in the Nile Delta
331	Return from Egypt. Alexander crosses the Euphrates at Thapsacus and then crosses the Tigris; defeat of Darius III at Gaugamela; surrender of Babylon by Mazaeus and Susa by Abulites; Alexander defeats the Uxians, overcomes the Persian satrap Ariobarzanes at the Persian Gates, and enters Persepolis
331/0	Symbolic destruction of Persepolis

330	Alexander marches against Darius, whose forces are at Ecbatana. Flight of the Persians; arrest and death of Darius at the hands of his own generals and courtiers. Alexander dismisses the allied troops – some at Ecbatana, others at Hecatompylus
autumn 330	Philotas affair; execution of Parmenion in Ecbatana
winter 330/29	Defeat of Satibarzanes; Alexander in Arachosia
329	Arrest and death of Bessus
329/8	Campaigns in Bactria and Sogdiana; capture of the Rock of Ariamazes
328	Death of Cleitus in Maracanda; capture of the Rock of Sisimithres; Alexander marries Rhoxane
327	Failure of Alexander's experiment with *proskynesis*; the Conspiracy of the Pages (Hermolaus); death of Callisthenes
327/6	Swat Campaign and capture of Aornus (Pir-sar)
May 326	Battle at the Hydaspes River
September 326	The Macedonian army returns to the Hydaspes
October–November 326	Departure of the Hydaspes fleet; Mallian campaign. Alexander near death
mid-325	Subjugation of Sindh
autumn 325	Beginning of the march west Gedrosian march
beginning of 324	Alexander in Carmania
March 324	Return to Susa
May/June 324	Alexander at Opis
June/July 324	Harpalus in Athens
July/August 324	Proclamation of the Exiles' Decree
October 324	Death of Hephaestion in Ecbatana

end of 324	The Cossaean campaign
spring 323	Alexander returns to Babylon
June 11, 323	Death of Alexander

KING LISTS

THE ACHAEMENID KINGS OF PERSIA

560–530	Cyrus the Great
530–522	Cambyses
522	Smerdis (Gaumata or Bardiya)
522–486	Darius I
486–465	Xerxes I
465–424	Artaxerxes I
424	Xerxes II
424/3	Sogdianus
423–404/3	Darius II
404/3–359	Artaxerxes II
359–338	Ataxerxes III (Ochus)
338–336	Artaxerxes IV (Arses)
336–330	Darius III (Artashata; Codomannus)
330–329	[Artaxerxes V: Bessus]

ARGEAD KINGS OF MACEDONIA

393–369	Amyntas III
369–368	Alexander II
368–365	Ptolemy of Alorus (regency)
365–359	Perdiccas III
359–336	Philip II
336–323	Alexander III
323–317	Philip III
323–310	Alexander IV

SOURCES

LOST SOURCES AND APPROXIMATE PUBLICATION DATES

336–323	*Ephemerides* or *Royal Journal*
334–329	Callisthenes of Olynthus, *Deeds of Alexander*

soon after 323	Onesicritus of Astypalaea, *Education of Alexander*
	Nearchus
310–305	Cleitarchus of Alexandria
	Marsyas of Pella
before 300	Chares of Mytilene
	Medius of Larissa
	Ephippus of Olynthus
285–283	Ptolemy son of Lagus
270s	Aristobulus of Cassandreia

EXTANT SOURCES

late first century BC	Diodorus of Sicily
middle of first century AD	Quintus Curtius Rufus
early second century	Plutarch, *Life of Alexander*, *De fortuna Alexandri*
middle of second century	Arrian, *Anabasis of Alexander*
second/third century	Justin, *Epitome of Philippic History* (Pompeius Trogus)

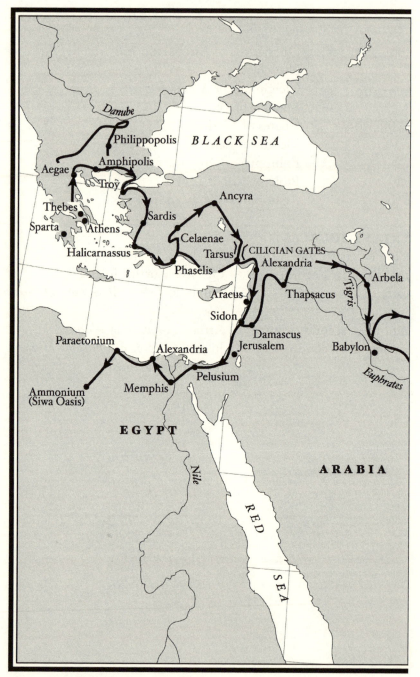

MAP I. *Alexander's Empire.*

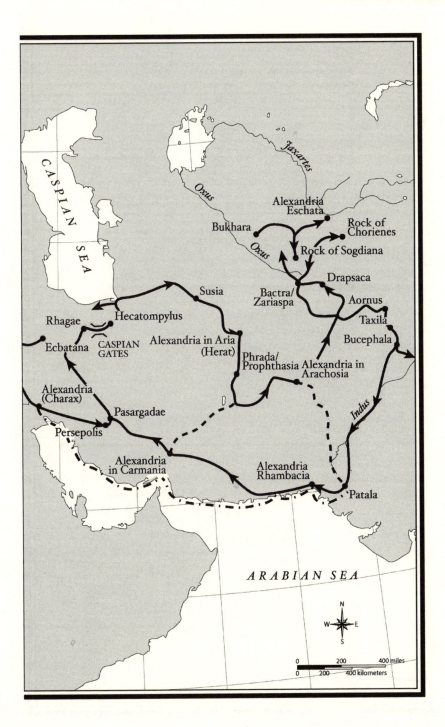

CASPIAN SEA

CASPIAN GATES

Oxus

Oxus

Jaxartes

Indus

Alexandria Eschata

Rock of Chorienes

Bukhara

Rock of Sogdiana

Drapsaca

Bactra/ Zariaspa

Aornus

Susia

Taxila

Rhagae

Hecatompylus

Bucephala

Ecbatana

Alexandria in Aria (Herat)

Phrada/ Prophthasia

Alexandria in Arachosia

Alexandria (Charax)

Pasargadae

Persepolis

Alexandria in Carmania

Alexandria Rhambacia

Patala

ARABIAN SEA

N
W   E
S

0   200   400 miles

0   200   400 kilometers

MAP 2. *Greece and Macedonia.*

INTRODUCTION

CHAPTER ONE

✺ ✺ ✺

I N 325 BC, ALEXANDER SAILED OUT FROM THE INDUS DELTA INTO
the Ocean, the vast body of water which, according to ancient
thought, encircled the world. Here he sacrificed bulls to Poseidon
and, after pouring libations, hurled the golden cup and bowls into
the sea as a thank-offering. The scene was hauntingly reminiscent of the
ceremony conducted on the Hellespont in 334. In less than ten years, the
Macedonian army had conquered the vast territories of the Achaemenid
kings, including the fringe areas of the Punjab and the Indus, the most
formidable empire of the ancient world. It had followed the path of
unbroken victories from the familiar confines of the Aegean to the
edge of the earth, overcoming everything in its way: armies, terrain, cli-
mate, all invariably hostile. Now the conquerors prepared to return to
the west – some by sea, others along the coastal deserts – to consolidate
their victory and contemplate the magnitude of their accomplishments.
Little did they know that within two years their beloved king would be
dead and their labors seemingly wasted. Most of those who returned
to Europe were impoverished, their health broken by years of physical hardship. Others, if they did not die on campaign, were destined
never to see Macedonia again, embroiled instead in the bitter struggles

I

of Alexander's successors. The average soldier, whose efforts brought wealth and fame to his king and a small group of Companions, was left only with the scars of combat and slowly fading memories of that glorious adventure in the east.

The age of Alexander the Great marks a turning point in world history. The defeat of the Greek city-states (*poleis*) by Alexander's father, Philip II, at Chaeronea in 338 BC and the consequent formation of the League of Corinth, which forged an alliance of Greek states under the Macedonian king as *hegemon* or supreme military commander (and director of foreign affairs), put an end to the debilitating, internecine wars of the fourth century. But with peace came war; for it was undesirable that a finely tuned war-machine such as the Macedonian army, now augmented by troops from the new allies and by growing numbers of mercenaries, should lose its edge as well as its livelihood. To reintegrate these fighting forces into their respective states would have economic as well as political consequences. And to create a league without a military purpose – that is, to create a new definition of "us" without identifying "them," the "other" against whom one must be on guard – denied the forcibly united Greek world its *raison d'être*. Indeed, from this point on, the Greek world was destined to subordinate its cherished system of independent *poleis* to a series of alliances (often reincarnations of this same league) and the overarching authority of kings.

Fortunately, the common enemy was not far to seek, and a mandate for the League was easily formulated. For more than two centuries, the Greeks who dwelt on the Aegean littoral had lived in the shadow, if not always under the direct authority, of the Persian king. The Greeks of Asia Minor had been incorporated first into the Lydian kingdom and then, between 547 and 540, into the Persian Empire of Cyrus the Great. For it was Cyrus who terminated the reign, and perhaps even the life, of the wealthy king, Croesus.[1] An ill-conceived and poorly executed rebellion at the beginning of the fifth century gave the Persians a pretext for attacking those Greeks who lived beyond the Strymon River, particularly the Athenians and Eretrians, who had given brief but half-hearted aid to the rebels in 498. The Athenian victory over Darius I's forces at Marathon in 490 and the paradoxical expulsion of Xerxes' huge invading force ten years later are well known. Indeed, these events led to the first serious union of Greek states, the so-called Delian League. But the effectiveness of this league and the commitment of its members depended entirely on the reality of the Persian danger. As this receded, especially after the Greek victory at the Eurymedon (c. 468), and once the official war against the barbarian was terminated by the terms of the Peace of Callias (449), the Delian League evolved into an Athenian empire, which compelled military service and the payment of tribute, and found a political and military counterweight in the Peloponnesian League, led by Sparta.

This shift in power led to the Peloponnesian War, a drawn-out affair (431–404) that ended in the total destruction of the Athenian Empire and of the balance of power in the Greek world. And, although Sparta emerged as the dominant *polis*, it had achieved this position by accepting financial aid from Persia and by abandoning its traditional isolationism. Soon it became clear that the Great King could act as arbiter of Greek affairs and guarantor of peace treaties, especially those, such as the Peace of Antalcidas in 387/6, that came to be designated as a "Common Peace" (*Koine Eirene*).[2] Hence, it was no misrepresentation to speak of the Great King as "the common enemy of all Greeks" (Dem. 14.3), one who could "sit on his throne playing the arbitrator for the Greeks in their wars and corrupting their politicians with gold" (Plut. *Ages.* 15.1). The extent of Persian intervention is doubtless exaggerated, but there was sufficient evidence of subversive activity that contemporaries were quick to see the gilded hand of the King or his satrap behind virtually every action, just as today the conspiracy theorist attributes every international crisis to the machinations of the CIA. Not surprisingly, then, came the reports that the assassination of Philip II, which brought Alexander the Great to the throne in 336, had been masterminded and financed by the Persian Court.

Whether the accession of Alexander accelerated the decline of Persia is uncertain. Philip II had a reputation for proceeding with caution and consolidating his gains before moving on. His conquests may at first have been restricted to Asia Minor, and his destruction of Achaemenid power might have been partial or slow in its completion. It might, on the other hand, have produced a more lasting union of east and west. It was not, however, his fate to lead the expedition, and Alexander's accomplishment was the direct result of his own methods. For better and for worse, the world was changed in a few short years, even if the consequences of these changes took three centuries to manifest themselves fully. Notions of a benign conquest that brought culture and moral elevation to the benighted barbarians, suggested by Plutarch at the height of Roman power and further developed against the backdrop of the British Empire and its pretensions about "White Man's Burden," are now dismissed as relics of a misguided age and poor historical method.[3] But an exchange of ideas between east and west did occur, and under Roman domination the language of the eastern empire was Greek, through which some of the most influential ideas of the Near East were disseminated throughout the Mediterranean world.

This book is not about the impact of Alexander's conquests but rather the means by which these were effected, from the formulation of policy to the generation of propaganda and the attainment of its ends by military means. Propaganda both justifies and facilitates action, but it can be a double-edged sword. In Alexander's case the Panhellenic cause and the inferiority of the barbarian were stressed from the very beginning, and even if many saw through the transparency of the vengeance motif, most were prepared to accept the view that barbarians were slaves by nature, cowardly and effeminate. What served the needs of conquest in the early years confounded the attempt to stabilize and consolidate the newly won empire in the years that followed.

HOW DO WE KNOW? SOURCES FOR ALEXANDER THE GREAT

CHAPTER TWO

❋ ❋ ❋

ANCIENT HISTORIANS HAVE LONG HAD TO CONTEND WITH the fact that their knowledge of the past is based on limited, often secondary and unreliable evidence. Statistical analyses fail for want of sufficient data; historical interpretation falters on the broken ground of textual corruption, authorial bias, and the unintentional but misguided superimposition of Roman ideas and institutions on Greek subjects. Documentary evidence is often lacking, or spotty, and almost always in need of at least partial restoration. And such documents as survive are those recorded on nonperishable material, such as stone or metal, or on papyri which have survived as a result of unusual climatic conditions. But, whatever the form of these primary documents, they rarely if ever survived because of the intrinsic value of the information they contained. Rather, inscriptions on marble or limestone were reused as building material, as doorposts, lintels, foundation stones, or steps. Where their inscribed sides have been exposed to the elements or the tread of human feet, their messages have generally been obscured, if not entirely obliterated. In other places, stones have been cut into two or more pieces and their information scattered and partially lost. Histories survived on papyri in many cases because someone found a more important use for the writing material and recorded bills of sale, land registers, or other accounts on the reverse side. Other evidence survives on palimpsests, texts that have been erased so that the medium could be reused; but traces of the ink remain and these texts are sometimes legible under ultraviolet or infrared light.

Although the works of some forty contemporary or near-contemporary Alexander historians have been lost, we nevertheless have a substantial collection of the fragments of their histories,[1] along with a surviving corpus of information ranging from a few contemporary inscriptions and coin types to works of art.[2] To these we may add sources from the period of the "Successors," which made use of Alexander's image and mystique; and we have a relatively large number of extant sources (written between 300 and 500 years after the king's death). The extant sources are supplemented by the works of writers who cannot be regarded strictly as historians and biographers – geographers, ethnographers, antiquarians, tacticians, lexicographers, and writers of anecdotes and philosophical and rhetorical treatises. Although the amount of surviving information may seem minuscule in comparison with what is available to, say, U.S. Civil War historians, by the standards of ancient history the Alexander sources are indeed numerous.

THE MAJOR LOST HISTORIANS

It is virtually certain that the royal chancery kept a record of some kind – in the form of a journal or diary – of day-to-day events. But modern scholars question how much detail it contained and how useful (especially for the military historian) its contents were. The authorship of the *Ephemerides* is attributed to Eumenes of Cardia or Diodotus of Erythrae, the latter perhaps a pseudonym. Where other writers claim to be quoting from the journal, the information is banal, dealing with the king's eating, drinking, and sleeping habits. The work may, at least, have preserved an accurate itinerary and may have been consulted by the man who has been called Alexander's "official historian." This was Callisthenes of Olynthus, a kinsman of Aristotle (Alexander's former tutor), who appears to have recommended him for the task. He served as a combination war correspondent and propagandist and appears to have sent his history (*Alexandrou Praxeis* or "Deeds of Alexander") back to the Greek world in annual installments. To him we may ascribe a good deal of the Panhellenic sentiment that pervades the accounts of the early years and the rather heroic image of the young king. But Callisthenes fell into disfavor as a result of his opposition to the introduction of *proskynesis* and he was executed in 327 for his alleged involvement in the conspiracy of Hermolaus. The last events recorded by his pen appear to belong to the year 329. His value as a military historian has been impugned by Polybius – though one might add that Polybius was critical of most who wrote before him – and his treatment of Alexander's leading general, Parmenion, bordered on character assassination. Nevertheless, traces of his work can be found in most surviving Alexander historians.

Three others who participated in the conquest may have begun to compose histories during Alexander's lifetime. Chares of Mytilene, who was the king's chamberlain and usher (*eisangeleus*), may have kept notes (if he did not write entirely from memory) for a work that would focus primarily on what went on at court.[3] Onesicritus of Astypylaea and Nearchus the Cretan are best known for their service with the fleet, which sailed down the Indus River to its mouth and, from there, followed the coast, sailing into the Persian Gulf and up the Tigris River. They made conflicting claims, each appropriating for himself the rank of admiral of the fleet. Nearchus exposes the mendacity of Onesicritus, who was merely the chief steersman of Alexander's ship, but exaggerates his own achievement.[4] It appears that they published very soon after the king's death, and Nearchus is on record as having read an account of his voyage to Alexander during his final days.[5]

The works of Callisthenes, Onesicritus, and Nearchus were used by Cleitarchus of Alexandria, arguably the most sensational (and also the most popular) of the lost historians. Cleitarchus did not accompany the expedition, but he did have access to both written sources and eyewitness informants. Furthermore, his father, Dinon, was an author of *Persika* and familiar with the affairs of the Persian Empire in the fourth century BC. Bringing together diverse sources and flavoring his work with a liberal dose of rhetoric and moralizing, Cleitarchus became the best known of the first generation Alexander historians. Cicero, in a letter to his brother, Quintus, shows that Cleitarchus' work was still popular in the late Republic. Not surprisingly, most of the major surviving histories of Alexander are based on Cleitarchus. But, whereas Cleitarchus was often critical of the king, two other participants in the campaign wrote accounts that defended the king's actions and omitted certain episodes that placed him in an unfavorable light.[6] These were Ptolemy son of Lagus – a former general and, at the time he wrote his work, the king of Egypt – and Aristobulus of Cassandreia, an engineer with an interest in geography and antiquities. Both were used in the second century AD by Arrian and they constitute the apologetic tradition concerning Alexander.

Numerous other lost accounts are known from fragments and citations only. These include the works of surveyors (*bematistai*), flatterers and gossip-mongers, hack poets and rhetoricians. Some were bitterly hostile, others hagiographers; virtually all were more credulous than critical. Several were dismissed as worthless by Alexander himself. For example, when Choerilus of Iasus composed an epic poem in which Alexander appeared as Achilles, the king remarked: "I would rather be Thersites in Homer's *Iliad* than the Achilles of Choerilus."[7] Such stories, nevertheless, made their way into the extant sources, though generally their contributions are bracketed and treated with caution.

THE MAJOR EXTANT SOURCES

The surviving histories of Alexander can be divided into two groups: the popular tradition (often called the "Alexander Vulgate," though this term is more confusing than helpful), represented by Diodorus of Sicily, Pompeius Trogus (whose work survives only in summaries and in the epitome of Justin), Quintus Curtius Rufus, and (to some extent) Plutarch;[8] and the apologetic tradition preserved in Arrian (and the derivative *Itinerary of Alexander*).

The earliest extant source for Alexander is the seventeenth book of Diodorus' *Bibliotheke* (a universal history). This was, in fact, a double-sized book: despite the fact that the sections dealing with the events of 330/29–327/6 are lost, the surviving text runs to about 175 pages in the Loeb Classical Library format, compared with the roughly 130 pages for Book 16 and 100 pages for Book 18. It was Diodorus' practice to follow a single primary source for each section of his work, and for his account of Alexander he used Cleitarchus, though as elsewhere he supplemented this source with information from other writers.[9] Nevertheless, his history not only is stylistically Cleitarchean but also contains numerous passages that are virtually identical (allowing for the differences between Greek and Latin) to corresponding sections of Curtius.

Not much later, another writer of world history, a Romanized Gaul from Vasio (modern Vaison-la-Romaine), Pompeius Trogus, devoted Books 11–12 of his *Philippic History* to Alexander, basing his work either directly on Cleitarchus or on the intermediary writer of the first century BC, Timagenes of Alexandria. Trogus' history has been lost, largely on account of the success of Justin's abbreviation, though the epitome does not do justice to the original.[10] W. W. Tarn rightly asked: "Is there any bread at all to this intolerable deal of sack?" His answer was "Not much,"[11] but, used with caution, the source is of greater value to the historian than Tarn was willing to concede.

It appears that Trogus was read by Q. Curtius Rufus, who was indebted to him stylistically. He wrote the only full-scale Latin account of Alexander, treating his subject in ten books and basing his history on Cleitarchus, but adding valuable details from Ptolemy. Of his ten books, the first two are lost, as are the end of Book 5 and the beginning of Book 6, as well as substantial parts of Book 10.[12] The historian may be identical with one (if not both) of the known Curtii Rufi of the first century AD. Suetonius names a Quintus Curtius Rufus in a list of grammarians and rhetoricians who belong to the late Republic and early Empire. (It is, of course, tempting to regard the author of the *History of Alexander* as a rhetorician, considering the nature of the work.) Tacitus and Pliny the Younger know a soldier and politician of the same name, a man who rose from obscurity to hold the praetorship in the reign of Tiberius and was proconsul of North Africa at the time of his death in AD 53.

Plutarch (AD c. 50–120), the famous philosopher and biographer, belonged to the local nobility of Chaeronea, the very place where Philip II defeated the Athenians and Thebans in what some have portrayed as the last stand of "Greek freedom." We may use the word "freedom" advisedly – for it was a loaded term in antiquity just as it is today – but Plutarch, despite gaining Roman citizenship, took his Boeotian origins seriously. For our purposes, Plutarch is best known for his *Life of Alexander*, one of the *Parallel Lives* (Alexander was paired with Caesar), of which all but those of Epaminondas and Scipio survive. But he also provides valuable information, and interpretations, in his *On the Virtue and Fortune of Alexander* I–II and the *Sayings of Kings and Commanders*. It is important to remember, however, that Plutarch was writing biography and not history, that he emphasized *ethos* over *erga* or *praxeis*, and that he repeated stories that elucidated a man's character even when he suspected their historicity.[13]

It is the last of the major extant historians, Arrian of Nicomedia, who enjoys the best reputation, especially among military historians.[14] Lucius Flavius Arrianus Xenophon was a Bithynian Greek whose family obtained Roman citizenship in the middle of the first century AD, if not earlier. Born in the last decade of that century, or perhaps as early as AD 85, Arrian held a number of political offices under the emperor Hadrian, but eventually became a citizen of Athens. In his writings, and to a certain extent in his life, he modeled himself on his namesake Xenophon, and his *Anabasis Alexandrou*, in seven books, resembles Xenophon's account of the Ten Thousand in no small way.[15] The influence of Arrian's work can be seen in the *Itinerarium Alexandri*, an anonymous work composed around AD 340 and dedicated to Constantius II.[16] But in the tradition of Alexander history, Arrian's account, based on Ptolemy and Aristobulus, stands alone as a work of *apologia*. Military historians have in general praised him, although his use of terminology is often vague and inconsistent.

SOURCE CRITICISM

Source criticism (*Quellenforschung*) has, in recent times, been treated with a measure of disdain, and it has been dismissed as old-fashioned and pedantic. Indeed, the method is susceptible to abuse. Some have regarded the slightest disagreements in detail between extant authors as evidence of the use of different primary sources, failing to take into account the methods and aims of the surviving authors. Ancient writers felt no qualms about plagiarizing the works of their predecessors, but that does not permit us to regard them all as slavish copyists. Similarly, all our surviving Alexander historians wrote when Rome dominated the world; two of them, Curtius and Pompeius Trogus,[17] compiled histories in Latin from Greek sources. Some Roman elements (*color romanus*) have crept into their accounts either by accident or by design. Hence, it is as important to understand the life and times of the extant writers as it is to know the circumstances under which the lost primary historians worked. Those who abbreviated, such as Diodorus and Justin, omitted some events entirely and distorted others through ignorance. Nevertheless, scholars must reject the view that there are "good" sources, which can generally be trusted, and "bad" ones, whose evidence is completely worthless. And what is true of the extant sources is equally true of the lost ones on which the former are based. The highly valued Arrian may serve as a lesson to readers. He prefers the evidence of Ptolemy and Aristobulus because, although they were contemporaries of Alexander and participants in the actual expedition, they wrote after the king's death and felt no need to flatter Alexander or distort the truth. But Arrian follows this observation with two stultifying remarks: that Ptolemy was a king, and it would be more shameful for kings than others to tell lies; and that, on occasion, he reports stories that *may be true* – the corollary is, of course, that they may not be – because they are too good to pass up.

Good source criticism is thus a matter of detective work. One collects the reported evidence and then makes an assessment of the credibility of the witness. Everything that can be determined about the source (life, social and political background, biases, etc.) may help in determining whether the witness is telling the truth or misrepresenting it. There is, additionally, the obvious question of whether the report is given by an eyewitness or by someone who has obtained it second-hand (or third-hand, for that matter), or whether the report may have been subjected to censorship of sorts. Was the original author free to tell the truth? Was he pressured to remain silent, or even to lie?[18] These considerations are further tempered by the fact that, since the information does not come directly from the witness (either orally or in his own hand), there is the risk of errors occurring in the process of transmission, especially when this process spans centuries and millennia. What is textual (i.e., scribal) error, and what is attributable to the author himself? Sometimes explanatory remarks (glosses), written into the margins of manuscripts, become incorporated into the text through the actions of a subsequent copyist, who may have believed that the marginal note represented a portion of the original text but had been omitted by accident. Sometimes an editor simply believed he was more knowledgeable than the author and changed what he regarded as error, thus obscuring the details.[19] The good detective will, in turn, compare the versions of several witnesses (when this is possible). In the end, however, the source-critic, if he or she wants to write history, must present the evidence before the court of scholarly opinion, and thus becomes an advocate, attempting to present the evidence (and the case) as cogently as possible. It may indeed be an old-fashioned approach, but hardly one to be disdained.

THE MACEDONIAN BACKGROUND

CHAPTER THREE

EOGRAPHICALLY, MACEDONIA BELONGS TO THE CONTI-
nental Balkans rather than Mediterranean Greece.[1] The
plains of Lower Macedonia, formed by the Axius (Vardar)
and Haliacmon rivers, extend to the Thermaic Gulf; to these
we may add the valleys of the Strymon and the Nestus, which came
under Macedonian control as the kingdom began to dominate the north
Aegean coast. But the river valleys lead from north to south, and they
brought a steady flow of migrants from the landlocked regions of the
Danube basin down into the warmer and more appealing climes of the
northern Mediterranean. In the west the mountains offered only limited shelter against the Illyrian tribesmen and the Epirotes farther south;
in the southeastern sector, Mt Olympus and the Peneus River (more
specifically the gorge of the Vale of Tempe) formed a natural barrier
between Macedonia and the Hellenized world.[2] The Macedonian people were scattered amongst the highlands, the various cantons of what
we call Upper Macedonia, and the aforementioned plain. In the lower
regions the kingdom began to develop, but the highlanders remained
fiercely independent and faithful to their regional barons. Hence the

formation of the state, effected by Philip II in the fourth century, was a remarkable achievement.

In 513, the European campaign of Darius I, which incorporated the Thracian region into the Persian Empire, organizing it into the satrapy of Skudra, reduced the kings of Macedon to vassalage. A daughter of Amyntas I is said to have married the Persian Bubaces, and there are institutions at the Macedonian court which appear to be modeled on Persian ones.[3] To the Greeks of the south the Macedonians were barbarians, and it was Alexander I who first evinced the Greek ancestry of the royal house (the Temenids or Argeadae) by tracing his descent from the Argive Heracles; thus he gained admittance to the Olympic games, but his epithet, Philhellene ("fond of the Greeks" or "friend of the Greeks"), speaks volumes about the perceived differences between Macedonians and Greeks. Certainly there were cultural and linguistic similarities, and Macedonian society and the names of the aristocracy conjure up the world of Homer. But the differences were sufficient to cause the Greeks to view them as foreign well into the Hellenistic age.[4] Nevertheless, the royal family and the aristocratic houses were educated in Greek. Archelaus I (regn. 413–399) was an admirer of Greek culture: Euripides came to Macedonia at the king's invitation and wrote *The Bacchae* and *Iphigenia in Aulis*, plays which reflect some of the savagery of the north. Socrates, too, was invited to the king's court, but to his credit (as far as other intellectuals were concerned), he declined to come.[5] Politically, however, the Macedonian state was weak and a backwater. Perdiccas II, the successor of Alexander Philhellene, survived the ambitions of the fifth-century Greek powers by vacillating in his support for Athens and Sparta.

The reign of the above-mentioned Archelaus saw the development of Pella as the capital and a system of roads that improved communication and military mobilization. But the true rise of Macedon was still half a century away. Archelaus' successors were numerous, weak, and ephemeral, and even Amyntas III, the father of three kings and grandfather of two more, walked a tightrope between the Illyrian menace in the west and the growing power of Thebes to the south. His rule, which stretched from 392 until his death in 369, was shaky at times – in fact, it was briefly interrupted by the Illyrians – and a hostile tradition depicts him as a cuckold and victim of a conspiracy by his wife Eurydice. His eldest son by Eurydice, Alexander II, ruled briefly (369–8) before being assassinated, and there followed a period of regency by Ptolemy of Alorus (his brother-in-law) on behalf of the young Perdiccas III, who gained the throne in his own name in 365. But in 360/59, Perdiccas and some 4,000 prominent *hetairoi* were killed in a disastrous battle against the Illyrians under King Bardylis. This brought to the throne the youngest son, recently a hostage in Thebes, Philip II.

The odds against Philip's political survival in 360/59 were overwhelming: his army had been all but destroyed in the Illyrian campaign, and what remained was sadly in disarray; the leaders of neighboring states plotted the kingdom's dismemberment, in some cases supporting pretenders to the throne, such as Argaeus; and three half-brothers (sons of Amyntas III and Gygaea) were prepared to challenge Philip's claims. The situation was further complicated by the fact that Philip's right to the throne was questionable: Perdiccas III had left a young son, Amyntas, but in a time of national crisis, the Macedonians had either elected Philip as their king or awarded him the regency only to promote him to the kingship within two or three years.[6] Yet Philip not only survived, he prospered. And in the twenty years that followed his accession, he unified the Macedonian state, consolidated power in the north, and made himself master of the Greek world.

A brief summary of Philip's political marriages, taken by Athenaeus from Satyrus' *Life of Philip*, although not entirely in chronological sequence, provides a reasonably full account of his political expansion:[7]

Philip had a fresh wedding with every campaign. In his *Life of Philip* Satyrus states, "In the twenty-two years of his rule Philip married the Illyrian Audata, by whom he had a daughter, Cynnane, and he also married Phila, sister of Derdas and Machatas. Then, since he wished to extend his realm to include the Thessalian nation, he had children by two Thessalian women, Nicesipolis of Pherae, who bore him Thessalonice, and Philinna of Larissa, by whom he produced Arrhidaeus. In addition, he took possession of the Molossian kingdom by marrying Olympias, by whom he had Alexander and Cleopatra, and when he took Thrace the Thracian king Cothelas came to him with his daughter Meda and many gifts. After marrying Meda, Philip also took her home to be an additional wife along with Olympias. In addition to all these wives he married Cleopatra, with whom he was in love; she was the daughter of Hippostratus and niece of Attalus. By bringing her home as another wife alongside Olympias he made a total shambles of his life."[8]

For modern scholars, this is probably the most overworked passage on the life of Philip II, and rightly so. Although, in fact, Philip married Philinna (358) long before Nicesipolis (352 or 346), the survey shows that Philip consolidated his borders on all sides, striking out in the direction of Thrace and the Black Sea before making his first "nonpolitical" union.

Despite Philip's talent for bribery and diplomacy, the true basis of his power was the reformed Macedonian army. By introducing a new style of fighting, one that involved infantrymen fighting in dense formation and wielding the fifteen- to eighteen-foot pike called the *sarissa*, Philip was able to put large numbers of troops into the field at moderate expense. The new weapons, along with the rigorous training of the troops, proved to be decisive. For no hoplite army could come to grips with an opposing formation from which five overlapping layers of pikes protruded to a maximum of twelve feet. The *sarissa* heads alone measured almost two feet and sliced through shields and armor like swords attached to hardwood poles. The hoplite whose shield was transfixed and dislocated by one *sarissa* soon found himself bloodied by another. It is a curious fact of history that military leaders are slow to adapt to change. Instead they do what they did in the past because it worked then, and it is assumed that it will work again. Major-General J. F. C. Fuller aptly remarked that, in Greek warfare, "changes in armament were due solely to compulsion, because, throughout, valour disdained inventiveness."[9] Such conservatism was costly and, although the Phocians had some success with artillery against the Macedonian phalanx, the Macedonian juggernaut rolled over Greek opposition in a relentless series of victories.

Successful on the battlefield, Philip was nevertheless careful to control Greek affairs rather than rule openly. In the Sacred War (356–46), he posed as the champion of Apollo, and in the battle of the Crocus Field (352), he even had his men wear laurel wreaths as signs of their service to the god, a modest precursor of the Crusader's cross. He acquired offices, such as the archonship of Thessaly, and exercised power by controlling the votes of the Amphictyonic League, much like a majority shareholder. Even after concluding the Peace of Philocrates in 346, he prudently avoided interference in affairs south of Thermopylae. But it was Athenian fear of Philip's growing power, especially in regions that bordered on the Hellespont and threatened the Black Sea grain supply, that drew him into further conflict. And in 338, the fate of the Greek world was decided on the battlefield near the Boeotian town of Chaeronea.

Ever since he began negotiations to end the Sacred War – talks that led to the Peace of Philocrates in 346 – Philip had hoped not merely to make peace with Athens but to win her as an ally. Although he had entered the Sacred War on the side of the Thebans, who were failing to make headway against the Phocians, and although Athens and Sparta were actually backing Phocis, Philip was concerned not to increase Theban power. But fears of Macedonian expansion drove Athens into the arms of Thebes and in 339 Philip entered central Greece and seized control of Elateia. The move terrified the Athenians, who believed that an invasion of Attica was imminent. They formed an alliance with Boeotia and prepared to resist the Macedonian army, which numbered 30,000 infantry and 2,000 cavalry, at Chaeronea. The battle was fought on 4 August, 338, with the Macedonian army facing south and extending its wings on the left to the Cephisus River and on the right to the foot of the Chaeronean acropolis. Opposite the right, where Philip commanded the infantry, were the Athenian hoplites; the Thebans and the elite Sacred Band held the wing opposite the Macedonian left, where Alexander led the Macedonian cavalry. Much has been made of the young prince's pivotal role at Chaeronea, but few draw attention to Diodorus' remark that Philip stationed beside him "his most accomplished generals."[10] Advancing in oblique formation, Philip's left wing made first contact with the enemy and then began an orderly feigned withdrawal. So convincing was this maneuver that the Athenians prematurely boasted that they would chase the king all the way back to Macedonia.[11] But as the Athenians pushed forward, a gap formed near the right wing where the Theban advance was impeded by a marsh;

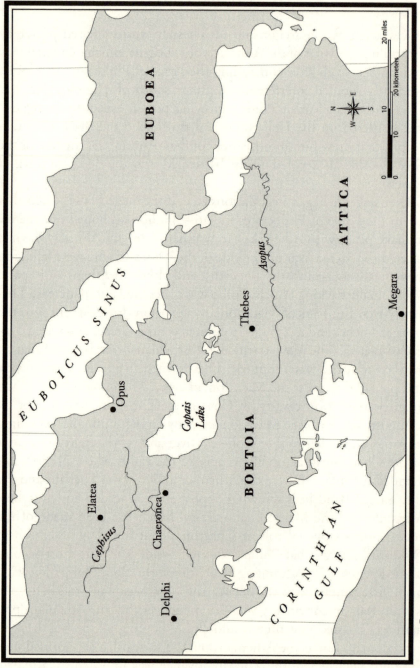

EUBOEA

ATTICA

Asopus

Thebes

Megara

EUBOICUS SINUS

Opus

Copais Lake

BOETOIA

Elatea

Chaeronea

Cephisus

CORINTHIAN GULF

Delphi

20 miles

20 kilometers

10

10

N E
W S

0
0

MAP 3. *Boeotia.*

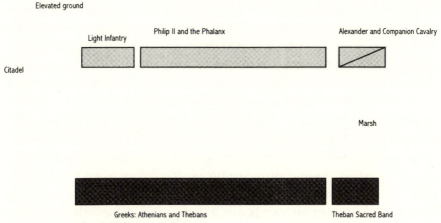

FIGURE 1. *Battle of Chaeronea: Phase I.*

Alexander was able to exploit the opening with his cavalry. Pressured at the point where the gap had formed and hemmed in by the Cephisus, the Thebans paid a heavy price, and the Sacred Band made a valiant but ultimately hopeless defense. On the Athenian side, over 1,000 were killed and twice that number captured. Theban losses will have been comparable.[12]

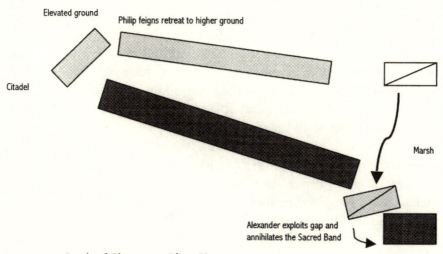

FIGURE 2. *Battle of Chaeronea: Phase II.*

The victory at Chaeronea and the formation of the League of Corinth (338/7) marked the pinnacle of Philip's military and political career. His demise had nothing to do with war or politics. Instead he and his heir, Alexander, became embroiled in domestic quarrels.[13]

The events that brought Alexander to the throne are, for the most part, well documented; their interpretation has, however, been a matter of dispute since ancient times. Military genius and diplomatic skill brought Philip II to the head of the Greek world. The might of his armies was matched by the power of his personality. Although disfigured by the loss of an eye in 354 and prone to fits of drunkenness, he nevertheless possessed an irresistible charm that arrested even his most stubborn detractors. All except his fourth wife, Olympias. The furor that attended Philip's seventh and final marriage to a young Macedonian girl named Cleopatra can be understood in purely human terms. The victor of Chaeronea, now in his mid-forties, was undergoing what we today would call a "midlife crisis." He had been captivated by a girl young enough to be his daughter, though by ancient standards more than old enough to be his wife. The Macedonian kings were, or at least could be, polygamous, and marriages were generally for the sake of heirs and political alliances. That does not rule out infatuation (or even genuine love), and it does not follow that Philip's motives could only have been political, as many have suggested. In the third century AD, Athenaeus of Naucratis observed that entire households had been overturned on account of women, drawing attention first and foremost to the case of Philip of Macedon. Alexander himself may have been embarrassed by the spectacle of his father as the bridegroom, besotted by love and drink, but it was the insult implicit in the toast by the bride's guardian that was the cause of all the trouble.

In the summer of 337, after securing the cooperation of the Greek states to the south, Philip returned to Macedonia to prepare for his great expedition against Persia. An affair of the heart intruded in a way that he had never imagined or intended. It was probably during October, the favored wedding month in Macedonia, that he married the young Cleopatra, the niece and ward of a certain Attalus. At the wedding-feast, which (it is important to note) Alexander attended, Attalus gave voice to his own ambitions by offering a prayer that the union would produce *legitimate* heirs to the throne. It was a tactless utterance, and ultimately fatal. Philip may indeed have hoped for other sons without ever wishing to disinherit Alexander. But scholars have assumed that Attalus' prayer and Philip's wishes were one and the same, and that the reference to legitimacy implied that Philip and others regarded Alexander as a bastard, apparently drawing attention to the foreignness of his mother. In response to the insult, Alexander hurled his drinking cup at Attalus, who responded in kind, but when Philip, in a drunken stupor, drew his sword and lunged at his son, the episode took on different proportions. Alexander fled to Epirus, where he deposited his mother with her brother, Alexander I, and then continued north to the kingdom of the Illyrians, with whose help he hoped to assert his claims to the throne.

If the wedding night was not a happy one, for Philip the following day must have brought a painful sobriety. Justin, who abbreviated the history of Pompeius Trogus, says that Philip had divorced Olympias on a charge of adultery (*stuprum*), patent nonsense that has, however, taken in more than one modern scholar. That the charge of *stuprum* should be found in the work of a historian writing at the time of Augustus' moral legislation is hardly surprising. The truth is that Philip had no need of divorce in order to take another wife, and in all likelihood the later rumor that Alexander had been fathered by Zeus-Amun gave rise to the charge of infidelity.[14] If the charge had been true, and the actual divorce had taken place, it would have been truly surprising to find Alexander, dishonored and disinherited, participating in the nuptial celebrations of his father. Philip must have known that he could not safely undertake an expedition in the east, leaving a house divided in Macedonia, and it is virtually certain that he never intended to do so. Up to that fateful moment at the wedding feast, father and son had enjoyed a harmonious relationship. Doubtless, they had disagreed from time to time, as happens even in the best relationships between fathers and sons, but there is nothing in the evidence to show that Philip was anything but proud of Alexander, whom he expected to succeed him.

His conduct at Chaeronea had made him the darling of the troops, as much as of his father. According to Plutarch:

> As a result, *as one would expect*, Philip was exceedingly fond of his son, so much so that he rejoiced when the Macedonians addressed Alexander as king and Philip as general [emphasis added].[15]

The biographer then goes on to contrast this harmony with the dissension created by Philip's marriage to Cleopatra. This picture is entirely consistent with everything we know about Philip and Alexander up to this point. It is a bitterly insecure mind that rejects the historicity of this gesture of genuine paternal affection. There is, moreover, a tendency in modern historical writing to dismiss those who believe that historical individuals can display warmth and goodness as naïve, with the corollary that clever scholars expose every act of the powerful man as deceitful and motivated by jealousy, fear, or hatred. Hence we have made monolithic villains of our modern tyrants – Hitler and Stalin in particular – and strained to expose Philips, Alexanders, and Caesars as their predecessors and role models. Furthermore, it was Alexander, accompanied by Antipater and, perhaps, Alcimachus, who brought the Athenian dead and Philip's terms to Athens. If there remained any doubt about Alexander's position, it was made clear by the Philippeum, set up at Olympia in 338, a statue group comprising Philip himself, his parents (Amyntas and Eurydice), his wife Olympias, and Alexander.[16]

The months that followed the wedding fiasco saw every attempt made to minimize the damage: Alexander was recalled from Illyria – indeed, a preemptive strike against the Illyrians followed soon afterward[17] – and Olympias was recalled to Macedonia to oversee the wedding of her daughter, also named Cleopatra, to her uncle, Alexander I of Epirus. But the insult at Attalus' hands and Philip's rebuke had made a deep impression on Alexander, whose trust could not easily be restored. His mother, who probably had reasons to dislike her husband, played upon his insecurities, but that is hardly sufficient to support the view, held already by some in antiquity, that Alexander plotted his father's murder. Those who are convinced of his guilt are the same ones who emphasize his precarious position at court. With so many political opponents, would Alexander have risked putting his right of succession to the test by eliminating the king? This would surely have played into his enemies' hands. Some have argued that he feared the unborn child of Cleopatra, but the fact is that this child had already been born a few days before Philip's death, and was a girl at that![18] For Alexander it would have been best if Philip had died on the campaign, where the army would have had few doubts about their new king and leader.

The details of the conspiracy against Philip are easily told. Pausanias of Orestis, a young man recently graduated from the corps of Pages and now one of the royal hypaspists, had been supplanted as Philip's favorite by another, also named Pausanias. Pederasty in military training was common enough in Greek states, especially Sparta and Thebes, and it was in the latter that Philip had served for some time as a hostage.[19] Hence we ought not to dismiss the story as scurrilous gossip, even if some of its details are overdramatized. The jilted Pausanias was alleged to have berated his rival and namesake, whom he called effeminate and promiscuous. The second Pausanias confided in Attalus, telling him that he would prove his bravery on the battlefield, and soon fell in a heroic defense of the king in a battle with the Illyrians (late winter 336). Attalus, for his part, invited the offending Pausanias to a drinking-party and there handed him over to his muleteers, who subjected him to gang rape. The matter was duly reported to the king, placing Philip in a dilemma, since Attalus, the perpetrator of the crime, was his "father-in-law" and had recently been selected to lead the advance party into Asia. Believing that he could placate Pausanias with other honors, and hopeful that Attalus' absence would put an end to the matter, Philip did nothing further to mollify him. In frustration, Pausanias decided to avenge himself not on Attalus but upon his perceived protector.

In October 336, Philip attempted a formal reconciliation with his Epirote family by celebrating the marriage of his daughter Cleopatra to Alexander I of Epirus. The festivities included a spectacle in the theater, where the statues of the twelve Olympian gods were brought in, accompanied by a thirteenth, that of Philip himself. In attendance were not only the Macedonians, but also the representatives of the various Greek states that were members of the League of Corinth and partners in

Philip's Persian enterprise. Here, in the theater, as he walked unattended by guards, he was accosted by Pausanias, who thrust a Celtic dagger into his ribs. The assassin was pursued and killed – some, of course, have regarded with suspicion the failure to take him alive – but the king died in a matter of minutes. If others had hoped to gain from the death, they were apparently ill prepared for it and taken by surprise. Alexander the Lyncestian, a son-in-law of the powerful general Antipater, was the first to hail Alexander as king. Others followed suit. The most dangerous rivals were either not at the gathering in Aegae (Vergina) or caught off-guard. Not so Alexander. He proceeded to round up rivals – the sons of Aëropus, Arrhabaeus, and Heromenes, as well as his cousin Amyntas son of Perdiccas – and, in the days and weeks to come, eliminated them on charges of complicity in the murder. To the thunderstruck crowd he proclaimed, with a measure of truth, that only the name of the king had changed. After the funeral rites had been celebrated, it would be business as usual.

Alexander's political opponents were now on high alert. They had little choice but to make their peace with the new king or flee the country. Amyntas son of Antiochus, a longtime friend of the deposed heir, Amyntas IV, took refuge in Asia with the Great King, as did Neoptolemus, a son of Arrhabaeus, who had been executed as a regicide. Parmenion, for his part, was forced to declare his loyalty to Alexander by sacrificing his son-in-law Attalus.[20] His conscience may have troubled him, but his career and the fortunes of his family prospered, at least in the short run.

The effects of Philip's murder were felt as far off as Greece to the south and Asia Minor. Satraps who had hoped to benefit from Philip's invasion now made their peace with Darius III, the governments of cities in Asia that had rid themselves of Persian garrisons now experienced counter-revolution, and amongst the Greeks of Europe there was the conviction that now, if ever, they must attempt to throw off the Macedonian yoke.

THE MACEDONIAN ARMY
Alexander inherited from Philip not only the task of conquering the Persian Empire but, more importantly, the army with which to do so.

The Macedonian army that crossed the Hellespont in 334 was essentially the same one that had served Philip in the years leading up to and including Chaeronea. Although half of the Macedonian forces were left behind under the command of Antipater, those who accompanied the new king included the most experienced of Philip's veterans. And they may also represent the majority of the troops who suppressed the Greek uprising of 335 and destroyed Thebes. Alexander's numbers on that occasion are given as 30,000, but almost half of these must have been allies.

The main offensive weapon of Alexander's army was the Companion Cavalry. These comprised, in 334, seven squadrons (*ilai*) and a royal squadron (*ile basilike*), in all 1,800 horsemen. If all *ilai* were of equal size, then the strength of an *ile* was probably about 225 men; but it may have been that the *ile basilike* was larger, with a corresponding reduction in the size of each of the other *ilai*.[21] Supplementing and working in tandem with these were five additional *ilai* of *prodromoi* (sometimes called *sarissophoroi*) and Paeonians; Plutarch (*Alex.* 16.3) speaks of Alexander leading thirteen *ilai* at the Granicus. We know that the *ilai* of the Companions were recruited on a regional basis, but the origins of the *prodromoi* are uncertain – they may have been Thracians, or perhaps Macedonians – except for the fact that they were distinct from the Paeonians. Later in the campaign, as reinforcements outnumbered losses, the strength of the *ile* was increased and it was divided into two *lochoi*. The standard unit appears to have become the hipparchy (although the term is used anachronistically before the military reforms). By the final years of the campaign there were five large hipparchies – possibly with a strength of 1,000 – as well as a cavalry guard (*agema*). The chief weapon of the Companions was the thrusting spear (*xyston*), rather than the javelin favored by the Persians, and if the *prodromoi* were, in fact, *sarissophoroi*, then it is unlikely (for practical reasons) that the cavalry *sarissa* was longer than nine feet.[22]

The Macedonian line was anchored by the *sarissa*-wielding infantrymen known in Alexander's time as the *pezhetairoi* (or *pezetairoi*), though some of the units were designed as *asthetairoi*. These were 9,000 heavy infantry divided into six units (*taxeis*), all recruited on an ethnic (i.e., regional) basis and led by generals from their local aristocracies or royal houses. The strength of each *taxis* was roughly 1,500 men, comprising either three units of 512 or six units of 256. The term *pezhetairoi* had originally been used of the elite troops, known in Alexander's time as the hypaspists (see below): Theopompus says that "the biggest and strongest of the troops selected from all the Macedonians acted as the king's guard and were called *pezhetairoi*."[23] But by the end of Philip's reign, or at the beginning of Alexander's, the term was applied to the heavy infantry. These were armed with the *sarissa*, which measured up to eighteen feet, and carried a smaller shield (roughly two feet in diameter), slung over the shoulder and secured by means of a *porpax* that allowed the forearm to pass through it but left the hand free to wield the pike.

Between the phalanx and the Companions, Alexander stationed the hypaspists (shield-bearers), 3,000 strong. These elite infantrymen, armed in the style of Greek hoplites (but with lighter linen corselets), acted as both an articulating force and as infantry support for the cavalry in the style of *hamippoi*. They were used also, often in conjunction with cavalry and the Agrianes, on campaigns that required speed and flexibility; usually they were among the first troops to scale the city walls of the enemy.[24] Unlike the battalions of the phalanx, the chiliarchies and pentakosiarchies of the hypaspists were commanded by men selected on the basis of merit rather than birth. Nevertheless, the responsibility for the entire hypaspist corps (the *archihypaspistes*) was entrusted to a nobleman, appointed by Alexander himself. During the Indian campaign, most likely when the army returned from the Hyphasis to the Hydaspes, they decorated their shields with silver and became known as the *argyraspides*. From that point on they were probably replaced by a younger group of hypaspists.[25]

On the left wing, which was assigned a defensive role and regularly held back (or "refused"), Alexander could deploy the 7,000 allied infantry (when they were not held in reserve behind the Macedonian phalanx) contributed by the member states of the League of Corinth, along with 600 allied cavalry. These were supplemented by 5,000 mercenary infantry, and the wing was secured by a force of 1,800 Thessalian cavalry. This entire force was normally under the command of

Parmenion, though Craterus began to emerge as his understudy. Both wings were covered also by javelin-men, of whom the Agrianes were the most formidable, slingers, and archers. The last group was divided between those from Crete and those of Macedonian origin.

It was, indeed, a luxury to have such a combination of specialized troops, but it could be argued that the Persian army was no less diverse. Nevertheless, it required both a tactician of Alexander's quality to coordinate the efforts of the army, and officers of the sort whose brilliance became clear during the course of the campaign – despite the fact that the historians tended to focus on Alexander and exclude many of the activities on other parts of the battlefield – to put the king's plans into effect. The king's recklessness and his practice of leading from the front are well known. Historian Adrian Goldsworthy observes:

> In this way he inspired his soldiers to heights of valour, but once the fighting began he could exercise little direct influence on the course of the battle. Instead he trusted his subordinate officers to control the troops in other sectors of the field. . . . [26]

For this reason, we may assume that Alexander's death in battle would have had less impact on the outcome for the Macedonians than Darius' would for the Persians.

Although the Macedonian army approached 50,000 men at the beginning of the campaign, it was smaller than that of the Persians on most occasions, and often vastly outnumbered. Alexander could not hope for a Cannae-style destruction of the enemy's forces. Instead, he was like a chess player, intent upon capturing the opponent's king; his aim was to win the battle *before* the enemy could use its numerical superiority to its greatest effect. Hence, he enticed the enemy into attempting a flanking move on its left wing, thereby separating the wing from the center left. This point he then attacked with his own right wing. The right hand of the phalanx fixed the enemy just beyond the center, while the Companions exploited the developing gap on the enemy left and wheeled to take the broken formation in the flank. The hypaspists acted as the hinge, keeping contact with both the phalanx and the cavalry and, once the flank attack began to throw the enemy into confusion, intermingling with the horsemen as the fighting turned to slaughter. But for the difficulties of the terrain at Issus, all three of Alexander's major battles against the Persians followed this general pattern.

SECURING THE EUROPEAN BORDERS

Philip's sudden death placed in jeopardy his military and diplomatic gains. The Athenians, and most vociferously Demosthenes, saw fit to challenge the mere "boy" who occupied the Macedonian throne; the orator went so far as to disparage Alexander as Homer's fool, Margites, thereby mocking the king's descent from the mythical Achilles.[27] Other states hastened to throw off the Macedonian yoke in a time of perceived weakness. Their assessment was wrong, and the error a costly one. Not so much for the Athenians, who were more prone to incite rebellion than to enact it, but rather for the Thebans. Incited by Demosthenes' rhetoric, deluded by promises of support, and misled by false rumors of Alexander's death in the north, they were destined to provide a bitter lesson to the Greek world. Their fate would be the prelude to the Panhellenic War.

Initial moves against Macedon were quickly suppressed, as Alexander cut "steps" into the side of Mt Oeta and forced the Thessalian League to proclaim him Philip's successor as the League's *archon*. The prompt action quelled discontent in central and southern Greece, freeing the Macedonian king to secure the northern borders in preparation for his Persian expedition. In rapid succession, he confronted the Thracians in the northeast and the Illyrians to the west. The first of these campaigns subdued the so-called autonomous Thracians in the Mt Haemus region and scattered the resistance of the Triballians, whose leader Syrmus took refuge on an island in the Danube. Those Triballians who had doubled back from the river and mounted further opposition were defeated in battle. A show of force across the Danube brought no small amount of booty as well as guarantees of good faith from the Getae;[28] it also compelled the Triballian leader to come to terms.

Farther to the west, Alexander sent Langarus, king of the Agrianes, to bring the Autariatae (who were derided as the least warlike of neighboring tribes) to heel, while he himself confronted the Illyrian chieftains,

Glaucias and Cleitus, at Pellium. This campaign, which gave early indications of Alexander's generalship and ability to improvise, also demonstrated the efficiency of the Macedonian infantry, perfected in both drill and battle under Philip's command. It would have been the final rehearsal for the Persian expedition, had not the disturbing news of Theban defection reached Alexander.

After his victory at Chaeronea, Philip had secured the citadel of Thebes, known as the Cadmeia, with a Macedonian garrison. In 335, during Alexander's lengthy absence in the north, rumors spread that the king had been killed in Illyria, encouraging the Thebans to rebel against Macedonian domination. Two members of the garrison, Amyntas and Timolaus, were caught off guard and dragged to their deaths. The assembled Thebans, incited by agitators, voted to throw off the Macedonian yoke and help liberate Thebes. According to Diodorus, they advocated the use of Persian subsidies to secure Greek freedom from the "true enemy." Alexander learned of the uprising when he was on his western borders and, making his way through Upper Macedonia, he crossed the Haliacmon River and arrived at Pelinna in Thessaly. The march had taken him a mere seven days; six days later he was in Onchestus, south of Lake Copais in Boeotia.[29] When he drew up his army of over 30,000 before the gates of Thebes, keeping his troops close to the besieged garrison on the Cadmeia, Alexander is said to have attempted a negotiated settlement. The king demanded the extradition of Phoenix and Prothytes, who had (allegedly) fomented the rebellion; the Thebans countered with the unrealistic demand that Alexander surrender Philotas and Antipater. Philotas may in fact have been the *phrourarchos* of the Cadmeia, but the reference to Antipater is undoubtedly to Alexander's regent in Macedonia.[30] Even when this showed little sign of success, the king held back – or so it was alleged by those who sought to minimize Alexander's responsibility for Thebes' destruction – until the battalion of Perdiccas attacked prematurely and set in motion the battle that would lead to the city's capture.[31] The Theban defenders soon displayed the valor of desperation: 6,000 infantrymen were killed, and some 30,000 Thebans were sold into slavery.[32] The city was razed to the ground as an example to the rest of Greece. Although the Boeotian enemies of Thebes were doubtless inclined to show the defeated city no mercy, the blame for the city's fate must rest with Alexander, and there are signs that throughout the campaign he may have regretted his excessive severity. But as a prelude to the Panhellenic mission it served its purpose. What better place to start than with the Medizers at home?[33]

THE PERSIAN ENEMY

CHAPTER FOUR

THE PERSIAN EMPIRE IN THE FOURTH CENTURY

At the end of the fifth century, the rebellious brother of Artaxerxes II, known as Cyrus the Younger to differentiate him from the great founder of the dynasty,[1] led a mixed force of barbarians and Greeks into the heart of the Persian Empire. The troops that confronted the armies of the Great King included more than 10,000 Greek mercenaries, drawn from many parts of European Greece, each contingent with its own commander. Although their leader and paymaster, Cyrus, was killed on the battlefield of Cunaxa, not far from Babylon, the Greeks (whose own generals had treacherously been slain by the satrap Tissaphernes) managed to escape the victorious army and fight their way back through the mountains of Armenia to the Greek settlements on the Black Sea. Their story is told vividly by Xenophon, the man who claimed to have assumed command of the force after the murder of the generals. His *Anabasis* or "March Up Country" was known to educated Greek and Macedonian youths, and there is no doubt that Alexander, as a boy, was held spellbound by the adventures of the Ten Thousand and the exotic world of Persia.[2] But the *Anabasis* also played no small part in contributing to the view of the Achaemenid empire as decadent

and "ripe for the picking." This picture of Persia in decline, so long
accepted by modern writers, has now been revised through the efforts of
Achaemenid scholars.[3] But the observations made by Xenophon about
the inherent weaknesses of the empire proved to be true, and they were
brilliantly exploited by Alexander the Great.

Two passages, one recording Xenophon's own estimate of the empire's
strengths and weaknesses, the other allegedly preserving the words of
Cyrus himself, deserve closer attention. In the first, Xenophon observes,

> It was clear to anyone who paid close attention to the size of the king's
> empire that it was strong in terms of lands and men, but weak on account
> of the great distances of road and the dispersal of its forces, if someone
> made a quick military strike against it.[4]

In the second, Cyrus remarks to the Greeks, in the hope of encouraging
them to endure hardships on his behalf,

> Our ancestral kingdom stretches southward to the point where men
> cannot live on account of the heat, and northward to where the winter
> prevents habitation. All that lies between these limits is governed by my
> brother's friends (*philoi*). If we conquer, we shall have to put our friends
> in charge of these areas.[5]

The Persian Empire was thus a large but cumbersome structure, which
could be taken by an efficient army and which offered opportunities
for the enrichment of the conquerors, an empire to be coveted rather
than feared.

In reality, the conquest of Persia, though possible – as Alexander
himself would prove – was not a simple matter in the first decades of
the fourth century. Xenophon's declaration that Agesilaus, who had
been campaigning with a force of not more than 10,000 in 395 and
394, was recalled to Europe just when he was on the verge of striking at
the very heart of the Achaemenid empire amounts to little more than
wishful thinking, and the general perception of Agesilaus was one of a
"robber baron" who was making life difficult for Tissaphernes in Ionia.
But when the time came, and "the man and the hour had met" (to use

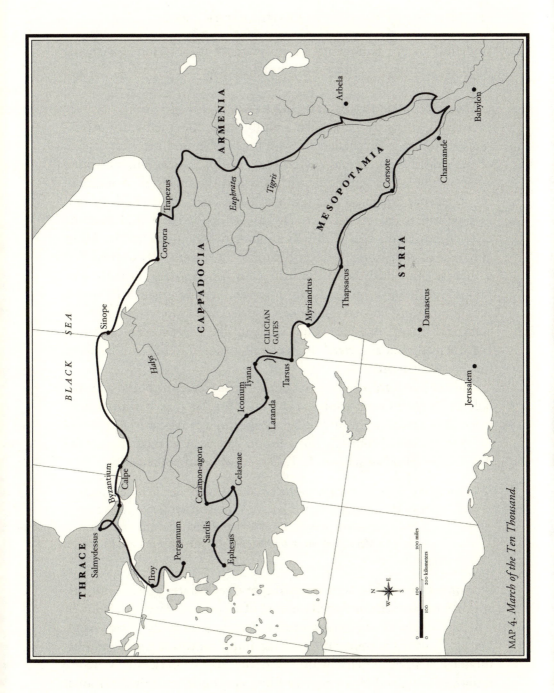

MAP 4. *March of the Ten Thousand.*

33

William Yancey's famous phrase in reference to Jefferson Davis), the truth of Xenophon's observations became clear.

COMMON ENEMY OF THE GREEKS

The death knells of the Persian Empire were thus premature. Artaxerxes II turned aside challenges from his brother and the great satraps of the west. Disparaged as militarily inept, his resolve blunted somewhat by advancing age, he nevertheless had the financial resources to buy mercenaries abroad and traitors in the Greek homeland. In tandem with first Sparta and then Thebes, he divided and weakened the Greek states, acting all the while as the guarantor of their local freedoms. When he died in 359/8, he left the throne to Artaxerxes III Ochus, who ruthlessly purged his family and the court of rivals and brutally suppressed rebellion in his lands. In doing so, he strengthened Persia for the moment but created conditions, particularly amongst the Phoenicians and Egyptians, that would facilitate the Macedonian conquest. For when Alexander arrived they were ill disposed to fight to the death for their Persian masters.

The military campaigns of the Great Persian Wars had been a dismal failure. Despite Greek euphoria, for the Persians they had been little more than an unsuccessful border war of the sort regularly suppressed in Near Eastern chronicles. But a lesson had been learned. The noted Assyrian and Persian scholar A. T. Olmstead rightly observed,

> From the very first contact with the Greeks, Persian monarchs had been well aware of the outstanding weakness of Greek statesmen – their susceptibility to bribes – and now that Xerxes had suffered a crushing series of military defeats Persian diplomacy, backed by the empire's gold must be brought into play.[6]

Not only bribery, but actual funding of Greek states at war with one another, became the preferred method of securing the western frontier. The late stages of the Peloponnesian War presented the Great King, Darius II, with the opportunity of regaining control of the Aegean littoral. Particularly hard hit by the loss of the coastal Greek cities were the satraps of Ionia and Hellespontine Phrygia, who coveted the additional revenues these would generate. The revolt of the tribute-paying states of the Aegean islands against Athens after the Sicilian disaster of 413 was doomed to failure if the Spartans could not bring aid; for even in its hour of crisis, the Athenian state was far from defeated and showed both the will to and the means of recovery. With the aid of Persian gold, Sparta could establish a naval presence in the east that would not only ensure the safety of the rebels but also offer the prospect of victory in the war. But in exchange for this victory, the Spartans – who had entered the war as the avowed liberators of Greece – would have to relinquish control of the Greeks of Ionia to their Persian paymasters.[7] The decision to ally themselves with the Persians – the treaty negotiations are described in detail by Thucydides – was politically embarrassing for the Spartans, but it guaranteed success. Spartan navarchs, especially the flamboyant Lysander, directed ever stronger fleets, manned in part by rowers who had been enticed away from Athenian service by higher wages. The partnership between Sparta and Persia was brokered by Darius II's son, Cyrus, whose concern to foster the friendship of Lysander was motivated in no small way by his aspirations to the Achaemenid throne. Hence, the Persians failed to heed Alcibiades' advice that it was not in their interests to support one side only.

> The Athenians sent ambassadors to Cyrus, using Tissaphernes as a go-between. Cyrus, however, refused to receive them, in spite of the entreaties of Tissaphernes, who urged him to follow his own policy (which he had adopted on the advice of Alcibiades) – namely, to guard against the emergence of any single strong Greek state by seeing that they were all kept weak by constantly fighting among themselves.[8]

In the event, Cyrus' schemes came to an abrupt end on the battlefield of Cunaxa, as we have already noted, and the involvement of Peloponnesian mercenaries turned Artaxerxes II against his former allies.

Now it was the Athenians who benefited from Persian gold, and Conon, the admiral who had gone into self-imposed exile after the disaster at Aegospotami (405), terminated the short-lived Spartan thalassocracy in the waters off Cnidus in 394. At about the same time, Agesilaus had returned to Greece to deal with the Corinthian War, after a fitful campaign in Ionia, driven out of Asia "by 10,000 archers."[9] The war in Greece dragged on until 387, when the Spartans again sought Persian aid in order to prop up their power and force a settlement on their opponents. This Peace of Antalcidas, more appropriately called the "King's Peace," revived once again the charge that Sparta was in league with the "common enemy of the Greeks."

> We may blame the Lacedaemonians because to begin with they went to war in order to liberate the Greeks, but in the end handed so many of them over . . . to the barbarians. . . . [10]

In some respects, Sparta's was a Teflon empire; for, despite its autocratic and narrow-minded policies, the opprobrium of Medism did not stick to it as it did to Thebes.[11] Who could cast blame on the defenders of Thermopylae and the victors of Plataea? For their part, after the Spartan army was broken in the battle of Leuctra (371), the Thebans imposed a new peace on the Greek world, again supported by Persia. Theirs were not the only ambassadors who found their way to Susa, but their actions were dutifully reported by the orators and historians. Most telling, however, was the Theban response to Alexander's appeal that they join the Panhellenic cause: instead they called upon all Greeks to side with them *and the Great King* in liberating Greece from the tyranny of the Macedonians.[12]

PANHELLENISM

The impact of the Persian Wars (i.e., the campaigns of Darius' general Datis in 490 and of Xerxes in 480/79) on the Greeks is hard to underestimate. This is especially the case with the Athenians, whose paradoxical defeat of the expeditionary force at Marathon and subsequent contribution to the decisive victory at Salamis served as the springboard for the growth of their power and the eventual creation of the Athenian Empire. In truth, it resulted in a distortion of modern views on the Persian Wars: what was for Greece a life-and-death struggle and a triumph of Greek arms and will over the barbarian was for Persia an unsuccessful border war, a check on western expansion. That Persia ever again contemplated the annexation of Greek territory is doubtful, but it served the purpose of the Athenians to portray Persia as an evil empire, ever close at hand and dangerous. Greek anxieties about Persia were probably not much different from those of westerners during the Cold War with regard to the Soviet Union and the Eastern Bloc, and equally contrived. These carefully nurtured anxieties were fertile ground for the development of notions of Panhellenism, Greek unity. Not that they were unaware of their common language, culture, and religion. To this, if nothing else, the Olympic, Pythian, Nemean, and Isthmian games bore ample testimony. But political union or coalitions of any kind were all but impossible to achieve unless imposed by force by a leading state or statesman, and even then for the avowed purpose of defense against a common enemy or an offensive war of retribution.[13]

The concept of Panhellenism is inextricably linked with the name of Isocrates, its most famous advocate. But the idea was clearly developed in the fifth century, probably in response to the Spartan decision to seek Persian aid in the war against Athens. Thus Gorgias of Leontini, the teacher of Isocrates, delivered an oration at Olympia (perhaps in 408) lamenting the fact that Greeks were wearing themselves out fighting one another, when they should be directing their hostility against the true enemy, Persia. Similarly, Xenophon, writing after the termination of Spartan supremacy by the Thebans, attributes Panhellenic sentiments not only to his hero, Agesilaus, but also to the Spartan navarch, Callicratidas, who is said to have remarked that

> the Greeks were the most wretched of beings, because they toadied to the barbarians for the sake of silver, and he said that, if he returned home safely, he would do everything in his power to reconcile the Athenians and the Spartans.[14]

For Isocrates himself, Greek unification and the avenging of Persia went hand in hand. That the Athenians should lead such a unified Greek undertaking was, of course, Isocrates' original intent, but he regarded the benefits to Greece as such that any unification, even if imposed upon the Athenians by Sparta or Macedon, was preferable to the current state of affairs and the debilitating warfare amongst the *poleis*. Whether Philip II was persuaded by these appeals or came upon the idea of a

Panhellenic crusade on his own, Isocrates was unable to say, but Philip clearly appreciated the value of such propaganda and professed a wish to lead rather than to rule Greece. It was a theme that served Macedonian interests, and therefore was adopted by Alexander on Philip's death. Yet, although many Greeks accepted slogans which gave a measure of respect to their own political humiliation, there were doubtless many who would have approved the comments of Plutarch in his *Life of Agesilaus* 15.4:

> Personally, I am not in agreement with the Corinthian Demaratus who claimed that the Greeks missed a very pleasurable experience in not seeing Alexander seated on Darius' throne. Actually, I think they might have had more reason to shed tears at the realization that the men who left this honor to Alexander were those who sacrificed the commanders of the Greeks at Leuctra, Coronea, and Corinth and in Arcadia.[15]

338–334 BC

Early in 338, Artaxerxes III Ochus, son and successor of Artaxerxes II, was poisoned by his Chiliarch, Bagoas. Greek and Roman writers were fond of depicting eunuchs as scheming half-men, flabby and beardless, and restricted to concocting mischief in the women's quarters. The physical description may be close to the truth: such figures appear on Assyrian reliefs and have been identified as eunuchs. But the influence of some eunuchs was not confined to the harem. Like the Byzantine Narses, Bagoas was a powerful individual at court and a competent military man.[16] He engineered the accession of Ochus' son, Arses, who reigned briefly as Artaxerxes IV, but eliminated the king's brothers and then Arses himself. He miscalculated, however, when he assumed that he could set up Artasata (Darius III), whom Greek writers called Codomannus, as his puppet. Darius III, although the Alexander historians portrayed him as a coward, was an experienced warrior, who had defeated an enemy champion in the Cadusian campaign of Artaxerxes III; at the time of his accession he was forty-four or forty-five years old and wise to the eunuch's machinations.[17] Suspecting treachery, he forced Bagoas to drink his own poison.

Intrigues at the court, especially those resulting in a change of ruler, are generally accompanied by uprisings in the provinces; for the peripheral regions are encouraged by the perceived weakness of the central government. The Egyptians, only recently reintegrated into the empire, were induced once again to rebel, this time by a certain Chababash, whose name suggests he was not a native Egyptian.[18] The dates of Chababash's rule have been much debated, though it is certain from an inscription on a sarcophagus lid of an Apis bull that his reign extended into a second year. Since Isocrates speaks of stability within the Persian Empire in 339 and we know that at Issus in late 333 Egyptian troops served under the satrap Sauaces, it is most likely that the Chababash interlude in Egypt followed the intrigues of Bagoas, which put Arses (Artaxerxes IV) on the Persian throne. This period coincided with Philip's decisive victory at Chaeronea, the formation of the League of Corinth, and the organization of the Panhellenic war against Persia. If the Egyptian rebellion was triggered by the weakness of Arses, it was almost certainly suppressed by the new king Darius III in 336.

In the spring of 336, Philip had sent an advance force of 10,000 Macedonians to Asia Minor under the command of Parmenion, Attalus, and a certain Amyntas, perhaps the son of Arrhabaeus. Their presence, and the apparent initiation of the war against Persia, induced the Carian satrap Pixodarus to seek an alliance with Philip II, in the expectation of Macedonian success, at least on the coast of Asia Minor. But, by the fall of 336, Philip had been assassinated, Egypt recovered for Persia, and Pixodarus had found a new son-in-law in Orontopates. Indeed, the latter's position as satrap of Caria suggests that Darius did not trust Pixodarus entirely. For the Macedonians, a window of opportunity had opened and closed. Whether Darius had sent gold to Macedonia to secure Philip's assassination is unclear: Alexander found it convenient to level the charge against his opponent in 332, knowing that many in his camp and in the Greek world would regard it as plausible, if not dead certain.

Should Darius have taken measures to preempt Alexander's invasion? Was he capable of doing so? These are difficult questions to answer. On the one hand, he may have found it difficult to secure a new fleet capable of contesting the crossing of the Hellespont. On the other, he may not have thought it necessary. Perhaps he was encouraged by the poor showing of the advance force, which Memnon had managed to hold in check, and by the reassertion of the pro-Persian element in cities such as Ephesus when the news of Philip's death became known. News of rebellions in Europe must also have provided grounds for optimism. Certainly, Darius had little reason to assume that the untried Alexander would have much more success than Agesilaus had some sixty years earlier, and he must have believed that the armies of a coalition of satraps from Asia Minor would suffice to repel the invader.

It is a common mistake to assume, from hindsight, that Alexander's conquest of Persia was inevitable or that the satraps and their king must have viewed the Macedonian invasion with deep foreboding. The Persians had learned the value of Greek hoplites, and they had a plentiful supply of them – though as it turned out they were reluctant to use them to maximum effect. Their skilled horsemen by far outnumbered the invader's cavalry. Only too late would they discover that their own cavalry, armed with javelins and bows, were no match for the "shock tactics" of the dense wedges of Macedonians and Thessalians. But all that was yet to come, with neither side sufficiently experienced in the techniques and weaponry of their opponents.

CONQUEST OF THE ACHAEMENIDS

CHAPTER FIVE

❋ ❋ ❋

I N THE SHORT INTERVAL BETWEEN HIS ACCESSION AND THE START of the Asiatic campaign, Alexander suppressed rebellion in the south and unrest on his northern borders – all with terrifying ease. A rapid move into Thessaly silenced the first grumblings of discontent, and in the following year (335 BC) he arrived at the gates of Thebes, dispelling by his very presence rumors of his death in the north. A single act of terror – the destruction of the city and the enslavement of its population – served to impress upon the Greeks the futility of opposition. The Spartans refused to join the League, just as they had after Chaeronea, but theirs was for now a passive resistance. When they did finally attempt to reassert themselves, they found few allies and no military success.

SETTING THE STAGE

In 334 Alexander's army crossed the Hellespont from Sestos to Abydus on 160 warships and an assortment of cargo craft. That Alexander did not build a boat-bridge was probably a matter of economics – his finances were an ongoing concern at the beginning of the expedition[1] – and the recollection that Xerxes' "chaining" of the Hellespont was regarded as hubristic. Instead he used every symbol in the Panhellenic arsenal. At Dium in Macedonia he staged games in honor of the Muses and the Olympian gods. Still on the European side, he propitiated Zeus the god of safe landings and made apotropaic sacrifice to Protesilaus, the first man in the great expedition against Troy to die on Asian soil, hoping to avert a similar fate. In the middle of the passage he slaughtered a bull and poured libations into the sea in honor of Poseidon and Nereids. And, when he reached the opposite shore, he hurled his spear into the soil, claiming Asia as "spear-won land." The dramatics were duly recorded and recited throughout Greece. Alexander was following in the foot-steps of the leaders of the Trojan War, continuing the endless struggle between East and West. For thus Herodotus had described the origins of the Great Persian War, and in similar terms the Spartan king, Agesilaus, had set out for Asia by conducting sacrifices at Aulis, as Agamemnon had done centuries before.[2]

Even the practicalities yielded to the pressure of propaganda. Before reviewing his troops on the Asian side, Alexander made a deliberate detour to the site of ancient Troy, sacrificing at the tombs of Achilles and Ajax, and depositing a suit of armor at the Temple of Athena. There he removed what came to be known as "the sacred shield of Athena," which was subsequently carried before them by the hypaspists. Some claim that this same shield later saved the king's life in the town of the Mallians (near modern Multan), during his descent of the Indus River. Stories of Alexander's activities at Troy were quick to circulate, empha-sizing his descent from Achilles on his mother's side. Others alleged that Hephaestion sacrificed at the tomb of Patroclus; but most proph-esied the king's impending greatness. But the public displays at Ilium were part of the official Panhellenic propaganda rather than personal statements, and the story that Hephaestion saw himself as Patroclus to Alexander's Achilles is almost certainly late, created after the two had died prematurely in 324 and 323.[3] Alexander will not have forgotten that the Athenian orator Demosthenes had referred to him not as the young Achilles but as Homer's fool, Margites. The Macedonian king was no longer a boy, animated by dreams of Homeric heroes – though many reputable scholars would have it so – but the leader of all Greeks in a war of vengeance. And so he was portrayed by his "official" historian Callisthenes.

Nor were the Panhellenic elements restricted to the Homeric tradition. Just as the destruction of Thebes in 335 had been justified by the past and continuing Medism of the Thebans, so too Gryneum on the coast of Asia Minor had paid the ultimate price for Medism. In the Troad, the fallen statue of Ariobarzanes, former satrap of Hellespontine Phrygia, was seen as an omen of victory. Perhaps his symbolic prostration had been arranged by Alexander's own men, or perhaps the pro-Macedonian party had defaced the statue in anticipation of liberation from Persian rule. If the latter is the case, it represents one of the few instances of Greek enthusiasm for the expedition. In truth, the Greeks of Asia Minor did not throw open their gates to the "liberating" army. Most were under oligarchies, propped up by Persian authority, politically secure and economically prosperous. Indeed, the Greeks had experienced liberation often enough to know that they were simply being asked to exchange one master for another.[4] The city of Ephesus had placed a statue of Philip II in its temple of Artemis in anticipation of Philip's campaign, but after the successes of Memnon against Parmenion and Calas, and the death of Philip himself, the statue was again dragged down. The support of the Ionians for the Panhellenic war was reactive, awaiting the outcome of battle and the coercive presence of Macedonian arms, rather than a key to the overthrow of Persian power. One cannot blame these Greeks. Liberation meant deposing a ruling group and disenfranchising many of its supporters: murder, exile, and the confiscation of property were the concomitants of political change, and in the Greek world memories were long and every offense, no matter how slight, was the cause of undying hatred. Nor was this the only problem. Pro-Persian garrisons controlled their cities, thousands of Greek mercenaries served with Memnon of Rhodes, and a substantial portion of the citizenry manned the Persian fleet. Those who did, indeed, favor revolution stood to lose much if Alexander failed.

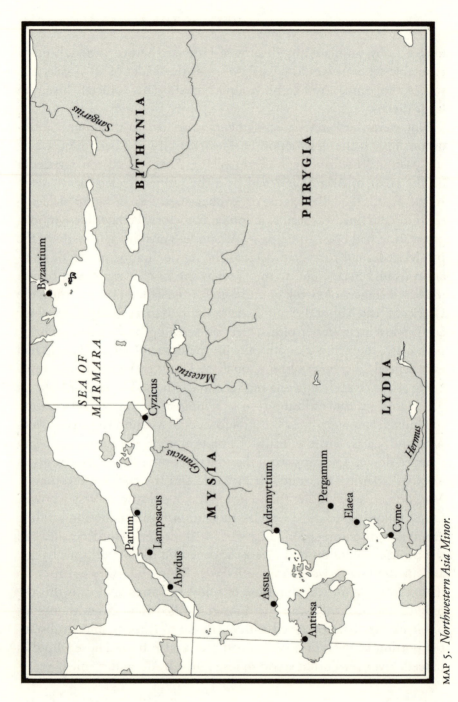

BITHYNIA

PHRYGIA

Sangarius

Byzantium

SEA OF
MARMARA

Maestus

Cyzicus

LYDIA

Granicus

Hermus

MYSIA

Parium

Lampsacus

Abydus

Adramytium

Pergamum

Elaea

Cyme

Assus

Antissa

MAP 5. *Northwestern Asia Minor.*

44

FIRST ENCOUNTER

The army that crossed the Hellespont comprised barely 40,000 men, but it was augmented by the troops already in Asia. To meet the Macedonian threat, the satrapal armies of Asia Minor assembled at Zeleia in Hellespontine Phrygia. They had had ample warning of Alexander's coming, but little could be done to prevent the crossing of the straits; for the Macedonian advance force under Parmenion and Calas held the Asian shore, and the Persian fleet, diverted to service in Egypt, had not yet entered the Aegean. Rejecting Memnon's suggestion that they adopt a "scorched earth" policy, the satraps opted instead to hold the line of the Granicus River. The refusal to consider Memnon's strategy has been ascribed to Persian distrust of the Greek mercenaries. Indeed, the satrap of Hellespontine Phrygia, Arsites, may have distrusted Memnon because of his family connections with his predecessor, Artabazus, who had rebelled against Artaxerxes and fled to Macedonia in 352. Artabazus was a grandson of Artaxerxes II. He had married a sister of Mentor and Memnon, and these two had married in succession Artabazus' daughter, Barsine. Although Mentor was responsible for persuading Artaxerxes III Ochus to pardon Artabazus, neither Ochus nor Darius III restored him to his satrapy. Arsites may have been a member of the same family, but that does not preclude political rivalry.

Why did Alexander move in the direction of the Granicus and the satrapal capital of Dascylium? The simple answer may be that he had learned that the Persian forces had assembled near Zeleia and sought a quick, decisive engagement. But there are other factors to consider as well. By this time, his financial situation was becoming critical – he had left Macedonia twenty days earlier with enough money to maintain the army for thirty days[5] – and it was politically wiser to supply his army from the resources of the Persian satrap than to become a burden on the Greek cities he was claiming to liberate. Furthermore, there was no guarantee that he would win over the Greek cities without costly sieges, and this would aggravate matters. And, finally, he could look forwards to support from the pro-Macedonian city of Cyzicus, which lay east of the Granicus River. Arrian claims that the Persian satraps assembled a force of 20,000 cavalry and an equal number of Greek mercenaries.[6] Mistrusting the Greek infantry, they placed their horsemen on the bank, perhaps in the belief that they could overwhelm the enemy with javelins thrown from an elevated position.[7] But, tactically, the decision was unsound; for the cavalry could now neither charge (unless it chose to fight in the actual stream) nor maneuver, but instead became a stationary unit with little offensive punch. Alexander was quick to exploit the mistake, attacking the enemy even though it was already late in the day.

As was his practice, Alexander stationed the *pezhetairoi* in the center – six battalions comprising 9,000 infantrymen – and deployed the 3,000 hypaspists on their right, with the Macedonian cavalry next to them. On the left wing were the Thessalian and allied cavalry, and, we may assume (although they are not mentioned), the allied and mercenary infantry. The Persians, although they kept the Greek mercenaries in reserve, must have positioned light infantry on the banks as well; for it is inconceivable that they made no use of archers and other skirmishers against the advancing enemy. Alexander countered this formation by sending Amyntas son of Arrhabaeus[8] with a contingent of horsemen and hypaspists against the Persian left. Drawn to the point of attack, they weakened their center, providing Alexander with the opening he sought. The initial attack – military historian A. M. Devine calls it a "pawn sacrifice" – was followed by a more direct attack by Alexander and the remainder of the Companions, followed by the rest of the army, which entered the river *en masse*. Some have questioned whether the *sarissa* might have impeded the advance of the infantry, whose footing must have been precarious. On the other hand, the *sarissa* was the ideal weapon for dislodging the enemy from the banks above, and the advantages must have outweighed the drawbacks. But in the event, the battle was primarily a cavalry struggle, in which the weaponry and the hand-to-hand fighting techniques of the Macedonians prevailed. Once the Persian horse had been routed, the Greek mercenaries, who had been held in reserve, were vulnerable and sought terms of surrender. Alexander, however, meant to make an example of "traitors" and refused to negotiate.[9] A slaughter of the Greeks followed, and only some two thousand were finally spared but sent to hard labor camps in Macedonia.

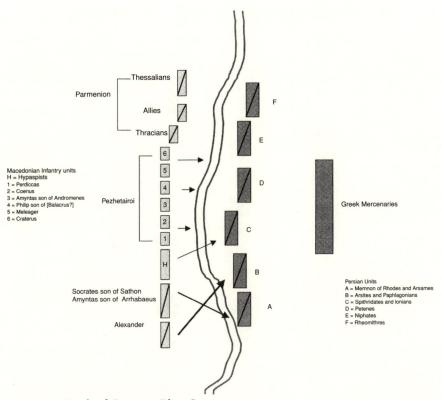

Macedonian Infantry units
H = Hypaspists
1 = Perdiccas
2 = Coenus
3 = Amyntas son of Andromenes
4 = Philip son of [Balacrus?]
5 = Meleager
6 = Craterus

Pezhetairoi

Parmenion
— Thessalians
— Allies
— Thracians

Socrates son of Sathon
Amyntas son of Arrhabaeus

Alexander

Greek Mercenaries

Persian Units
A = Memnon of Rhodes and Arsames
B = Arsites and Paphlagonians
C = Spithridates and Ionians
D = Petenes
E = Niphates
F = Rheomithres

FIGURE 1. *Battle of Granicus: Phase I.*

THE BATTLE OF THE GRANICUS RIVER: HISTORY AS PROPAGANDA

There is considerable disagreement among Alexander historians on the Persians' numbers, their strategy, and the details of the battle itself. Diodorus of Sicily gives an account that differs significantly from those given by Arrian and Plutarch (and even these two are not in perfect agreement). Arrian says the Persian force comprised 20,000 cavalry and 20,000 Greek mercenaries, and that, against the advice of Parmenion, Alexander attacked the enemy although it was already late in the day. Diodorus postpones the attack until the following day, saying that Alexander crossed the river unopposed at dawn and that the battle was fought on the eastern side with the river protecting the Macedonian

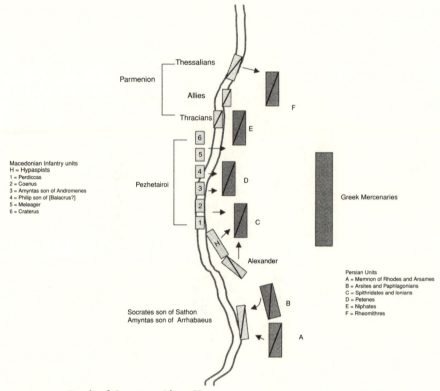

FIGURE 2. *Battle of Granicus: Phase II.*

right and the Persian left. He attributes to the Persians a force of 10,000 cavalry and 100,000 infantry, including some Greek mercenaries. Certain elements in the conflicting versions are simply irreconcilable. From a military standpoint Diodorus' account is implausible. Two points are particularly disturbing. First, how could an army of 40,000 to 50,000 have made an undetected crossing of the river, whether at night or at dawn?[10] Second, even if we accept the argument that Persians trusted more in their cavalry than their infantry, and that their aim was to kill Alexander himself, the Macedonian failure to coordinate the infantry and cavalry (which they did on every other occasion) is inexplicable. Historiographically, Diodorus' narrative contains elements of the "official" version as well as details that are unlikely to be true.[11]

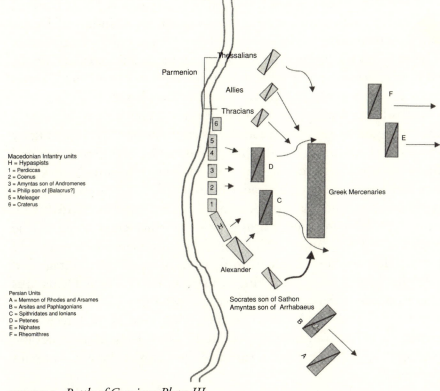

Macedonian Infantry units
H = Hypaspists
1 = Perdiccas
2 = Coenus
3 = Amyntas son of Andromenes
4 = Philip son of [Balacrus?]
5 = Meleager
6 = Craterus

Persian Units
A = Memnon of Rhodes and Arsames
B = Arsites and Paphlagonians
C = Spithridates and Ionians
D = Petenes
E = Niphates
F = Rheomithres

Thessalians
Parmenion
Allies
F
Thracians
6
5
E
4
3 D
2
1
C Greek Mercenaries
H
Alexander
Socrates son of Sathon
Amyntas son of Arrhabaeus
B
A

FIGURE 3. *Battle of Granicus: Phase III.*

The accounts of the battle of the Granicus are, however, uniform in their portrayal of Alexander as the daring and charismatic leader of the Panhellenic crusade. Alexander takes the lead personally in the attack on the Persian enemy. Impatient of delay, he rejects the advice of his experienced general, Parmenion, that they should postpone the attack until the following day and refers to the Granicus as a "mere trickle" compared with the Hellespont, which he has already crossed with great ceremony. What follows is clearly the work of Callisthenes of Olynthus, who proved to be an accomplished propagandist. After a quick survey of the terrain and the deployment of the opposing forces, the focus of the narrative is suddenly on the young king, who charges, as if possessed (*manikôs*), towards the enemy cavalrymen who occupy the riverbank.

Quickly, the account moves from armies in collision to single combat, as Alexander fells with his long spear (*xyston*) a son-in-law of Darius and then turns to deal with another of the Persian leaders, Spithridates. This man too is killed by Alexander, but his brother Rhoesaces is on the verge of striking the king when Cleitus (nicknamed "the Black") severs his arm with a single slash of his curved sword (*kopis*).

Callisthenes is not just selling the war to the Greek allies; he is manufacturing an image. Here is a leader worth following, here are military exploits worth sharing. His youthful impulsiveness becomes a virtue and his brush with death reveals him as the darling of fortune (*tyche*). The Greeks who had accepted his leadership out of fear and compulsion were now treated to a hero laboring on their behalf,[12] one who invited them to become his comrades-in-arms. This is further emphasized by the reference to Demaratus the Corinthian, a prominent Greek supporter of Macedon and the League, who fights in Alexander's entourage and offers his spear (*xyston*) to the king, who has broken his own. Demaratus later reappears at Susa, where he weeps to see Alexander seated on the Great King's throne.[13] By contrast, the punishment of the Greek mercenaries who had sold their services to the Great King underscores the message: enjoy the fame and fortunes of the victor or share the miseries of defeat.[14]

It may also have been Callisthenes who noted that the Thessalian cavalry fought with distinction on the left wing. These were by far the most prominent of Alexander's Greek allies; certainly they are praised again in the accounts of the battle of Issus. That they played a key role in the victory at the Granicus is supported by the Persian casualty list. We are told that Memnon, Arsites, and Arsames survived the battle – they were located on the Persian left wing – and that Alexander, in the center, came to grips with the Lydians, Rhoesaces and Spithridates, as well as Mithridates. But the dead included also Rheomithres, Niphates, and Petenes, who were stationed on the Persian right (see Plans 1–3), and it appears that the Thessalians did heavy damage here before turning the enemy in flight. Arrian's failure to mention the Thessalians may simply be the result of abbreviation, since he does not give a full account of the battle, but rather chooses to focus on Alexander's *aristeia*.[15] On the other hand, his primary source, the Macedonian Ptolemy, may have been less generous in his praise of the allied horsemen.

Alexander's actions after the battle of the Granicus are just as important as the measures he took to win it. In addition to the punishment of the mercenary "traitors," he paid particular attention to the funeral rites of those who fell in battle, and commissioned a group of equestrian statues by Lysippus for the twenty-five Macedonian *hetairoi* who fell – apparently all in the initial attack led by Amyntas son of Arrhabaeus. To the Athenians he sent 300 panoplies with a dedication: "Alexander son of Philip and the Greeks, *except for the Lacedaemonians*, [dedicate these spoils] from the barbarians dwelling in Asia." He could not resist a swipe at the Spartans who had refused to join the League of Corinth.

THE FIRST SIGNS OF A POLICY OF "INCLUSION"

Victory at the Granicus failed to incite widespread defection; for the false start of 336 had made the Greek *poleis* circumspect, and they chose to await, rather than anticipate, the unfolding of events. Nevertheless, Sardis, the satrapal capital of Lydia, was surrendered by Mithrenes. It would have been a difficult city to besiege, possessing strong natural defenses and more likely to succumb to treachery than siege or assault. Alexander retained Mithrenes in his entourage and later appointed him satrap of Armenia, a fact that should not go unobserved, since it shows that from the beginning the king was conscious of the need to rely on Persian officials in the administration of the empire. In Aeolia he established democratic governments – to replace pro-Persian oligarchies – through the agency of Alcimachus (perhaps a brother of Alexander's Bodyguard, Lysimachus). The cities of Miletus and Halicarnassus were, however, taken by siege, though the latter showed far greater resistance. Again the king relied on political measures. The old queen, Ada, who had been ousted from power by her brother Pixodarus, was reinstated as ruler of Caria. Alexander allowed himself to be adopted by her, thus winning the goodwill of the Carians while reserving a claim to the rule of the satrapy for himself. Nevertheless, Ada needed Macedonian military power to secure the citadel of Halicarnassus, which held out until the winter of 334/3.

Though still actively playing the Panhellenic avenger, Alexander opted for a policy of accommodation or "inclusion," his actions clearly modeled on those of Philip II in Greece. Philip had been progressive in his approach to the defeated. He had extended to foreigners the rank of *hetairoi* (Companions), who not only served in roles similar to the *proxenoi* of the Greek states but also served in his army. Demaratus of Corinth, who appears as one of the Companion Cavalry at Granicus, will not have been an exception. Other *hetairoi* had been granted land in Macedonia, and their sons were promoted to high offices in the kingdom, as were the sons of the Thessalian Agathocles or the Mytilenaean Larichus. Philip had also sealed political alliances through marriage or adoption. Alexander was thus far from revolutionary. He simply applied the practices of Philip to his new empire. Instead of integrating Europeans, he did so with barbarians, though, in the early years, this was done with caution. Mithrenes received no political office until 331, and Ada was, after all, the aunt of the younger Ada, whom Philip had planned to marry to the mentally deficient Arrhidaeus. Alexander recognized that there were many fronts on which war could be fought. It was not until later that he also learned that conflicting policies confused and alienated his own supporters.

It is an interesting coincidence that, just as Alexander showed the first signs of orientalism, his official propaganda would make use of a Persian image. In the winter of 334/3 the Macedonian army was able to round Mt Climax on the seashore only because the sea had withdrawn. Callisthenes depicted this as an act of obeisance. The sea was performing *proskynesis* as for one who was destined to be Great King of Asia. This was deliberate borrowing from Xenophon's *Anabasis*, where it was alleged that the waters of the Euphrates at Thapsacus had receded to allow Cyrus' men to cross, as if it were doing *proskynesis* for the future king.[16] Readers would have recognized the parallel instantly, and they would have approved. After all, it was an omen of barbarian submission. Later, when Greeks and Macedonians were asked to perform *proskynesis*, the idea was less appealing.

As a final gesture, intended to promote the goodwill of the men and sell the Panhellenic campaign, Alexander sent those Macedonians who had recently married – including the officers Coenus, Meleager, and Ptolemy son of Seleucus – back to Macedonia for the winter. They would rejoin the army at Gordium in the following spring, bringing fresh recruits. Coenus' brother, Cleander, had been sent to the Peloponnese that same winter and returned with allied reinforcements. Success is a powerful recruiting tool. When the campaign recommenced in 333, most of western Asia Minor was in Macedonian hands, administered by Alexander's satraps and garrisoned by his troops. The modest aims of earlier Greek expeditions had already been attained, and the army had yet to confront Darius in person.

First Winter in Asia (334/3 bc)

During the winter of 334/3, the Macedonians who had been left behind in Phrygia with Parmenion arrested a Persian agent named Sisines. He had been sent by the chiliarch Nabarzanes to the Phrygian satrap Atizyes, not knowing that the latter had been forced to flee his satrapy. When he was apprehended Sisines was carrying a letter to Alexander the Lyncestian, offering him handsome rewards if he assassinated the Macedonian king. The agent and his letter were sent to the king, who was at this time at Phaselis. After interrogating Sisines – in all likelihood the Persian knew a smattering of Greek, for he had spent a period in exile in Macedonia during Philip's reign – Alexander sent Amphoterus, brother of the reliable Craterus, in disguise to Parmenion's camp with orders that the old general arrest the Lyncestian.

Alexander Lyncestes, it will be recalled, had not shared the fate of his brothers, Arrhabaeus and Heromenes, who were executed on the charge of complicity in the murder of Philip II. The evidence against them is not given by the sources, and it is possible that there was little. Their links with a rival faction and, perhaps, support of the claims of Amyntas son of Perdiccas (III) were sufficient to require their elimination. Alexander Lyncestes, however, was the son-in-law of Antipater and had been the first to declare his namesake king, no doubt on Antipater's advice. This not only saved his life, but also gained him the generalship (*strategia*) of Thrace in 336. This important official would have been subordinate to the regent of Macedon in Alexander's absence, and the king appears to have had second thoughts about the wisdom of leaving too much power in Antipater's hands. Instead he was replaced by a certain Memnon and taken on the expedition to Asia as one of the king's Friends (*hetairoi*). But, when the satrapy of Hellespontine Phrygia was given to Calas son of Harpalus, the king appointed Alexander Lyncestes to the now-vacant office of hipparch of the Thessalian cavalry. In this capacity, he was capable of doing great damage – perhaps even turning the tide of battle – if he chose to defect at a critical stage of a battle with Darius.[17] Hence, any contact with the enemy (whether he had initiated it or not) was treated as high treason. The Lyncestian's connections with Antipater, many of whose adherents were prominent in the army and in the new administration of Asia Minor, saved him from immediate execution, and he was kept in chains awaiting the king's pleasure.

For the king it was a timely reminder that the festering problems that accompanied, or even caused, the death of his father endured. The Macedonian nobility, which controlled the vital posts in the army, was a network of kinsmen by blood and marriage and a breeding ground for future conspiracy. A Macedonian king ignored the wishes or complaints of the nobles at his own peril, and each arrest brought realignments within the aristocracy, new allies, and new political enemies. Amyntas son of Arrhabaeus was of particular concern. His father was doubtless the convicted regicide, his uncle the now-incarcerated Alexander, and one of his brothers a defector to the Persian cause. His last attested military action was at Sagalassus in Pisidia soon after his uncle's arrest.[18] What became of him, we do not know, and we may attribute his disappearance to more than mere chance.

THE SECOND YEAR OF CAMPAIGNING

Gordium in central Anatolia provided what we would today call a convenient "photo op." The famous Gordian knot, virtually unknown before Alexander's invasion, offered too great a publicity stunt to be ignored. According to the prophecy, whoever undid the complicated knot which secured the yoke to the wagon of Midas (or his father, Gordius) was destined to become "ruler of Asia." By ancient usage, this must have referred only to Asia Minor, though it soon came to take on greater meaning. The intricacies of the knot confounded even the king, and failure would have been construed as a bad omen. But Alexander, with a degree of cynicism, drew his sword and slashed through the thongs. There was, after all, no specific requirement that it be "untied." Those who so chose considered the prophecy fulfilled. Others, like the historian Aristobulus, denied the story and claimed that Alexander had removed a pin that held the loops of the knot together.[19] For Alexander it was sufficient to have averted failure. The man who on other occasions was alleged to have been motivated by a sense of fair play had no compunctions about doing what was expedient.

With Celaenae and Phrygia secured by Antigonus the One-Eyed (who was to become a major player in the wars of the Successors but destined never to see Alexander again), the Macedonian army moved towards Cappadocia, only to turn south to the Cilician Gates. By now, Darius had begun to move his forces from Babylonia, expecting to confront the enemy on the plains of northern Mesopotamia. But Alexander was delayed by illness near Tarsus and then by the need to secure the Cilician coast. When the two armies met, on the narrow shores of the Gulf of Issus, it was not according to a set plan but in a hastily improvised encounter.

EXILES AND *CONDOTTIERI*

Despite the campaigns of Darius I and Xerxes, and Panhellenic propaganda, much of which developed in the days of the Athenian Empire,[20] the gulf between Greeks and Persians was not as great as one might think. The leader of the Greek alliance against Persia, Themistocles, later sought refuge with the Great King and was given the revenues from three cities to maintain himself. Pausanias, the victor of Plataea, had likewise intrigued with Xerxes. And, in the fourth century, there were Persian exiles to be found at the court of Philip II[21] and Greek mercenary adventurers in the service of both rebel satraps and the Great King himself. The Greek powers and their Macedonian successors had recognized the value of supporting rebels against the Persian King, and the mercenaries and their leaders were willing to fight for either side, as long as they were guaranteed wages. In spite of the treachery of

Tissaphernes and the perils of the Ten Thousand, Greek mercenaries, most of them political exiles, continued to serve in the East, often fighting against armies that included substantial contingents of their own kind.[22] Between 366 and 360, a coalition of rebels conducted the so-called Great Satraps' Revolt, placing great reliance on Greek mercenaries and military leaders from the Greek mainland. But the satraps were as venal as the soldiers they hired and soon betrayed one another and again submitted to the authority of the Great King.

One of the leading men caught up in the confusion of the satrapal revolt was Artabazus, a son of Pharnabazus and Apame (daughter of Artaxerxes II), whose family had long administered Hellespontine Phrygia. Artabazus had married a sister of the Rhodian *condottieri*, Mentor and Memnon, and fathered nine sons and eleven daughters, many of whom were to play prominent roles in the history of Alexander. At some point around 352, he and his family sought refuge with Philip II in Pella, and it was perhaps during their extended sojourn there that Alexander first became acquainted with Barsine, who was destined to become his mistress in 333/2. It was through the agency of Mentor, who served Artaxerxes as commander of the coastal region, that Artabazus and his family were pardoned. When Mentor died at some time after 340, his mercenary forces at least were entrusted to his brother Memnon. Hence, in 336, when the advance force under Parmenion and Attalus crossed into Hellespontine Phrygia, Memnon led the forces sent to dislodge them. Though he was outnumbered, perhaps two to one, he was able to keep the Macedonian force in check. When Alexander himself invaded Asia in 334, Memnon appears to have been little more than a Greek mercenary captain.

The defeat at the Granicus left the defense of western Asia Minor in the hands of Memnon the Rhodian and his Persian relatives. The most prominent of the satraps and the Great King's kinsmen perished in the engagement or committed suicide soon afterward. When the attempts to hold Miletus and Halicarnassus proved futile, Memnon and Pharnabazus turned their attention to the Aegean islands, with a view to spreading counter-revolution and creating an uprising in Greece behind Alexander's back. That diversion was aided initially by the disbanding of the League's fleet under the command of Nicanor. Nevertheless, a small fleet under Proteas defeated a squadron of ten Phoenician ships led by Datames in the Cyclades. As security for his own office, Memnon sent his wife and children to Darius as hostages;[23] they were subsequently captured at Damascus, along with other prominent Persians. How effective Memnon was in his new role is difficult to determine. Certainly he did win back some Greek cities for Persia, if only temporarily, but he died of illness in early 333.[24] The statement that Darius pinned all his hopes on the efforts of Memnon may contain an element of truth, but allowances must be made for the bias of Greek historians.

Others members of the Artabazus clan continued to resist Alexander, especially Thymondas son of Mentor and Artabazus' own son Pharnabazus. The former would soon bring mercenaries to Darius at Issus (i.e., Sochi) and the latter was destined to become Memnon's successor in the Aegean sphere of operations. They were joined also by exiles from Macedonia: Neoptolemus son of Arrhabaeus, who died in the fighting at Halicarnassus, and Amyntas son of Antiochus, who must have gone first to Memnon before joining Darius at Sochi and fighting at Issus. To these we may add some other Greek mercenary captains. Charidemus of Oreus, who had fought against Philip II and earned Athenian citizenship, sought refuge with the Great King after Alexander's sack of Thebes; he was the one implacable enemy of Macedon with whom Alexander could not be reconciled.[25] At that time, Chares and Ephialtes also joined the resistance to Macedon in Asia Minor. Two other notable mercenary leaders, Bianor and Aristomedes, appear to have served in Asia for some time before the invasion of 334.[26] Patron the Phocian and Glaucus the Aetolian appear as prominent mercenary captains during Darius' final retreat, but we do not know much about their backgrounds or if they chose to fight for Persia for anything more than financial gain.

BATTLE OF ISSUS (333)

Darius' decision to enter Cilicia and place himself astride the Macedonian lines of communication, although it caused Alexander momentary anxiety, was tactically unsound. Rightly had his Greek advisers — whether it was Charidemus or Amyntas son of Antiochus who counseled him to remain in Mesopotamia – urged him to fight on ground that allowed him to deploy his greatest asset, his numbers, particularly the large contingents of cavalry. Instead the Persians found themselves on terrain restricted on the one side by mountains and on the other by the sea (the Gulf of Issus). Alexander's prolonged inactivity – some of which was attributable to illness – was mistaken by Darius for cowardice, or at least diffidence. And we should not be fooled by hindsight into thinking that Alexander's victory was a foregone conclusion. In fact, the Persians had realistic expectations of victory, and even in the Macedonian camp there were some who questioned Alexander's prospects.

We are told that, when Alexander was at Mallus, he learned that Darius was on the plains of Sochi with his army. Upon hearing the news, he hurried south, traveling through Castabulum and Issus and past the Pillar of Jonah.[27] It was clear that he was hastening towards Syria and a confrontation with the Persians. Darius, meanwhile, believing that Alexander was avoiding battle, crossed the Amanus range (Bahçe Pass) and took possession of Issus. Here, it was claimed by Alexander's propagandists, they killed and mutilated the Macedonian prisoners. And they were now securely established in the Macedonian rear. It was only when he reached Myriandrus that Alexander discovered the true position of Darius' army, and then only because he had been delayed by bad weather. Otherwise, there might have resulted a farcical situation in which Alexander arrived in Sochi only to discover that his enemy was now in Cilicia. News of the Persian march forced the Macedonians to return to the narrows that led back into Cilicia. On the following morning, they marched out against the enemy, who had now taken up a position on the Pinarus River. Alexander brought his army forwards in a marching column until the terrain allowed him to deploy the various units in a battle line. Neither side had the option of riding around the wings of the other. In order to take the enemy in the flank the wings would have to be destroyed.

The identification of the Pinarus River is a much-debated and seemingly insoluble problem. The Deli Çay appears to be too far north of Myriandrus for Alexander to have reached it in time to do battle before sunset;[28] its banks present no significant obstacles and the battlefield

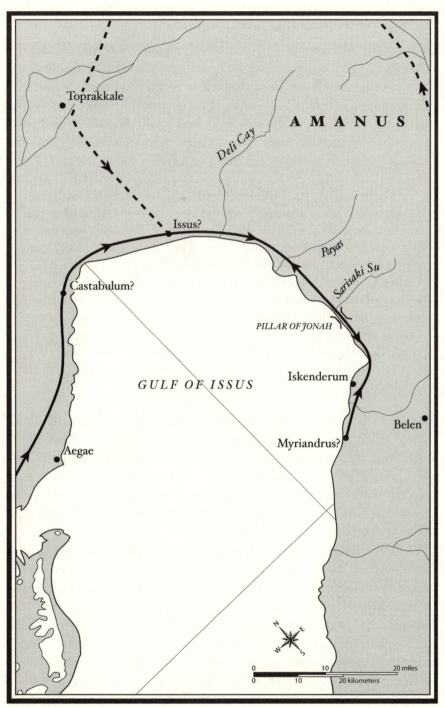

TOPRAKKALE

AMANUS

Deli Cay

Issus?

Payas

Castabulum?

Sarisaki Su

PILLAR OF JONAH

GULF OF ISSUS

Iskenderum

Belen

Aegae

Myriandrus?

N
W E
S

0   10   20 miles
0   10   20 kilometers

MAP 6. *Gulf of Issus.*

from the hills to the sea extends some 6 kilometers, more than double the 14 stades (2.5 km) estimated by the eyewitness historian, Callisthenes.[29] On the other hand, the Payas (which is favored by many scholars)[30] offers some 4 kilometers of battle frontage and obstacles that would make a cavalry attack of the sort described by the Alexander historians impossible. Perhaps the most likely location is the Kuru Çay. It is worth quoting the observations of the intrepid traveler, Freya Stark:

> The Deli Chay has been identified with Pinarus, where the battle was fought; and I rather wondered why the more southerly Kuru Chay had not been chosen, giving as it does a ten- instead of fifteen-mile march between the start at dawn and the opening of the battle, and crossing the plain at a slightly narrower place, more like the fourteen hundred [sic] stadia of Polybius. This measurement, I take it, refers to the narrowest section of the plain, which widens with every torrent that pours out of its defile in the range. This opening and shutting of the ground explains Darius' maneuver. He stationed about twenty thousand men on the ridge "that opened here and there to some depth and had, in fact, bays like the sea; and, bending outwards again, brought those posted on the heights to the rear of Alexander's wing."[31]

The main disadvantage of the Kuru Çay is that it amounts to little more than a trickle today (which may not reflect the conditions of antiquity) and scarcely deserves the term *potamos* ("river"). On the other hand, it is a suitable distance from the Pillar of Jonah and from Issus to constitute a decent day's march from either direction, very close to Callisthenes' estimate of 14 stades in width from hills to sea, and suitable for the type of battle described by the sources.

Despite the limitations of terrain, Darius deployed his forces in a way that best suited the topography. He was prepared to await the Macedonian infantry attack on the north side of the river, which today, as in antiquity, forms a rocky bed and uneven ground that would be disruptive for soldiers advancing in formation, especially those wielding eighteen-foot sarissas.[32] Where the ground was smoother, he constructed a palisade, presumably an abatis. On his right wing, by the sea, Darius massed his horsemen, a move which forced Alexander to transfer the Thessalian cavalry behind the infantry lines to his own left. And, indeed, there was hard fighting on that wing before the breakthrough on the right decided the engagement. In the center, the *pezhetairoi* confronted the Greek mercenaries, flanked on each side by barbarian troops known as the *Kardakes*,[33] and on Alexander's right certain Persian units had infiltrated the hills, intending to strike at the Macedonian flank. Isolated by some of the Agrianes and the light horsemen, these were compelled to remain little more than spectators.

The battle plan followed what was to become a familiar refrain: the infantry fixed with their impenetrable wall of sarissas the enemy center, while the cavalry on the left wing played a defensive role. With the Companions on the right, Alexander attempted to overpower the opposing flank and drive into the middle, where Darius himself was located. But in this battle topography was to play its part. The hypaspists and the first two units of the phalanx strained to keep touch with the cavalry as it surged ahead, and a gap occurred to the right of the Tymphaean *taxis* commanded by Ptolemy son of Seleucus at exactly the point where the terrain was most difficult. Here it was that the heaviest Macedonian losses occurred: some 120 notables and Ptolemy himself fell in this part of the engagement, where there was a particularly violent clash between Greeks and Macedonians.[34] Although the *Kardakes* on the Persian left were easily rolled up by the charging Companions and hypaspists, the Greek mercenaries exploited the gap and inflicted casualties on the phalangites. But, by this time, Alexander had routed the Persian left and pushed hard upon the Greeks in the center. Darius, seeing that his line was broken, turned to flee, sending panic throughout the army and even the cavalry on his right, who up to now were holding their own in a fierce struggle with the Thessalian and allied horse. The Great King's brother, Oxyathres, is depicted as fighting valiantly, his courage serving unintentionally to highlight the perceived cowardice of Darius. In truth, the Persian king had little choice, and capture on the battlefield might have brought the war to a sudden conclusion, but his flight and his abandonment of his own family in the camp were grist for the propaganda mills.[35]

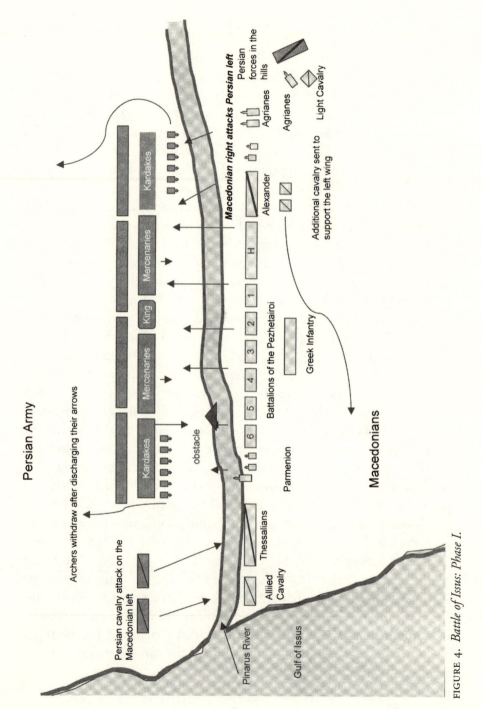

Persian Army

Macedonians

FIGURE 4. *Battle of Issus: Phase I.*

62

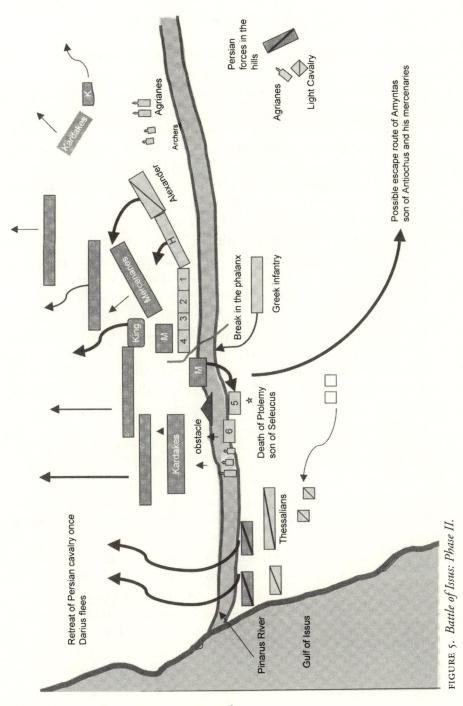

Retreat of Persian cavalry once Darius flees

Pinarus River

Gulf of Issus

Thessalians

Death of Ptolemy son of Seleucus

obstacle

Kardakes

King

M

M

4 | 3 | 2 | 1

Break in the phalanx

Greek infantry

Mercenaries

Alexander

H

Kardakes

K

Agrianes

Archers

Persian forces in the hills

Agrianes

Light Cavalry

Possible escape route of Amyntas son of Antiochus and his mercenaries

5

6

FIGURE 5. *Battle of Issus: Phase II.*

As a rule, Persian emperors did not die on the battlefield – the dynasty's founder, Cyrus the Great, killed by the Massagetae in 530, is the notable exception[36] – but their presence was seemingly required to inspire the troops. Xenophon reported that they occupied a position in the center in the belief that this was both the safest place and the best suited for sending instructions to either wing.[37] Nevertheless, the presence of the Great King could also be a liability, since he became the focal point of the battle. The younger Cyrus had moved directly against his brother at Cunaxa in an attempt to win the battle by killing the king. Although it was Cyrus who was slain, the strategy was employed by Alexander at both Issus and Gaugamela.[38] By jeopardizing Darius' safety and forcing him to flee, Alexander could win a speedy victory and bring about the collapse of Persian resistance. Troops who were holding their own, or even overpowering their opponents, abandoned the field once they learned of their king's flight. Hence, Alexander sought to overcome Darius before his forces were enveloped by the superior Persian numbers.

Despite the loss of men and territory, the military defeat at Issus had not been crippling – for which reason several scholars have argued that Alexander should have followed up his victory by pursuing the king into the interior of the empire – but the capture of his family in the abandoned camp was both a personal blow and a political embarrassment. Eastern rulers regularly took their women with them on campaign.[39] The origins of this practice may have been varied – perhaps concerns about usurpers legitimizing their claims through levirate marriage caused them to keep their women with them[40] – but it appears that by the fourth century the primary concern was the projection of the royal image. Even on the battlefield, or rather particularly in such an instance, the king needed to be seen in all his splendor. Just as in his royal chariot he stood out amongst the warriors, so too in the camp his royal tent represented the palace with the court in attendance and all the trappings of royalty on display. To Greek writers it was a sign of decadence that Persian kings and satraps could not do without the luxuries attendant upon wealth and power. But they clearly misunderstood the vital role of symbols and protocol. Although the women and the possessions of other notables were sent to Damascus for safe-keeping, the presence of Darius' family near the battlefield expressed a confidence, either real or feigned, that the king wished to convey to his army. In retrospect, we may be tempted to view Darius as vainglorious and deluded, and to dismiss him as a braggart whose actions on the battlefield failed to match his bluster. Darius too must have known the outcome of Cunaxa, which could have been nothing but encouraging.

Defeat and flight made captives of the king's mother, wife, and daughters, as well as of his young son, Ochus. These were treated with kindness and respect by the conqueror – although the relationship between Alexander and Darius' wife, the elder Stateira, was perhaps not quite as the propagandists made it out to be. The Great King's family would remain in the Macedonian camp as hostages: that they were not ransomed at the first opportunity merely attests to their value and the high stakes that were involved. Furthermore, after the battle, Parmenion had been sent ahead to capture a treasure of over 3,000 talents and the families of Persian notables, whom Darius had left (as if in safe hands) in Damascus, among them three daughters of the former king, Artaxerxes III, and Memnon's widow, Barsine, who was destined to become Alexander's mistress.[41]

PERSIAN NAVAL POWER

Recently, several scholars have argued that Alexander's failure to pursue Darius eastward was a strategic error. Alexander should have hunted the Achaemenid king down before he was able to field another army. But this strategy fails to take into account the threat of the Persian fleet and the danger of extending the lines of communication and supply. Alexander's decision to turn south and secure the Phoenician coast is entirely consistent with his strategy of defeating the Persian navy by land. Ever since he disbanded the allied fleet at Miletus, it had been Alexander's plan to destroy Persian naval power by seizing the ports of the Aegean and eastern Mediterranean. Ancient ships could not operate far from land, nor could they remain at sea for a long time, for they carried limited supplies of food and water. Long periods at sea also caused them to become waterlogged, which decreased their speed and maneuverability. But the real weakness of the Persian fleet was its composition. It was made up entirely of ships and rowers from subject states, often, as in the case of the Phoenicians, commanded by their local kings or members of the royal families. Hence, by securing the coastal cities, Alexander encouraged the Persian allies to defect, thus weakening the fleet and adding to the Macedonian military strength. Some of the crews from Asia Minor may have decided to continue the struggle, for there were still large numbers of Greeks who opposed Alexander, but the defection of the Phoenician and Cypriote kings was decisive. Furthermore, the destruction of the Persian fleet would all but put an end to communication between the resistance in Asia Minor and the disaffected in Greece, primarily the Spartans. And it would limit the transfer of Greek mercenaries to Asia to fight for Darius. The conquest of the coast, from Cilicia to Egypt, was thus vital to the security of the Macedonian forces and the speedy conclusion of the war.

The first stages of the program were relatively easy. The northern cities were quick to recognize Alexander as their new overlord, bringing the conqueror crowns of gold. At Sidon, Straton son of Tennes[42] was deposed by Alexander for his pro-Persian leanings and replaced with a scion of the royal house named Abdalonymus. But the Tyrians, trusting in their location, refused Alexander access to their city. His claim that he wished to sacrifice to Melqart, whom the Greeks equated with Heracles, was a transparent ploy, and similar to the one used by Philip II in his campaign against Atheas the Scythian; the Tyrians told him he could do so at the temple of Melqart in Palaetyrus (Old Tyre) on the mainland. Sacrificing to Melqart in the new city was the prerogative of the Tyrian king, and Alexander was effectively asking for recognition as such. This would have meant only that Azemilcus (or someone appointed in his place) would be forced to accept Alexander as his overlord. That Alexander was ignorant of the implications, as Ulrich Wilcken suggests, strikes me as implausible. If no one else, his new Sidonian friends would have alerted him to the custom and its implications.[43]

The Tyrians hoped to become independent of both Persia and Macedon by becoming a neutral, open city. This was something Alexander could not countenance. But the siege of Tyre was more than a test of wills, an indication that Alexander would not let anyone stand up against him. It was a simple strategic necessity. History offers a splendid parallel from the age of the Crusaders. It was the ability of the Latins to keep control of Tyre, when Saladin had rolled up the Crusader forces and overwhelmed their castles after the disaster at the Horns of Hattin (1187), that ensured the survival of the Crusader states for another century. Not without reason was Conrad of Montferrat, who held the city, called the savior of the Latin East.[44] It was the best port in the eastern Mediterranean and a vital link with the west. In Alexander's time, the Tyrians were also able to call upon the Carthaginians in time of need. Ironically, the siege of Tyre best illustrates the effectiveness and importance of Alexander's maritime policy.

THE SIEGE OF TYRE (JANUARY–JULY/AUGUST 332)[45]

The new city was situated on an island half a mile offshore, and its 2.75-mile circuit of walls extended to a height of 150 feet. These would have to be reached and assaulted by a force that, at the time, was deficient in naval power. Alexander had commissioned a new fleet, but it was fighting under the direction of Amphoterus and Hegelochus in the Aegean. The Tyrians, on the other hand, although they had contributed to the Persian fleet, still retained some eighty triremes in their two island harbors: the Sidonian harbor, which faced north, and the Egyptian harbor, sited somewhat to the southeast. Hence, Alexander's first option was to construct a mole directly westward towards the city, using the stones from Old Tyre as well as timber from the neighboring forests. As laborers he impressed natives of the coastal region, though clearly many of the soldiers themselves were forced to help with the work. But the building would have to be done in full view of the enemy, and within range of their catapults and missiles. Artillery mounted on the city's walls was supplemented by that on board the Tyrian ships, and the Macedonians were forced to construct siege-towers to defend the workers and return fire against the walls and down upon approaching ships. Nevertheless, the defenders were tireless and imaginative, sending smaller craft to attack the workmen, divers to undermine the stability of the causeway, and a fireship to destroy the Macedonian towers.

The deciding factor in Alexander's siege of Tyre, despite the brilliant work of his engineers and the Herculean labor expended on the mole, which was widened to 200 feet and soon sported new siege-towers that matched the height of the Tyrian walls, was the acquisition of a substantial naval force. In the aftermath of Issus, the surrender of the Phoenician cities had led to a wholesale defection of the Phoenicians and Cypriotes from the Persian fleet. At Sidon, Alexander was able to collect 224 ships,[46] with which he could not only conduct a blockade of Tyre and its harbors but also attack the more vulnerable portions of the city walls. For although the mole progressed steadily towards the island – despite the depth of the water, which reached three fathoms – the opposing walls were at that point impervious to battering rams, having been reinforced by a second wall. Furthermore, the defenders were able to concentrate all their attention and firepower on the assault force on the mole. The addition of a naval force thus heightened the odds of success and added to the consternation of the Tyrians. Using rams mounted on ships – often two ships were lashed together and supported a superstructure to protect the rams and their operators – Alexander was able to create a breach in another sector. Landing ramps, similar to the "crows" later used by the Romans against Carthaginian ships, were lowered to allow the hypaspists and members of Coenus' battalion to enter the city. Thus was ended the siege, which was at the time in its seventh month.[47]

The ensuing slaughter was mitigated only by the Sidonians, who spirited many of the Tyrians away to the safety of their ships. For Alexander it was not only a warning to others who might contemplate resistance (some 2,000 of the captured men were crucified), but also a reward for his men who had labored long and suffered much in the months of siege. Some 6,000–8,000 Tyrians died during the actual fighting; a further 30,000 are said to have been sold into slavery, and as many as 15,000 may have been saved by their fellow Phoenicians.[48] King Azemilcus and the notables of the city took refuge in the temple of Heracles (Melqart) and were pardoned by Alexander.

The punishment meted out to the Tyrians appears to have had little impact on the population of Gaza, or at least on the garrison which chose to resist. Gaza was a rich city, situated at the end of the southern trade route (some 160 miles south of Tyre), and inhabited by a people ethnically different from the Phoenicians.[49] Built on a *tel*, or mound, some 250 feet high, the fortifications of the city were difficult to assault or mine. Indeed, simply getting there was a feat in itself, since water for the army was scarce – with few rivers of any size – and had to be provided by the fleet. Supplying the army with water was easier on the march than when it had settled down for the siege.[50] Here it was that Alexander's closest friend, Hephaestion son of Amyntor, made the first of his recorded contributions to the campaign: not only did he convey the siege-engines from Tyre on twenty Athenian ships (which had been retained after the dispersal of the allied fleet) but also he must have served as the king's quartermaster-general, perhaps the only military office for which he was truly suited.[51]

What induced the Gazeans to hold out when the other Palestinian centers capitulated is unclear. It is perhaps simplistic to explain the stubborn resistance of the city in terms of the unfailing loyalty of its commandant, the eunuch Batis, and to suppose that he trusted too much in the natural and manmade defenses of the city. We are told that the place held a large Persian force, supplemented by Arab mercenaries, and that Batis had stockpiled provisions with a view to withstanding a siege. In all probability, this was part of a larger defensive strategy put in place by Darius after the disaster at Issus. There has been a tendency to depict Darius as a broken man after Issus, reduced to negotiating a settlement with Alexander in order to recover his family and prepared to cede vast portions of the empire to the invader. In fact, although Darius was desperate to ransom his family, he was not prepared to offer any more than he had already lost and was determined not to lose any more territory before the negotiations were completed. So much was clear to his opponent as well. Instead, the Persian king was counting on delaying tactics and counterstrikes in the West to buy him time until he could assemble another army.[52]

After Issus, Persian forces moved into Anatolia, intent on recovering lost territory there, while Pharnabazus and the fleet commanders were doing their best to aid the defiant Spartan king, Agis III. At least 4,000

Greek mercenaries who escaped from Issus joined Agis, and a similar number had turned south to Egypt. This force, led by Amyntas son of Antiochus, went first to Tripolis to acquire ships for transport and then, having destroyed those they could not use, sailed to Cyprus in search of new recruits and, it is reasonable to assume, funds for the continuation of the campaign. Thereafter they sailed to Pelusium in Egypt, and it is not unlikely that they made a stop at Gaza to report, and likewise get an update on the affairs of the Persian king. His whereabouts were kept strictly secret, but it is likely that his satraps, generals, and garrison-commanders had instructions to hold out against the invader. Amyntas is depicted as a soldier of fortune whose only motivation in going to Egypt was to take advantage of Darius' misfortunes and enrich himself. But it may well be that he was speaking the truth when he declared that he had been sent to hold Egypt in lieu of the satrap Sauaces, who had been killed at Issus.

Our interpretation of Amyntas' activities depends, to some extent, on the manner in which he escaped from the battlefield of Issus. Clearly Amyntas and his mercenaries did not retreat with Darius – considering their position in the battle line this would have been virtually impossible – but fled to the hills and from there to Tripolis.[53] Hence, one might argue that in the future they acted without consulting Darius. Contrary to the generally accepted view, Amyntas' contingent escaped through the gap that formed in the phalanx, and where the heaviest Macedonian casualties occurred, and followed the coastal road via Myriandrus (see Plan 5).[54] Hence they must have moved quickly, or else stealthily through the hills, to avoid Parmenion's force (which included the Thessalian cavalry), which was sent, probably on the following day, to capture Damascus. Arrian reports that Alexander did not pursue Darius until after the mercenaries had been driven back from the river,[55] but if these mercenaries included Amyntas' group it is hard to see how they could have escaped to the hills, since the area to their left would now have been closed off by two battalions of *pezhetairoi* and the hypaspists. Nevertheless, Darius may have given the mercenaries further instructions once he learned of their escape to Tripolis or Cyprus. Fugitives from Macedonia must have believed that their cause was better served by Persian victory than by independent action.

At Gaza, Alexander set about constructing a ramp leading up to the city, which as an undertaking did not rank far behind the building of the mole at Tyre. The difficulty of building a ramp to a height of 250 feet was complicated by the fact that the city was surrounded by deep and loose sand, which caused the wheeled siege-equipment to bog down. On the other hand, when the Macedonians finally did reach the walls, the nature of the terrain actually helped with the sapping of the walls. But just as the single mole at Tyre had allowed the defenders to concentrate on a narrow front, so the ramp at Gaza proved insufficient, and Alexander was forced to build ramps surrounding the fortress. A complete build-up of earthwork around the city was almost certainly impossible in the two months that the siege consumed, and it is more likely that Alexander built a number of ramps to allow him to attack from different directions simultaneously. Three times the walls were breached before the city could be taken, and in the assault, Neoptolemus, a kinsman of Alexander on his mother's side, distinguished himself. He would not go unrewarded, for in 330, when Nicanor son of Parmenion died of illness, Neoptolemus assumed command of the hypaspists, the infantry guard.

EGYPT

In Egypt Alexander met with no resistance, and it appears that in Memphis he was recognized as the legitimate successor of the Pharaohs. The ease with which he gained control of the country is explained both by its long history of opposition to Persian rule and by the chaotic conditions in Egypt in 332. Originally conquered in 525 by Cambyses, son of Cyrus the Great,[56] Egypt remained a satrapy of the Persian Empire until the rebellion of the Libyan prince Inarus in 461. This uprising was soon crushed by Persian forces, despite support for the rebels from the Athenian fleet operating in the eastern Mediterranean. Inarus was captured and crucified, and Persian domination reaffirmed. But after the death of Darius II, the Egyptians rebelled again and this time maintained their independence until they were defeated by Artaxerxes III in 343. The last Pharaoh of the Thirtieth Dynasty, Nectanebo, fled to Nubia, although a tradition, which found expression in the form of the *Alexander Romance*, claimed that he sought refuge at the Macedonian court, seduced Philip's wife Olympias in the guise of the ram-headed god, Amun, and fathered on her Alexander. Hence, Alexander returned to Egypt in 332 not as conqueror but as the country's rightful ruler.[57]

When the Persian satrap Sauaces died at Issus and the fortunes of Darius were in decline, Mazaces, who had been left behind to administer the satrapy, must have decided to recognize the supremacy of Alexander. The Egyptians could not be forced to remain loyal to Persia, as was clear from the revolt of Chababash[58] at the time of Darius' accession and their rejection of Amyntas son of Antiochus and his mercenaries, who may have hoped to preserve Egypt for Darius. Alexander's capture of Gaza and march to Pelusium settled the question once and for all. Some modern scholars have debated whether Alexander was actually crowned in Memphis, but the fact remains that he was depicted as Pharaoh on Egyptian monuments and his name appears in a royal cartouche, accompanied by the titles "son of Ra," "beloved of Amun," and "Lord of the Two Lands."[59]

From Memphis Alexander sailed to the canopic mouth of the Nile, where he put plans in motion for the founding of the city of Alexandria, destined to be the second city of the Mediterranean after Rome. He then marched with some of his forces to the Oasis of Siwah, near the Qattara Depression, where the oracle of Amun-Re was located. The Greeks had long been familiar with the oracle and the god, whom they equated with Zeus. Alexander's visit to the oracle has been the subject of controversy from the very first. What was its purpose? Was it merely to gain confirmation of his legitimacy as Pharaoh by gaining the sanction of the priests at Siwah? Or was Alexander intent upon being recognized as a god? If the latter, then one wonders why he took so long to exploit the oracular utterance, and why, according to a number of anecdotes, he ridiculed the notion that he was divine.[60] Cambyses' allegedly disastrous expedition to Siwah shows that he too thought it necessary to gain recognition as Amun's son.[61] Furthermore, it soon became clear to Alexander that his Macedonians found the purported divinity of their king objectionable. Hence, we may assume that the gesture was directed entirely at the Egyptians.

More interesting is the question Alexander put to the high priest concerning the punishment of his father's murderers. This may have been little more than a clever ploy: by seeming to be concerned about his filial duties towards Philip, the king receives the unexpected (or so it would seem) news that his true father is Amun. But perhaps Alexander was also looking for an opportunity to bring closure to the purge of his Macedonian enemies, thereby reducing tensions within the army. The last of the regicides may have been Amyntas son of Antiochus, who perished earlier. He had been associated with Amyntas (IV), son of Perdiccas III, whom Alexander had killed at some point before the Theban campaign. Alexander the Lyncestian, brother of the convicted regicides, Arrhabaeus and Heromenes, had also been in custody for two years (unless Diodorus is right in placing his arrest shortly before the battle of Issus).[62] Nevertheless there remained men such as Hegelochus son of Hippostratus, a relative of Alexander's bitter enemy, Attalus, who held important offices in the Macedonian army and were both the object of suspicion and themselves fearful of reprisals.[63]

FAILURE OF NEGOTIATIONS

Since the capture of his family on the battlefield of Issus, Darius had attempted to settle affairs by diplomacy. Although the sources disagree on the number of exchanges between the two kings, there is a logic of sorts in the version provided by Curtius. The initial offer, which involved only the ransoming of Darius' family and no territorial concessions, reached the Macedonian camp at Marathus. This was rudely rejected, but the arguments of Alexander's letter were clearly intended for his Greco-Macedonian audience, for it reaffirmed the underlying principles of the expedition.

> King Alexander to Darius: Greetings. The Darius whose name you have assumed wrought utter destruction upon the Greek inhabitants of the Hellespontine coast and upon the Greek colonies of Ionia, and then crossed the sea with a mighty army, bringing war to Macedonia and Greece. On another occasion Xerxes, a member of the same family, came with his savage barbarian troops, and even when beaten in a naval engagement he still left Mardonius in Greece so that he could destroy our cities and burn our fields though absent himself. Everyone knows that my father, Philip, was murdered by assassins whom your people had seduced with the expectation of a huge Persian reward. The wars you

Persians undertake are unholy wars. You have weapons and yet you put a price on your enemies' heads – just as you, the king of a great army, recently wished to hire an assassin to kill me for 1,000 talents. Hence I am not the aggressor in this war, but acting in self-defense. Furthermore, the gods support the better cause: I have already brought most of Asia under my control and defeated you in person in the field. You should not expect anything from me in view of your failure to observe the conventions of war towards me, but if you come to me as a suppliant I promise that you shall have your mother, your wife and your children without ransom.[64]

The response, made public by Alexander's propagandists, was nothing less than a restatement of the original grievances that were used to justify the war, adding the charge that Darius had resorted to paid assassins.[65] Darius' second appeal to Alexander offered territorial concessions – he was willing to cede Asia Minor west of the Halys River and to give one of his daughters in marriage – but since these amounted to less than he already possessed, the conqueror swept the proposal aside. It is significant, however, that this second offer came after the fall of Tyre. Alexander might have reacted differently if the city had proved impregnable. Despairing of a negotiated settlement, Darius prepared once again for war, and his military preparations were aided by Alexander's decision to secure Egypt. In fact, Darius made one final attempt to secure peace, this time as Alexander returned from Egypt in the spring of 331. But again he offered his opponent only what he had already taken by conquest – the lands south and west of the Euphrates, to which were added the hand of a daughter in marriage and 10,000 talents for the hostages – and diplomacy failed once again. Parmenion, as the story goes, claimed that he would be inclined to accept the offer. "So would I," remarked Alexander, "if I were Parmenion."[66]

From Egypt the Macedonians marched north again, stopping briefly at Tyre and then continuing to the crossing of the Euphrates at Thapsacus. This had been bridged by an advance force despite a half-hearted attempt by Mazaeus to prevent the action. Mazaeus' task may in fact have been to lure the Macedonian army to the plains beyond the Tigris, the crossing of which he also failed to contest, despite the obstacles it presented to troops attempting to ford the river. What has sometimes been described as negligence may have been part of the grand scheme that sought a decisive battle on terrain that suited Persian numbers and tactics. Whatever the truth is concerning Persian numbers, there can be no doubt that Darius' army vastly outnumbered that of his enemy, especially in cavalry, the most formidable branch of the Persian military; for the interval in which Alexander had secured the Mediterranean coastline had given the Great King time to summon the finest horsemen of Bactria and Sogdiana, Arachosia and India, to say nothing of the Scythians (the Dahae, Sacae, and Massagetae), who like the Mongols of later times were virtually born in the saddle (or, more precisely, on the saddle blanket). The encounter would prove to be decisive, but not as Darius imagined.

Gaugamela

The final clash of the great armies took place in summer 331, under conditions that favored the Persians. Here was the battlefield that they should have sought in 333, and the Persian numbers were greater than before, with sizable contingents from the eastern satrapies. Darius had marched his army from Babylon to the Tigris, which he followed upstream before fording the river south of Arbela. From here he continued to the Bumelus River and occupied the plain beyond it, taking care to clear the terrain of any obstacles that might impede the movement of his cavalry.[67] It was to the cavalry that Darius looked for victory, using its numerical superiority to effect a double envelopment. In the event, the attempt to outflank the right wing of the Macedonians proved fatal; for, by drawing cavalry forces away from the Persian left, Bessus and his horsemen created a gap for Alexander to exploit. Hence by penetrating the enemy line and putting pressure on Darius himself while the Persian horse attempted its encirclement, Alexander was able to rout the Persian center.

Alexander drew up his forces much as he had done at Issus. The various *taxeis* of *pezhetairoi* occupied the center; to their right were the hypaspists, 3,000 strong, forming a link between the heavy infantry and the Companion cavalry, which would form the main striking force. On the left, adjacent to the battalion of Craterus, who had charge of the infantry on the left of the line, Alexander positioned the allied

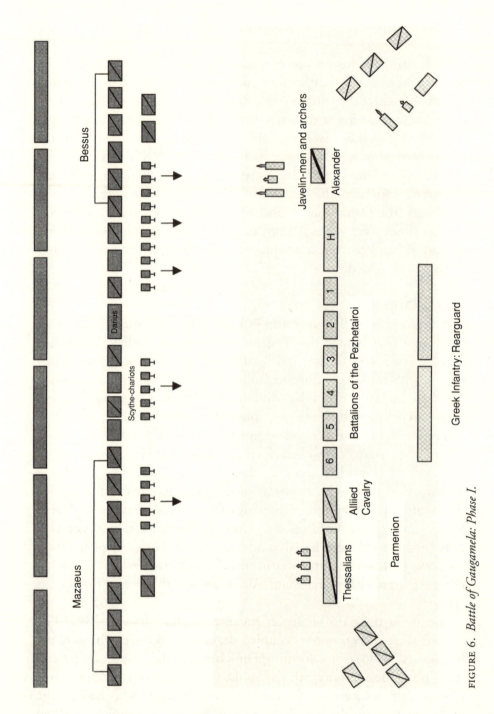

Mazaeus

Bessus

Darius

Scythe-chariots

Javelin-men and archers

Alexander

H

6 5 4 3 2 1

Battalions of the Pezhetairoi

Allied Cavalry

Thessalians

Parmenion

Greek Infantry: Rearguard

FIGURE 6. *Battle of Gaugamela: Phase I.*

76

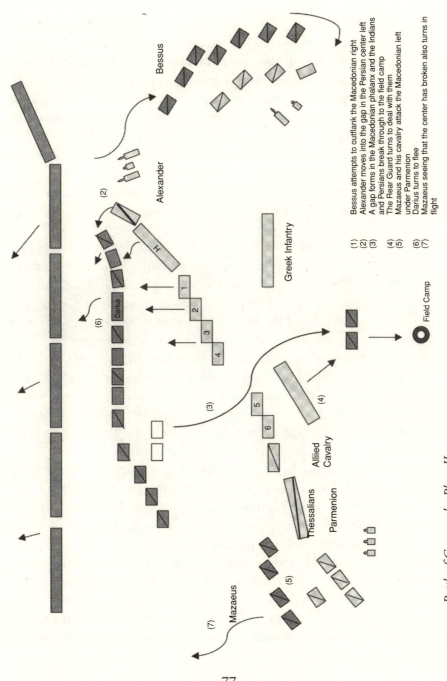

Bessus

Alexander

Greek Infantry

Darius

(2)

(6)

H

1
2
3
4

(3)

5
6

Allied
Cavalry

(4)

Field Camp

Thessalians

Parmenion

Mazaeus

(5)

(7)

(1) Bessus attempts to outflank the Macedonian right
(2) Alexander moves into the gap in the Persian center left
(3) A gap forms in the Macedonian phalanx and the Indians
    and Persians break through to the field camp
(4) The Rear Guard turns to deal with them
(5) Mazaeus and his cavalry attack the Macedonian left
    under Parmenion
(6) Darius turns to flee
(7) Mazaeus seeing that the center has broken also turns in
    flight

FIGURE 7. *Battle of Gaugamela: Phase II.*

77

horse, under Erigyius, and the Thessalian cavalry. Here Parmenion held supreme command, protected by the squadron from Pharsalus. Additional cavalry were located on each wing, their lines angled backwards in anticipation of the Persian flanking maneuver. Not only were the cavalry on both wings refused but, by leading from the right and advancing *en échelon*, Alexander forced the enemy right, controlled by Mazaeus, to advance in order to engage its opponents. On the Macedonian far left were the Thracians under Sitalces, the allied cavalry, led by Coeranus (perhaps Caranus), the Odrysians under the command of Agathon, and Andromachus' force of mercenary cavalry. Here, as in the accounts of other battles, the allied contingents received little attention from the historians.

The plan was a good one, though somewhat ragged in its execution. By refusing the wings, the Macedonians drew the Persian horse away from the center, where Darius directed affairs, protected by a guard of *melophoroi* (guards who had golden apples on the ends of their spears in lieu of buttspikes) and the best of his forces.[68] As Bessus' horsemen wheeled to engage Aretes and Menidas on the Macedonian far right, drawing the Bactrians after them, a gap (or at least thinning of the ranks) was created to the left of the Persian center. This Alexander was not slow to exploit, driving the wedges of the Companions into the spot where the enemy had weakened and bringing the hypaspists and the nearest battalions of the *pezhetairoi* into contact with the Persian line. The bristling sarissas of the phalanx pinned down the enemy line, while horsemen followed by hypaspists wheeled from right to left, rolling up the battered flank of Darius' army. But the swiftness with which Alexander's cavalry knifed into the developing gap drew the right side of the Macedonian infantry line forwards too quickly, creating a tear in the formation between the phalanges of Simmias and Polyperchon (the second and third battalions from the left). Here Darius might have counterattacked with devastating effects, but the Indian and Persian cavalry rode right through the opening and continued forwards to attack the Macedonian field camp.[69] They were, however, soon cut off and slaughtered by the forces held in reserve, who turned to rescue the baggage camp.

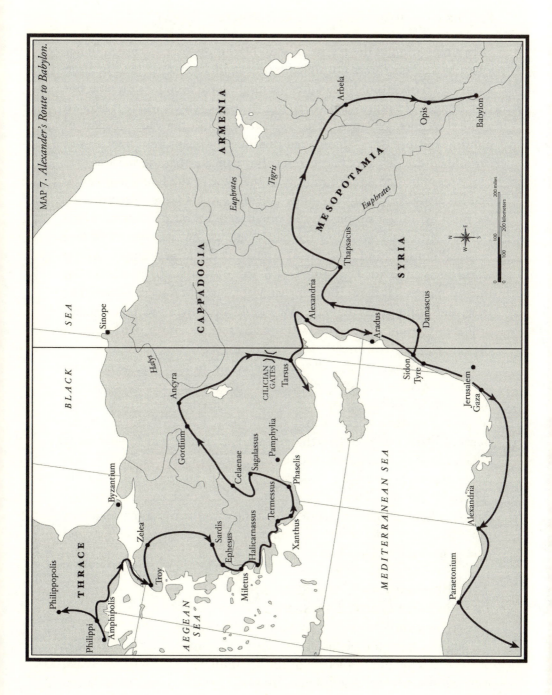

MAP 7. *Alexander's Route to Babylon.*

79

In a repetition of the events at Issus, Darius once again turned to flee when he saw his forces crumpled by Alexander's charge. Had he been able to hold his ground, the outcome might have been far different, but the strength of his army had been drawn to the wings, where it labored while the center collapsed. His own safety – and the vain prospect of fighting another day – demanded that he avoid capture. Flight would certainly mean defeat in battle, but capture meant that the war was lost. Once more he fled, ignominiously in the view of the Greek sources, as first his army and then the empire collapsed in his wake. Nevertheless, we must avoid the simplistic and unfair conclusion of military writer Bill Fawcett that Darius lost the battle because he "was unable to face personal danger" and "lost two battles and the largest empire in the world because he was a coward" (2006: 10). Instead his flight was similar to, and more vital than, the extraction of General Douglas MacArthur from the Philippines in 1942. We should bear in mind that Darius, unlike modern heads of state, was actually present on the battlefield, in the thick of the fighting.

Alexander's pursuit was allegedly halted by an urgent message from Parmenion, who was struggling against the cavalry of Mazaeus. But by the time Alexander approached the Macedonian left, Mazaeus' advance had been checked and the Persians had withdrawn on the news of Darius' flight. The charge that Parmenion had fought badly at Gaugamela, which appears to have originated with Callisthenes, was doubtless made after the Philotas affair and the murder of the old general.[70] For the defeated Persian king, the escape route led first to Arbela, where he collected some of his fractured army, and then across the Zagros range, following the valley of the Great or Upper Zab and emerging south of Lake Urmia.

THE PERSEPOLIS CAMPAIGN AND THE PANHELLENIC CRUSADE

The collapse of Persian military power at Gaugamela sealed the fate of the empire: from the plains of northern Mesopotamia, the royal cities of the Achaemenids, replete with the accumulated wealth of 230 years, were within easy striking distance. To say that Darius took consolation in the fact that Alexander would now find himself distracted and weighed down by the spoils of victory is to put a brave face on the disaster.[71] Darius, who had fled to Ecbatana in Media, knew that there was little hope of collecting yet another army, much less of defeating the Macedonians in battle. But hope and the solitudes of Central Asia were all that remained for him.

Mazaeus, the former satrap of Cilicia and Syria, who had fought with distinction at Gaugamela, hurried to Babylon to prepare the city's official surrender to Alexander. The conqueror's entry into the ancient capital is described at length by Curtius, celebrated in a painting by Charles le Brun, and recreated in all its imagined splendor in Oliver Stone's otherwise unspectacular film, *Alexander*. It was indeed a defining moment, and Alexander's first meaningful encounter with the rulers of the empire. As satrap he installed his noble adversary, Mazaeus, although his powers were tempered by the imposition of a garrison in the city and a variety of Macedonian overseers. Similar arrangements were made in Susa (the old center of Elam), where Abulites retained his satrapy, under the watchful eye of the *phrourarchos* (or commandant) Xenophilus.[72] The "conquest" phase of his campaign was drawing to a close. Persepolis was only lightly defended, as Darius looked in vain for fresh levies in Ecbatana. Madates, the hyparch of the Uxians and a relative of Darius III by marriage, resisted the Macedonian advance, but the Uxians themselves were more intent upon their habitual collection of tribute (akin to the *hongo* charged by African tribes in return for free passage through their territory)[73] than upon saving Darius' empire. In the event, their opposition was not only futile but costly; for Alexander arranged for Craterus, along with Tauron and the archers, to seize the heights to which it was thought the Uxians might retreat, before directing his forces against them. Their escape route blocked, many were slaughtered in the initial engagement or as they attempted flight on the mountainous terrain.

A far more serious threat confronted the invaders at the Persian (or Susian) Gates, where the satrap of Persis, Ariobarzanes, had blocked the pass with some 25,000 men.[74] A direct charge was repulsed with heavy casualties. The similarity of the situation to the Greek defense of Thermopylae in 480 was doubtless emphasized by the Alexander historians – if not by Callisthenes, then certainly by Cleitarchus. And the circumventing of the Gates by a force guided by herdsmen is also reminiscent of the treachery of Ephialtes in Greece. There is no reason to suppose that the incident did not take place, but the idea of the past repeating itself in reverse was surely seized upon by contemporary writers. Once he had cleared the pass, defeated and killed Ariobarzanes, and bridged the Araxes River, Alexander was allegedly met by a crowd of mutilated Greeks. Here it is virtually certain that history has taken a back seat to fiction. The dramatic purpose of the episode is unmistakable, and the existence of such a band of unfortunates must be rejected.

The story of these pathetic victims of past atrocities is reported only by those authors who based their histories on Cleitarchus, and this episode is truly worthy of his reputation for tasteless exaggeration. To dismiss it as bad history is enough, but it is also an example of storytelling at its worst. Yet, as always, there have been those who have accepted the story as genuine. Where, one wonders, would these unfortunates have come from? Victims of which king's cruelty? Captured mercenaries from the time of the so-called Great Satraps Revolt, perhaps? But at a time when the value of Greek mercenaries was keenly understood by the Great King, it is hard to imagine that their talents would be wasted and their bodies abused.[75] Clearly, they are little more than a storytelling device: living reminders of the purpose for which Alexander had led the forces of the allied Greeks against Persia, they are the victims of the very atrocities that the Panhellenic crusade sought to avenge. Like the wretched Odysseus, who slaughters the suitors of Penelope after suffering further abuse in the guise of a beggar, they give a sense of purpose and immediacy to the capture of Persepolis and the torching of its palace. We, who have experienced the deceit of "eyewitnesses" relating to a U.S. congressional committee tales of babies thrown from incubators in Kuwaiti hospitals, can testify to the persuasive power of invented crimes.[76] Nothing promotes hatred like fear and anger, and nothing inspires men to take up arms and mete out punishment more than hate. But, as effective as the plight of Euctemon, Theaetetus, and their disfigured companions is, the episode was designed to animate the reader rather than the troops in the field.

It was apparently in the camp, which Alexander had established a mere two stades (about 1,200 feet) from the city, that the king proclaimed to his commanders that

> no city was more hateful to the Greeks than Persepolis, the capital of the old kings of Persia, the city from which troops without number had poured forth, from which first Darius and then Xerxes had waged an unholy war on Europe. To appease the spirits of their forefathers they should wipe it out. . . . [77]

It is significant that the king allowed his soldiers to ravage the town but exempted the palaces, the most obvious symbols of Persian power. But even here there were sufficient spoils for the troops, who had been denied the opportunity for plunder in Babylon and Susa.[78] In the case of the palaces, there was the matter of removing the treasures that had been amassed there, and Alexander would have postponed any decision on their fate until the eve of his departure. In the meantime, since the deteriorating conditions in Greece, where the Spartan king, Agis III, was organizing resistance to Macedonian leadership, detained him, he occupied his men with a campaign in Persis.[79] During their absence, the vast amounts of coined and uncoined gold and silver were crated for transport to Ecbatana to finance the remainder of the expedition.

It is hardly surprising that, as a final dramatic touch, Cleitarchus attributed the burning of Xerxes' palace to the actions of the Athenian courtesan, Thaïs – a woman who was to become the mistress of Ptolemy son of Lagus, founder of the Ptolemaic dynasty, and the mother of a Cypriote queen.[80] The setting is a drinking party, followed by the typically Greek *komos*, in which partygoers proceeded through the streets by torchlight. Like Philip, who acts one way under the influence of alcohol only to feel regret in his more sober moments, Alexander is induced by the woman to burn the very palace that Parmenion had advised him to spare; it was unwise, he argued, for a man to destroy his own property.[81] Whether the actual burning of the palace was the result of policy or whim, the story of Thaïs and her drunken band constitutes a fitting conclusion to the lengthy pretense of the Panhellenic enterprise.

Nevertheless, Alexander's actions at Persepolis are important, for they have a direct bearing on his relationship with both the Greek allies and the conquered Persians. Was his destruction of the palace an irrational act or one of policy? As long as Darius was alive, the war would continue. Indeed, until such time as Alexander could win recognition as Great King of Asia (or some suitable equivalent), the war was destined to continue. The conqueror found himself on the horns of a dilemma: how could he be, simultaneously, avenger of the Greeks and legitimate successor of the Great King? The latter was a position he had yet to secure, despite having sat on the Imperial Throne at Susa. The former role required him to make a significant gesture of retribution that would, at the same time, signal the end of the Panhellenic war.[82] It was not until after Darius' death, when the Macedonian army had reached Hecatompylus, that Alexander agreed to dismiss the allies. But Persepolis, which was the perceived source of Persian might and the font from which the barbarian hordes poured forth, cried out for punishment. Alexander's action was thus symbolic. It must, however, have represented a setback to his policy of winning the hearts of the Persian nobility. Other subject states may have regarded Persepolis as a symbol of oppression, and shed few tears, but Alexander had long before determined to make some of the Persian nobles partners – some might say puppets – in his new regime.[83]

EMPIRE IN TRANSITION

When Darius learned of the death of his wife, Stateira, and of the honors accorded to her by Alexander, he naturally assumed that the Macedonian king had been intimate with her and that his treatment of her after her death reflected his desire for her while she lived. But a faithful eunuch, who had escaped from the Macedonian camp and was, indeed, the bearer of the news of her death, assured his master that Alexander had not taken advantage of his captive but had shown her nothing but the honor due to a queen. When he realized this, Darius allegedly prayed that, if the gods did not grant him victory and the empire was to change hands, the throne should pass to Alexander, who conquered his enemies not only on the battlefield but in his kindness as well. The story is utter fiction. Stateira died in childbirth or as the result of a miscarriage at least eighteen months after her capture at Issus. If she was carrying someone's child, it was not Darius', and it is hard to imagine how anyone could have been sexually intimate with her without Alexander's knowledge. The king's claim that he had seen her only once, when she was captured at Issus, and never again thereafter smacks of "protesting too much." He certainly did not have any reservations about making the captive widow of Memnon his mistress, and he is said to have remarked that the sight of the Persian queens was a "torment to the eyes," whereby he did not mean that he found them unattractive. Rumor held that Stateira was the most beautiful woman in Asia, just as Darius was the most handsome of men, but here too there is an element of ruler cult to be considered. We shall never know the truth about the queen's death or whether she visited Alexander's bed or he hers. Darius' prayer was in any case superfluous, for the nature of the Persian Empire was such that the conquest of the Great King was the most important step towards the rule of his empire.

It was the unity of the Persian Empire that offered Alexander the greatest advantages. Its system of roads made the movement of troops as easy for the invader as for the defender; its financial structure meant that the resources that had been put in place for the purpose of defense could now be used by the victor against the imperial forces. Furthermore, the stability of the imperial structures and the tolerance that Achaemenid rulers had shown to the defeated contributed more than anything else to Alexander's success. By maintaining these structures and by interfering only minimally in the patterns of administration and day-to-day life, he facilitated a smooth transition of power. It was the power elites, not the native populations, that mattered, and by retaining as many of them as possible in positions of authority, he made them willing to accept a new ruler. As Pierre Briant, the leading authority on Achaemenid Persia, observes: "As soon as the royal military was conquered, local leaders found themselves with a simple choice (which their ancestors had known since the conquests of Cyrus): to negotiate with the victor a way to maintain their dominant position within their own society."[84] It was a familiar refrain: "The king is dead, long live the king." And, as long as the change of leadership caused little or no disruption to the system, it was acceptable to those whose approval was most needed. To the common man it mattered little to whom he paid his taxes, as long as his life did not change for the worse. The Achaemenid policies of multiculturalism and religious toleration did little to promote loyalty to the rulers of the empire. Instead they "rendered unto Caesar what was Caesar's" without much concern for Caesar's identity or origins.[85]

Alexander had conquered Darius when he defeated his armies at the Granicus, at Issus, and at Gaugamela; he had secured his empire by retaining the ruling structures and, as far as possible, the rulers themselves. Since the highest political offices had been held by Iranians – most of whom could claim kinship of one sort or another with the Great King or the families of the conspirators against Smerdis[86] – a change in leadership at this level had little impact on the subject peoples. But the offices below the level of satrap were critical, and it was important to appear to be respectful of local traditions and religion. Alexander had recognized this at the very start, although openly he continued to play the role of Panhellenic avenger. By the time he covered Darius' corpse with his own cloak, Alexander was *de facto* the Great King of Asia. His quarrel from then on was with rivals for the throne.

RESISTANCE ON
TWO FRONTS

CHAPTER SIX

❦ ❦ ❦

❦ ❦ ❦

T HE DEFEAT AND DEATH OF DARIUS ENDED THE CONQUEST
phase of Alexander's campaign. The four Achaemenid capitals
were in his possession, along with their treasuries; the Greek
allies had been dismissed, with bonus pay; satraps, *strategoi,*
phrourarchoi, and *gazophylakes* had been appointed; and he could claim
the eastern satrapies as his by right of conquest. The struggle for legitimacy continued, however, and it was necessary to overcome any rival
claims. The period from 330 to 328 was one in which Alexander fought
to establish his legitimacy and authority.[1]

THE USURPATION OF THE ROYAL TITLE BY BESSUS
If Alexander had hoped that the death of Darius would bring the war
against Persia to an end, he was soon disappointed. Those who had
betrayed their king fled into Bactria via Margiana (the Merv Oasis)
and attempted to rally the splendid horsemen of Central Asia and their
local barons. Bessus, a relative of Darius (though we do not know how
close the relationship was), wore the tiara upright, in the style of kings,
and took the name Artaxerxes (V).[2] Politically, it was a major setback
for Alexander, who was himself posing as the "legitimate" successor of

Darius, having assumed the trappings of Persian royalty. For this reason, too, in an act of piety, he had ordered that the dead king be given a state funeral;[3] Bessus, as regicide and usurper, could expect no mercy. This he clearly understood, but he was doubtless disappointed by the lack of support he received in his own satrapy. The struggle that ensued was not one for independence but rather a question of loyalties and acceptance of authority; for, ultimately, the nobility owed their offices and estates to the Great King.

Satibarzanes, perhaps an accomplice of Bessus,[4] had been spared by Alexander and permitted to return to his satrapy of Areia, albeit with Anaxippus and forty mounted javelin-men (*hippakontistai*) to oversee his affairs. Encouraged by Bessus' usurpation, Satibarzanes killed the Macedonian escort and openly rebelled. The betrayal of trust diverted Alexander from the direct pursuit of Bessus and drew him southward. He defeated the rebels in the vicinity of Artacoana (probably near modern Herat), where he founded Alexandria-in-Areia.[5] But Satibarzanes and his supporters fled, intending to resist in the land that is today synonymous with guerrilla warfare.

Alexander himself paused at Phrada (modern Farah, north of Lake Sistan), where he faced the second serious conspiracy of his reign. The first, in 334, was exposed while the conspirator himself was not in Alexander's camp, and his arrest was carried out quickly and secretly. Alexander the Lyncestian was kept in chains for the next three years, and by avoiding the bad publicity that might result from the trial and execution of a prominent and well-connected nobleman, the king was able to avoid bringing the matter to a head until a more convenient time. Alexander Lyncestes had no strong links with Philotas – indeed, the family and adherents of Parmenion may have played an important role in counterbalancing the power of Antipater and his supporters – but, as it turned out, Philotas' arrest in 330 provided the king with the opportunity to revive old charges and finally rid himself of a political enemy.

THE PHILOTAS AFFAIR AND THE MURDER OF PARMENION

When Alexander set out for Asia, he left Antipater in charge of affairs in Europe, exercising a kind of *bailliage* in the king's absence. At the same time, the Macedonian army had become nothing less than a peripatetic state, with the *hetairoi* as courtiers and advisers and the senior officers as the executive body. Assemblies of the army were held sporadically and then only to sanction publicly an action by the king that might be viewed as autocratic or arbitrary. The seven-man group of Somatophylakes constituted, among other things, a "Secret Service" of sorts, and the hypaspists provided the police force. Political elevation, that is, promotion up the military ladder, was usually at the expense of another, who was relegated to an administrative post or removed from office on the suspicion of misconduct or treason. The punishment for the latter was invariably execution. The political world of Alexander's camp was fraught with danger, particularly for the leadership: historian Elizabeth Carney rightly observes that "Macedonian kings tended to die with their boots on."[6] As a result, there was no menace too slight to be ignored and no form of negligence that could not be construed as complicity. This was the trap into which Philotas' lack of judgment led him.

In the fall of 330, Dimnus, an otherwise unknown *hetairos* from Chalaestra, either hatched or participated in a conspiracy to kill Alexander, the details of which he confided to his lover, Nicomachus. This man, however, revealed the plan and the names of the conspirators to his brother, Cebalinus, who hastened to bring the matter to the king's attention. He happened upon Philotas and asked him to inform Alexander, but Philotas ignored the report, even when Cebalinus approached him on the following day. Philotas is later alleged to have said in his own defense that he had not taken the charges seriously, coming as they did from the brother of a male prostitute. But, when Cebalinus finally informed the king, through the agency of Metron, one of the pages, the decision was made to arrest both Dimnus and Philotas.

There has been a tendency to judge, quite wrongly, the seriousness of the plot and the extent of the danger by the status of the conspirators themselves. That in itself may have been Philotas' mistake, but it should not be repeated by modern scholars. Great men have often met their ends at the hands of insignificant agents or even for relatively minor causes, and nothing gives offense as easily as personal insult. What it was that motivated Dimnus and his co-conspirators, we shall probably never know. The conspirators were, for the most part, undistinguished,[7] with the notable exception of Demetrius the Somatophylax. According to Curtius, a certain Calis (probably "Calas") confessed that he and Demetrius had planned the whole affair. If this was, in fact, the case and Demetrius' alleged role was made known to Philotas, his failure to pass on the information becomes more difficult to explain. Whether the conspirators were lesser or greater men, Philotas' inactivity amounted to culpable negligence. Was he trying to protect Demetrius? No personal connections between the two are attested, and his name did not come up during Philotas' interrogation, although other friendships – those with Amyntas son of Perdiccas and the sons of Andromenes – were held against him. Perhaps his political enemies were right: Philotas failed to expose the conspirators because he secretly hoped their plot would succeed.

Nothing could be learned from Dimnus himself, who either commit-ted suicide or was killed resisting arrest. Historian Ernst Badian sees this as evidence of a conspiracy to "frame" Philotas, and many have accepted his intriguing but implausible scenario: Dimnus' plot was a fiction and the revelation of its details to Philotas was an attempt to entrap him; Philotas conveniently took the bait and was charged with complicity in the plot. Dimnus' death was thus a cover-up: "Dead men tell no tales."[8] But the objections to this theory are manifold. How could Alexander predict that Philotas would fail to pass on the information?[9] What of the alleged role of Demetrius the Bodyguard: was he too framed by the king? And what of the fact that Cebalinus did not in fact seek out Philotas but came upon him purely by chance?[10] Ten innocent men, in addition to Philotas and Parmenion, thus lost their lives – and the careers, if not the lives, of the sons of Andromenes were jeopardized – merely for the sake of eliminating a political rival. And no one in antiq-uity had any inkling of this, even when it was safe to speak the truth.

It appears virtually certain that a conspiracy against Alexander existed, and that one of its instigators was Demetrius the Bodyguard. That man could not have been executed without good cause, and certainly no one in the camp or amongst the historians spoke in his defense. Even Dim-nus, as a member of the *hetairoi*, cannot have been as inconsequential as many make him out to be. If Philotas' crime amounted to nothing more than negligence, that was still enough to warrant the arrest and execution of a lesser man. But it is more likely that his actions were not cavalier or thoughtless, and that his motives were hostile. His resentment of Alexander had come to light earlier, in Egypt, after the king's recognition as son of Amun. Furthermore, he attributed Alexander's success in the war to the skill of his father, and even himself. Nevertheless, the king had pardoned his actions and continued to place his trust in the old general and his son. Two years later he was less inclined to forgive, and he was pressured by his closest friends and most trusted officers to put Philotas on trial for treason. Alexander was clearly ready to abandon Philotas to his enemies, but the decision was complicated by Parmenion, who still had a large following in the army and remained with substantial forces in Ecbatana, astride the king's lines of communication. If Philotas could not be pardoned, then Parmenion too must die.

Condemned to death by the assembled Macedonian troops,[11] Philotas and the members of Dimnus' conspiracy were executed by the army, along with Alexander the Lyncestian, who thus ended three years of imprisonment, a broken man no longer able even to muster arguments in his own defense. Polydamas the Thessalian, a man trusted by Parmenion, was hastily dispatched to bring the order for the old general's execution to Ecbatana. It was left to Cleander, Sitalces, and Menidas to carry out the murder. As he read the letter containing the news of Philotas' execution and the charges against himself, he was struck down. That his executioners believed in his guilt is doubtful, but they did what was required of them.[12] Parmenion was killed not for what he had done but for what he might do.

If there were members of the *hetairoi* who supported Philotas and felt pity for Parmenion, they wisely remained silent. Those who had actively participated in Philotas' demise were rewarded with military advancement – that was, after all, what had motivated them first and foremost. The common soldiers foolish enough to voice their objections were formed into a disciplinary unit (the *ataktoi*); most, however, were experienced in the ways of Macedonian politics and recognized that changes were usually the result of casualties. But the conditions of service soon became more onerous and the stress of campaigning in the wilds of Central Asia led to further confrontations between Alexander and his men. The euphoria of the first years of the war was beginning to wear off as the demands increased and the rewards were less obvious.

RESISTANCE IN BACTRIA AND SOGDIANA

From Phrada (later known as Prophthasia or "Anticipation" because it was here that the conspiracy was revealed), Alexander moved south into the lands of the Ariaspians. These people lived near Lake Sistan and, because they had supplied the army of Cyrus the Great in a time of need, had earned the sobriquet "Benefactors" (*euergetai*). According to some sources, it was during his two-month stay amongst the Ariaspians that the king learned of the continued rebellion of Satibarzanes. The version given by Arrian is, however, more likely: he relates that Alexander had moved up the Helmand River valley and founded Alexandria-in-Arachosia (modern Kandahar) before moving on into Parapamisus, the region of the Hindu Kush. This range the Greeks identified with the Caucasus, and they regarded the Iaxartes River (Syr-darya) as the Tanais (usually identified with the Dnieper or Don) and considered it the dividing line between Europe and Asia. Hence Arrian speaks of the "European Scythians" living beyond the Syr-darya. Both the Amu-darya (Oxus) and the Syr-darya flow into the Aral Sea, but the Greeks were ignorant of its existence and believed the Oxus flowed into the Caspian, which in turn they considered a gulf of the outer Ocean.[13] Since it was known that Bessus was desolating the country beyond the Hindu Kush – specifically the area beyond the Shibar Pass, which he expected the Macedonians to use – Alexander advanced northeast beyond Kabul and founded another city in the vicinity of modern Begram and Charikar, Alexandria-in-the-Caucasus. Here he installed Neiloxenus son of Satyrus as military overseer, leaving also a Persian named Proexes as satrap of the Parapamisadae. It was at about this time, according to Arrian, that Alexander learned of Satibarzanes' return to Areia with some 2,000 horsemen supplied by Bessus. The king therefore left Artabazus behind with Caranus and Erigyius to deal with the rebel,

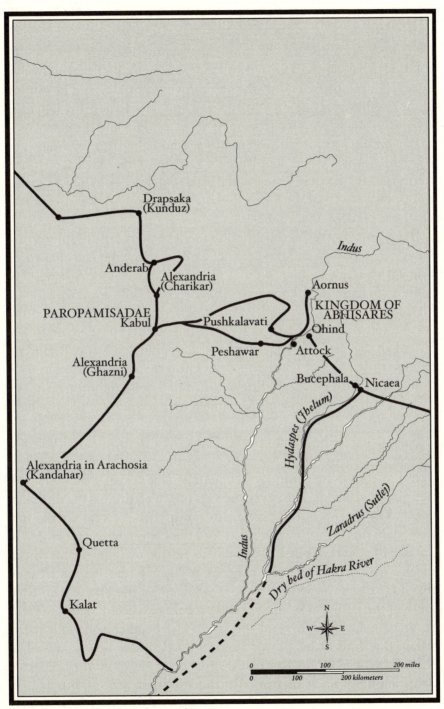

Drapsaka
(Kunduz)

Anderab

Alexandria
(Charikar)

PAROPAMISADAE
Kabul

Pushkalavati

Alexandria
(Ghazni)

Peshawar

Indus

Aornus

KINGDOM OF
ABHISARES

Ohind

Attock

Bucephala

Nicaea

Alexandria in Arachosia
(Kandahar)

Hydaspes (Jhelum)

Zaradrus (Sutlej)

Quetta

Indus

Kalat

Dry bed of Hakra River

N
W E
S

| 0 | | 100 | | 200 miles |

| 0 | | 100 | | 200 kilometers |

MAP 8. *Bactria and the Indus Lands.*

while he himself crossed the mountains via the Khawak Pass. Winter conditions had not fully abated and the crossing took a heavy toll on his horses, ill equipped to endure the hardships of Central Asia. The summit of the pass has an elevation of 11,650 feet, and it took the army sixteen or seventeen days to cross on account of the conditions and the narrowness of the terrain.[14] Eventually, Alexander reached Drapsaca (Kunduz) and Bactrian Aornus, where he planted a garrison under Archelaus son of Androcles. By the time he reached Bactra (Balkh), Bessus and his group had pushed north of the Oxus River (Amu-darya), in the direction of Nautaca (modern Shahrisabz).

It was probably at this time that Alexander heard of the suppression of the Areian rebellion and the death of Satibarzanes, who had challenged Erigyius to single combat only to die at the Macedonian's hand. The contest of champions, known to virtually every child from the story of David and Goliath, was still a feature of warfare. Although it did not act as a substitute for battle – as in the famous case of the Curiati and Horatii or the Spartan–Argive battle of champions – it was an important prelude to battle and tended to demoralize the army of the loser.[15] A little more than a year later, Erigyius died of illness, and this fact, along with his long friendship with Alexander, may account for the emphasis on his *aristeia*.

Bessus, retreating north of the Oxus, had destroyed the boats to prevent or, at least, delay Alexander's crossing. The Macedonians were forced to improvise: stuffing their leather tent covers with straw and using inflated bladders, they created rafts on which to cross the turbulent river.[16] The British in the nineteenth century (the "Great Game" era) were to do much the same thing to ford the Oxus and similar rivers. In the face of relentless pursuit, Bessus was unable to augment his forces, and his own supporters (the majority of his 7–8,000 Bactrians) soon abandoned him. Nevertheless, he was joined by the Dahae who lived south of the Iaxartes (Syr-darya) and probably expected to attract those Scythians who lived beyond the river. The Sogdianian nobles were, however, jealous of his power[17] and arrested Bessus now that he had been abandoned by his Bactrian contingent. Doubtless, they expected clemency, if not a reward, from Alexander for their actions. But news of

Alexander's massacre of the Branchidae made them apprehensive and distrustful.

Before learning of Bessus' arrest by his own men, Alexander resorted to another act of terror. Coming upon a town that surrendered to him voluntarily, he turned it over to his men for rape and pillage; the inhabitants were slaughtered and the town razed. The army had been through much hardship in recent months and the king set his troops free to satisfy their urges and blood lust. It would, he reasoned, send a message to the rebels that he meant business. But the measure, although it may have appealed to the soldiery, proved to be counterproductive; for it sent the wrong message to the native leaders who were at that moment hoping to win clemency by surrendering Bessus. Spitamenes, Dataphernes, Catanes, and other prominent local barons had arrested Bessus and were just now offering to extradite him. The news was welcomed by Alexander and he sent a force, led by Ptolemy, to accept the usurper's surrender. The damage had, however, been done. Those who betrayed Bessus did not come face to face with the Macedonians but left him to be picked up by the Macedonians.

Alexander's encounter with Bessus is instructive, showing once again the importance the king placed on symbols and propaganda. Bessus was placed on the roadside naked, chained and wearing a wooden collar,[18] as Alexander had instructed. Little attention has been paid to the fact that Alexander rode up to the captive in a chariot,[19] which signified his role as Great King. He was now ready to pass judgment on the rebel, regicide, and usurper, and Bessus could expect no mercy. All who rebelled against the authority of the Great King, especially regicides, deserved the harshest penalties of mutilation and execution. The exact details of Bessus' death are disputed. He may have been crucified, or torn apart by recoiling trees, or (what is most likely) mutilated before being sent to Ecbatana for execution; for it was customary to cut off the ears and the nose of a rebel.[20] But the savagery of both acts in the summer of 329 made a deep impression on the leaders of Bactria and Sogdiana.

The massacre in Sogdiana also deserves closer attention. Arrian says nothing about it,[21] but Curtius claims that the settlers of this town were descendants of the Branchidae, Milesians who had been resettled in the

Persian Empire by Xerxes in 479. Their crime had been to hand over to the Persians for plunder the temple of Apollo at Didyma. That the Branchidae were transplanted to Sogdiana is doubtful, and not supported by the evidence of Herodotus. But that some tradition to this effect had been known to Alexander's historians, particularly Callisthenes, is nevertheless possible. It appears that Callisthenes may once again have attempted to put Alexander's actions in a good light by relating that the victims were, in fact, descendants of those who had betrayed Greece and its gods.[22] Panhellenic motives are hard to explain at this juncture, and it may simply have been a convenient justification of terror. It is, however, interesting that, just before the incident, Alexander had dismissed some troops on the grounds of advancing age or ill health and retained others, many of whom may have served originally in the allied contingents.[23]

The fears of the Bactrians and Sogdianians were thus confirmed and what followed was a prolonged guerrilla war, in which the natives relied on the speed and efficiency of their horsemen (and their Scythian allies) and the safety of their mountain fortresses. Alexander had lost control of the propaganda war, he had failed to win the trust of the ruling elites, and he found himself confronted by an enemy that would fight on its own terms and strike where the Macedonians were weakest. To compare them with terrorists or the Taliban, as some do today, does them a disservice. Their fight was not motivated by religious fanaticism, nor were they part of a larger movement to destroy Macedonian power at its roots. One could not even claim that their goal was to save the Achaemenid Empire. They fought out of fear, for the preservation of their families and their way of life, which they believed the Macedonians had come to destroy. Nor would the capture of their leaders put an end to the resistance. New leaders were ready at hand; those captured or killed were martyrs, not failures. The fear of annihilation or enslavement had turned them into the one type of enemy Alexander had so far not encountered: the desperate, with a collective sense of purpose.[24] They could be weakened, but not conquered, by military means. Reprisals and intimidation through violence, in short, the repeated use of terror, were not the answer; for the East has long resisted the imposition of Western freedom. It was a lesson Napoleon, an admirer of the great Macedonian conqueror, was slow to learn when he applied similar principles to his conquest of Egypt. And it is a fact that military strategists and leaders of the West have yet to come to terms with. Alexander soon realized that he would have to find a political solution.

Having dealt with Bessus, Alexander rounded up large numbers of horses in Sogdiana in order to replace the cavalry mounts that had perished in the crossing of the Hindu Kush.[25] Then, after moving in a southeasterly direction to Maracanda (where he left a garrison), he advanced once again to the Iaxartes River (Syr-darya). Here a chain of settlements – one of which, at least, had been established by Cyrus the Great in 530 – demarcated the limits of the satrapy. These he appears to have garrisoned before he conceived of the plan to establish an outpost on the river, for Arrian (4.1.4) says that "the barbarians living near the river seized and killed the Macedonian soldiers who occupied the forts in their cities." Alexandria Eschate was intended to be both a defense against the barbarians north of the river and a base for a possible attack on the Scythians. Some scholars have seen this as a disruption of the economic patterns of life in the region and a threat to the Scythians, but it appears that there were other reasons for the uprising that followed. Fear and distrust of Alexander were certainly factors, especially after the earlier massacre in Sogdiana. Some may simply have reacted against the prospect of being transplanted from their homes to Alexander's new metropolis. The seven outposts that had revolted were attacked by Alexander, who entrusted the siege-work to various generals. Resistance was fierce, but the defenses and the defenders were not up to the task – though both Alexander and Craterus were wounded in the process. Once he overcame these forts, the king determined to make a show of military force against the Scythians who lived to the north of the river and to establish a larger fortified city, which would come to be known as Alexandria Eschate (Alexandria the Farthest, near modern Khojend).

Alexander's attack across the Iaxartes is reminiscent of his move against the Getae on the Danube in 335. There was never any thought of conquest. The campaign was strictly preemptive, a show of Macedonian strength intended to persuade the Scythians to recognize the borders of the province. The crossing of the river on rafts constructed of hides and bladders – rafts big enough to transport horses to the other bank – was a daring one, especially in the face of enemy fire. But the Scythians revealed the futility of trying to subdue a mobile force and a nomadic people. It was sufficient to demonstrate that the Macedonians had the capabilities, if called upon, to deal with so elusive an enemy. Despite the claims of some scholars that Alexander's frontier outposts on the river threatened the normal patterns of economic life, this can hardly have been the case. For the present the king wished to prevent military incursions, and to a limited extent he was successful. Alexandria Eschate would provide a refuge in case of invasion, but it was not a barrier to movement across the Iaxartes.

Some Scythians – the Massagetae and the Dahae – continued to support Spitamenes, who in Alexander's absence had attacked Maracanda. A relief force was sent under the command of Andromachus, Caranus, and Menedemus, along with a Lycian guide named Pharnuches.[26] Their undertaking was, however, marred by incompetence, and it appears that there was no clear chain of command. Ambushed at the Polytimetus River, the Macedonians were slaughtered by Spitamenes forces familiar with the terrain.[27] Pharnuches' chief qualification was, allegedly, his linguistic skill. But it is hard to believe that Alexander would have subordinated Macedonian officers to the leadership of a barbarian with limited military experience. He may, however, be identical with the father of Bagoas (the only attested Persian trierarch of the Hydaspes fleet), and thus a man of high standing in Alexander's entourage. The name is clearly Persian, and Pharnuches may have defected to Alexander in 334/3, when the Macedonian army secured Asia Minor.[28] Nevertheless, it is tempting to regard him as the father of the famous eunuch (who was thus also the trierarch). He owed his position to his son's influence, and the version that holds him accountable for the Polytimetus disaster may reflect some disapproval of Bagoas' role at the court. Such a view requires us to accept (what is obviously the case in other imperial societies) that eunuchs were more than harem-keepers and vile mischief-makers. There is, in fact, nothing that speaks against the view that the younger Bagoas exerted political power similar to that of his older namesake.

News of the Polytimetus disaster reached Alexander at the Iaxartes River. He hastened south with a portion of the army, leaving the rest to follow at a slower pace under the command of Craterus. When the two parts of the army reunited, Alexander turned once again to military reprisals against the rebellious population. Leaving a garrison of 3,000 men under the *phrourarchos* Peucolaus (possibly in Maracanda), he moved his army south of the Oxus to Bactra for the winter (329/8).

SPITAMENES

After the capture of Bessus, Alexander had summoned the local barons and regional leaders (*hyparchoi*) to a meeting at Bactra in the hope of bringing peace to the area; clearly he sought their recognition of his authority as the legitimate successor of Darius III. But the conference failed to materialize; for the Sogdiani and Bactriani were told by their political leaders that negotiations with the conqueror would not be to their advantage.[29] The most powerful of these leaders was Spitamenes, in all likelihood a Persian who, like Bessus, had connections with the Achaemenid royal house. Although he was responsible for extraditing the usurper, he did not come to terms with Alexander, and it is conceivable that he had coveted supreme power since the arrest of Darius in 330. Alexander's brutal tactics against the rebels had, furthermore, done little to endear him to the natives, who joined the nomadic Dahae and Massagetae in supporting Spitamenes. The destruction of the relief force at the Polytimetus must have increased both Spitamenes' prestige and the number of his adherents.

The rebels wintered among the Massagetae and, waiting for Alexander to return to Sogdiana, they launched raids into Bactria. There they employed tactics similar to those which had been successful at Maracanda in the preceding year. Luring the garrison commander, Attinas, into an ambush, they overwhelmed him and his force of 3,000. At Bactra itself, where Alexander had left a small force, including some Companions suffering from illness, as well as the royal pages, they inflicted casualties on the force that sallied forth and captured their leader, Peithon son of Sosicles. But the news of these successes caused Alexander to send Craterus against Spitamenes, who chased him and the Massagetae back into the desert.

At the beginning of the campaigning season of 328, Alexander, with the reinforcements that arrived over the winter,[30] returned to Sogdiana and laid siege to the so-called Rock of Sogdiana, where Ariamazes had taken refuge with a large band of followers. Alexander attempted, at first, to negotiate the enemy's surrender, sending to him Cophes son of Artabazus (whom Alexander had made titular satrap of Bactria–Sogdiana). Ariamazes, trusting in the security of his mountain fortress, declared that he would submit to the Macedonians when they produced "men with wings." The challenge was too much for Alexander, who sent men with ropes and pegs to climb to the heights above Ariamazes' position, and then told Cophes to point out to the rebel the "winged men" who had outmaneuvered him. Ariamazes agreed to an unconditional surrender, but he found no mercy at the hands of the king, whose mounting frustration led him to resort to further acts of violence: Ariamazes and his adherents were flogged and crucified; the majority of the captives were sold into slavery.[31]

The capture of the rock was followed by a sweep campaign in which Alexander divided his forces into five contingents in the hope of eliminating pockets of resistance. These units reunited in Maracanda, where Alexander was met by Pharasmenes, king of the Chorasmians, and a delegation from the Scythians who lived north of the Iaxartes. It was at this time that he was offered a Scythian bride, an offer he declined. As one scholar has remarked, "Scythian princesses were renowned for their virtue; but, in pastoral simplicity, they ate rancid butter, dried horse flesh, and were little addicted to personal hygiene."[32] Delightful as this image is, the Macedonians scarcely judged potential brides by such exacting standards, and Alexander's reasons for rejecting the offer were doubtless political.[33] Nevertheless, from this time on, Alexander must have given serious consideration to the idea of marriage as a political solution to the affairs of Central Asia.

THE CLEITUS AFFAIR

In summer 328, the strain of the seemingly endless campaigning in Sogdiana was taking its toll. At a drinking-party in Maracanda, Alexander killed Cleitus, the man who had saved his life at the Granicus River.

The catalysts are obvious enough – alcohol, combat fatigue, personalities – but there were larger issues at stake and long-suppressed resentment. Since the death of Darius III, Alexander had openly presented himself as the legitimate successor of the Great King. He had assumed Persian dress – abandoning only those elements that most offended his Macedonians, the conical tiara and the trousers – along with other trappings of Persian royalty. He had given splendid funerals to Darius and his wife Stateira, and he had punished with barbaric mutilation the usurper Bessus. Arrian remarks that Cleitus objected to both Alexander's orientalisms and the sycophancy of his courtiers, who exaggerated his achievements and ignored the contributions of the Macedonians themselves. It was, in fact, the last of these issues that animated Cleitus. The sad affair was a clash of generations and ideologies. Cleitus objected more to the elevation of Alexander to heroic – almost godlike – status than he did to orientalism. The king had ceased to be *primus inter pares* and not only had begun to play the role of absolute ruler but also was now accepting full credit for the accomplishment of the Macedonian army – as if there had been no merit in the works of Philip or Parmenion or Cleitus himself. The king's vanity rankled, but the obsequiousness of his flatterers, which Alexander encouraged, was beyond endurance.

To this may be added the claim, which we have no reason to doubt, that Alexander planned to leave Cleitus behind as satrap of Bactria and Sogdiana, replacing the incumbent Artabazus, who had asked to be excused on account of his old age. Strategically, the area was one of the most important in the entire empire, but for Cleitus the appointment was tantamount to being marooned on the outer fringes of the world. Only two years earlier he had been promoted to the command of half the Companion Cavalry. But the choice of Cleitus was probably a concession, to offset the appointment of Hephaestion as hipparch, a clear case of nepotism that fooled no one. By 328, even Alexander recognized that he had exercised poor judgment and instituted cavalry reforms. By making Hephaestion commander of what now became known as the "First Hipparchy," the king could demote his favorite without dishonor. In Cleitus' case, it was simpler to find him an administrative post. Again, no one was fooled, though Hephaestion, who probably recognized his own limitations, may have been content with a title that disguised his incompetence.

Thus, although the king's orientalizing policies were a source of tension, they did not constitute the major cause of Cleitus' displeasure. It should be noted that Alexander had not yet taken a Sogdianian wife, Rhoxane, nor had he attempted to introduce the Persian court protocol known as *proskynesis*. These things were still to come. Hence, it is fair to say that the argument that ensued had more to do with personal grievances and Cleitus' disapproval of the increased arrogance and autocratic behavior of Alexander. The actions taken against Philotas, Parmenion, and Alexander the Lyncestian may have been acceptable for the general good of the army and the campaign – but not for this: not for the personal aggrandizement of a king who paid more attention to his courtiers and sycophants than to his Macedonian *hetairoi*.

The "final straw" may have been the poem recited at the banquet by a Greek poet named Pierion (or Pranichus), which Cleitus claimed mocked a Macedonian defeat in the presence of the barbarians. In fact, it was a matter of tone and interpretation. Although many scholars believe that the poem related the defeat of Andromachus, Caranus, and Menedemus at the Polytimetus River at the hands of Spitamenes, this is highly unlikely. More plausible is Frank Holt's brilliant deduction that the subject of the poem was the heroism of the harpist, Aristonicus, who had been left with a small garrison, the sick, and a band of royal pages (*paides basilikoi*) at Bactra.[34] Not a warrior by trade, Aristonicus nevertheless fought gallantly against the barbarians and died heroically. At Delphi he was later honored with a statue, depicting him with a spear in one hand and his harp in the other. Aristonicus' last stand must surely have been the theme of the poet's song. Cleitus' objections merely show how thin-skinned the conservative Macedonians had become, how threatened by change, and how sensitive to their own honor.

For all the political undertones of the Cleitus episode, and indeed there were many, the clash between Alexander and his cavalry general was a classic display of what we today call post-traumatic stress disorder (PTSD), as has been noted by historian Lawrence Tritle.[35] Both Cleitus and Alexander exhibit the signs of the stress induced by prolonged combat experience, a desensitized approach to violence, and chronic alcohol consumption. These factors, compounded by ancient notions of honor, almost certainly contributed to the tragedy. In the heat of an argument, which saw the clash of male egos, deed matching deed, and the voicing of opinions best left unspoken, Alexander killed Cleitus in a fit of anger. Whether it was at the banquet or after Cleitus had left the tent and returned, whether it could be justified by the victim's ceaseless provocations, it matters little. The stress of campaigning was great, but even greater was the burden of command.

Nor should we treat Alexander's behavior at Maracanda as unique in the annals of history. Not only does Philip II's behavior on his wedding-night provide a (fortunately, less tragic) example, but other societies, where the heavy consumption of alcohol mixes unhappily with *machismo*, have staged similar scenes. A foreign account of a banquet put on by the Tsar records a confrontation between Peter the Great and his military commander Alexis Shein. Peter had left the room after a heated engagement:

> When he returned a short time later, his rage had increased to such an extent that he drew his sword out of its scabbard and, in front of the General-in-chief, struck the table and threatened: "Thus shall I strike you and put an end to your command." Foaming with righteous anger, he stepped up to Prince Romadanowsky and Mikitin Moseiwitsch; but as he sensed that they were excusing the general, he went into such a smouldering rage that, by repeated and undirected thrusts of the cold steel, he transported all the guests into a state of panic. Romodanowsky received a slight wound on his finger, another a cut to the head, and as he brought his sword backward he injured Mikitin Moseiwitsch on the hand.
>
> He aimed a far more deadly blow against the General-in-chief, who would doubtless have been stretched out in his own blood at the hands of the Tsar, had not General Lefort – probably the only one who would have dared the deed – clutched the hand of the Tsar and pulled it back and thereby prevented a wound. But angered by the fact that there was someone who prevented the fulfillment of his justified rage, the Tsar turned and dealt the uninvited interloper a hard blow on the back.[36]

The intervention nevertheless prevented Peter from murdering Shein as Alexander had killed Cleitus.

Alexander's court had not descended to the buffoonery of Mark Antony's "Inimitable Livers."[37] But the chaos that descended upon Peter the Great's parties blurred the lines between king and subject. As Robert K. Massie observed: "They forgot who the tall man with whom they were heatedly arguing actually was."[38] In Peter's case the formal boundaries between Tsar and subject were beginning, at least temporarily, to erode; at Alexander's court the outspokenness of *hetairoi* was at odds with the changing nature and the increasing aloofness of the Macedonian king. Hence Curtius Rufus has Alexander say: "I tolerated his scurrilous comments, his insults to you and to me, longer than he would have tolerated the same coming from me. The clemency of kings and leaders depends not just on their own character but on the character of their subjects, too. Authority is rendered less harsh by obedience; but when respect leaves men's minds and we mix the highest and the lowest together without distinction – then we need force to repel force."[39] No Macedonian king could have viewed his relationship with his *hetairoi* in this fashion before the conquest of Asia.

POLICY AS AN EXTENSION OF WAR BY OTHER MEANS

By the fall of 328, it was clear that Alexander was making inroads in Transoxiana, but a settlement continued to elude him as Spitamenes, supported by the Massagetae, waged a guerrilla war. In place of Artabazus, the king installed Amyntas son of Nicolaus as satrap, leaving him in Maracanda with Coenus and his forces. Hephaestion was sent across the Oxus to collect provisions, and winter quarters were established at Nautaca. Alexander himself made an excursion to Xenippa, causing a force of about 2,500 rebels who had taken refuge there to abandon the place.[40] By this time, Alexander had come to realize that terror (such as that employed against the Branchidae, the outposts on the Iaxartes, and Ariamazes) was ineffective;[41] and he pardoned the people of Xenippa. His clemency soon paid dividends.[42] Sisimithres, who ruled the region around Nautaca, had withdrawn with the families of the leading nobles to a fortress nearby and was preparing to withstand a siege. Alexander was, however, able to negotiate his surrender through the agency of Oxyartes.[43] Spitamenes, meanwhile, hard pressed by the contingents of Craterus and Coenus, fled with the Massagetae into the desert, but he was soon betrayed by his allies, who sent his head to their Macedonian pursuers. Like those who betrayed Darius in 330 and Bessus in the following year, Spitamenes' erstwhile supporters hoped to buy a respite from war, if not an actual peace.

In the region of Gazaba, Alexander accepted the surrender of Chorienes, who entertained the king when he returned from a punitive expedition against the Scythians. Among the girls who danced at the banquet were the daughters of leading nobles, including Rhoxane (whose name means "Little Star"), the daughter of Oxyartes. Alexander is said to have been smitten with her and asked her father for her hand in marriage. She may indeed have been as beautiful as the sources allege, but it must strike the reader as more than coincidence that the very man who had earlier surrendered to Alexander and persuaded Sisimithres to come to terms with the Macedonians should happen to be the father of the girl with whom Alexander happened to become infatuated. Political marriages are precisely that, arranged unions for political advantage, and if the groom is pleased with the bride (or sometimes the bride with the groom), this is considered a bonus.[44]

Arrian's claim that she was captured on the Rock of Sogdiana (which was defended by Ariamazes) is unlikely for a number of reasons. First, Ariamazes himself was crucified and those who had taken refuge were enslaved. Second, the capture of this fortress occurred before the Cleitus episode and it is significant that Cleitus in his criticisms of Alexander never once mentioned his marriage to Rhoxane; in fact, Curtius remarks that after the fate of Cleitus, even those who were inclined to view Alexander's marriage to Rhoxane with disapproval were afraid to speak out.[45] Finally, there is no strong connection between the Sogdianian Rock and Oxyartes, although the latter is associated with both Sisimithres and Chorienes, who may in fact have been the same individual.[46]

ORIENTALISM AND CONFRONTATION

Towards the end of winter 328/7, one of the most controversial episodes in the career of Alexander occurred.[47] It was becoming clear to the king that his orientalizing policies were proving decisive in his dealings with the barbarians. The retention of local officials, respect for their practices, and intermarriage had all begun to pay dividends. The decision to experiment with the Persian court protocol known as *proskynesis* was part of the same policy. Court ceremonial was quickly becoming a potentially divisive issue. The barbarian could not imagine approaching his king without the required gesture of obeisance; the Macedonian mocked the practice as subservient and demeaning, and Leonnatus' open ridiculing of a Persian elder was an affront to both the subject and the king.[48] Correspondingly, the Macedonian form of interaction with Alexander fell far short of what the Persians regarded as necessary to the dignity of the ruler.

For the Persians, *proskynesis* was a simple gesture of respect, which reflected sociopolitical hierarchies. Herodotus observes:

> When they encounter one another in the streets, one can tell from this sign if those who meet are of similar rank: instead of addressing one another they kiss each other on the lips, but if one is a little inferior to the other, they kiss on the cheeks, and if someone is considerably inferior in birth, he throws himself before the other and does obeisance.[49]

In its most ceremonial form, *proskynesis* emphasized the relationship between ruler and ruled. But even here, it is clear that physical abasement in front of the king was restricted to those of very low social standing, and Persian court officials are depicted as respectfully blowing a kiss towards the King, bowing the head only slightly. Numerous anecdotes relate how reluctant Greek ambassadors or exiles were to perform *proskynesis*,[50] just as western Europeans were later opposed to kowtowing to the Chinese emperor. Their argument was that such behavior was not only inappropriate for free men, but that the recipient of such veneration ought to be a god. Nevertheless, they knew full well that the Great King did not regard himself as a god – a fact conveniently forgotten by many writers, ancient and modern. Hence, it is certainly wrong to regard Alexander's experiment with *proskynesis* as a prelude to ruler cult. It was instead an unsuccessful attempt to blend Macedonian and Persian court practices.

The Macedonians were appalled. The more progressive thinkers (and these were probably few in number) accepted the need for duality in their king's interaction with Greeks and Macedonians on the one hand and barbarians on the other – as long as these roles were kept separate. The application of a mixed ceremonial, which applied equally to the conquerors and the conquered, was another matter. The elevation of Persians to political and military offices, the sight of the Macedonian king in Persian attire, and (most seriously, up to this point) the prospect of an heir to the throne who was of mixed blood, these were all regarded as betrayals and demotions in status. But for them to do obeisance in the Persian fashion to the man who had traditionally been *primus inter pares* – even if Alexander's response to Cleitus' complaints had placed this practice in abeyance – was intolerable. Greek intellectuals had long classified the subjects of the Great King as his "slaves" (*douloi*), and to this level the Macedonians refused to sink. Even more, they disdained the king's flatterers, who sanctioned the process by eulogizing Alexander as one who had surpassed the achievements of heroes and rivaled the excellence of the gods. The king may have welcomed such comparisons – it is hard to see how a young man dazzled by his own success could not have – but this does not mean that their words have any bearing on Alexander's reasons for experimenting with *proskynesis*.

To argue that the Macedonians rejected *proskynesis* because it implied Alexander's divinity is to place too much emphasis on the Macedonian misunderstanding of the practice. When, some time later, Hermolaus was charged with plotting against the king, he listed numerous grievances, the first of which was that Alexander had "begun to act not as a king with his free-born subjects but as a master with his slaves."[51] The allusion to the subjects of the Persian king as slaves (*douloi*) is clear. Later, Hermolaus criticizes Alexander for assuming barbarian dress and attempting to introduce Persian court practices. Finally he remarks:

"You wanted Macedonians to kneel before you and worship you as a god."⁵² Thus, Curtius elucidates the Macedonians' thought process: a Persian ruler treats his subjects like slaves and demands prostration, which is appropriate only for a god. But Alexander's understanding of affairs is equally well spelled out by Curtius, who puts in the king's mouth a speech that answers Hermolaus point for point. On the adoption of Persian ceremonial, he says:

> But Hermolaus claims that I am foisting Persian habits on the Macedonians. True, for I see in many races things we should not blush to imitate, and the only way this great empire can be satisfactorily governed is by our transmitting some things to the natives and learning others from them ourselves.⁵³

When he turns to the matter of his recognition as son of Jupiter (i.e., Amun), Alexander in no way associates it with *proskynesis* but rather notes that

> Jupiter held out to me the title of son; accepting it *has not been disadvantageous to the operations in which we are engaged.* I only wish the Indians would also believe me a god! For reputation determines military success, and often *even a false belief* has accomplished as much as the truth [emphasis added].⁵⁴

It may be argued that Curtius' is a set-piece rhetorical fabrication. But why, we must ask, when Alexander nevertheless emerges as the villain of this episode,⁵⁵ does the historian choose to make Alexander depict his "divinity" as a political tool, equally useful whether it is true or false? On the other hand, Curtius himself is no infallible witness, since in his earlier account of the introduction of *proskynesis* he explicitly states that Alexander wished thereby to be worshipped as a god.

> Alexander now believed that the time was ripe for the depraved idea he had conceived some time before, and he began to consider how he could appropriate divine honors to himself. He wished to be believed, not just called, the son of Jupiter, as if it were possible for him to have as much control over men's minds as their tongues, and he gave orders for the Macedonians to follow the Persian custom in doing homage to him by prostrating themselves on the ground.⁵⁶

But this is not the only occasion on which Curtius contradicts himself – in fact, there are numerous cases where the historian takes over the information in his primary source (Cleitarchus) in its entirety, and then adds contradictory (but often corrective) information from other authors. Such information often comes from Ptolemy, and he if anyone would have understood the utility of image and propaganda.[57]

The setting for the *proskynesis* experiment was a drinking-party in Bactra, apparently restricted to a chosen group of *hetairoi* and members of the king's entourage. These had been instructed by Alexander's chamberlain and historian, Chares of Mitylene (who is believed to have organized the ceremony, perhaps in collusion with Hephaestion), to drink a toast, perform *proskynesis*, and receive a kiss from the king. The form of *proskynesis* was clearly little more than a slight bow; otherwise it is hard to imagine that Alexander can have failed to notice Callisthenes' failure to perform the act. Plutarch's description of the ceremony is instructive:

> Chares of Mitylene says that once at a banquet Alexander, after drinking, handed the cup to one of his friends, and he, on receiving it, rose up so as to face the household shrine, and when he had drunk, first made obeisance (*proskynesai*) to Alexander, then kissed him, and then resumed his place upon the couch. As all the guests were doing this in turn, Callisthenes took the cup, the king not paying attention but conversing with Hephaestion, and after he had drunk went towards the king to kiss him; but Demetrius, surnamed Pheidon, cried: 'O King, do not accept his kiss, for he alone has not done thee obeisance'.[58]

The story is also told by Arrian, but the significant difference in Plutarch's version is the presence of the altar. It may be that the king allowed those who objected to the act to salve their consciences by assuring themselves that the gesture was directed towards the altar rather than throne. To all appearances, and particularly to the Persian subjects, the Macedonians had fulfilled their obligations to the king.[59]

CALLISTHENES AND THE CONSPIRACY OF HERMOLAUS
The true extent of Macedonian dissatisfaction can be gauged by the events that followed, the conspiracy and trial of the pages. It had been

customary at the Macedonian court since the time of Philip, if not earlier, for the sons of the aristocracy to be raised at the king's court. Here they were educated in the company of the king's sons, learned to ride, and accompanied the king on the hunt. Thus they were trained in both the military arts and the ways of the court. This practice may have had its origins in the Near East: certainly, the sons of the Persian nobility were raised in this fashion, as we know from the evidence of Xenophon.[60] It endured in the Hellenistic kingdoms and was adopted also by the Romans. Charlemagne, too, appears to have adopted the practices of the Romans, and the precepts of authors such as Isidore of Seville, who delineated the six stages of a man's life, influenced the courts of kings and other potentates and shaped the development of the knighthood. Hence, it is not entirely anachronistic to use the familiar language of the Middle Ages and refer to these youths as pages.[61]

In 327, not long after the abortive attempt to introduce *proskynesis*, an apparently insignificant incident gave rise to a dangerous conspiracy against the king. During a boar hunt, a page by the name of Hermolaus had rushed to strike the prey instead of leaving the honor to Alexander. For this act of *lèse-majesté* Hermolaus was flogged; for it was the king's prerogative to mete out such punishment. That Hermolaus was pained by this humiliation in front of the other pages and plotted revenge is understandable, and a conspiracy against the king resulting from such an act might have occurred at any time. But the background to the conspiracy is far more complex, and it appears that several of the pages may have been influenced by the views of their fathers.[62] Furthermore, their tutor, Callisthenes, was suspected of having incited Hermolaus to murder the king.

Until the Bactrian campaign, Callisthenes had been (at least openly) a staunch supporter of the king and his Panhellenic program. What it was that turned him against Alexander is not known. Perhaps his alienation from the king was due in part to the influence of Anaxarchus, a rival philosopher (though, strictly speaking, Callisthenes was more historian than philosopher), who is said to have consoled Alexander after the Cleitus affair and encouraged his emulation of heroes and gods. Compared with Anaxarchus, Callisthenes may have been considered a man of principle, as the later tradition implies, and his opposition to *proskynesis* may have been exaggerated to make the point. Certainly, his conduct vis-à-vis the king showed an excessive independence of spirit, if not downright disrespect. Such a man could be suspected as harboring ill will against the king, and of inciting treason. The discovery of Hermolaus' plot thus provided the Macedonians with a convenient excuse to implicate an unpopular courtier.

The plot itself was simple enough, though hardly easy to carry out: one night, when all the conspirators were scheduled to be on guard duty in front of the king's tent, they were to enter it and kill Alexander as he slept. This action was made more difficult by the fact that at least two of the Somatophylakes slept inside the king's chamber, and these too would have to be overpowered. Hence, the pages must have been eighteen years old, or very close to that age, in order to feel physically capable of carrying out so audacious a plan. But the plot was revealed by Charicles to Epimenes' brother Eurylochus, who informed the king in the hope of saving his brother's life. After their arrest, Hermolaus and his colleagues remained defiant, speaking out against the tyranny of Alexander. Although they did not implicate Callisthenes in the crime, even under torture, the connections between the traitors and the outspoken courtier were sufficient to ruin him. The pages were tried and condemned by the army and executed by stoning at the hands of their fellow pages. The nature of Callisthenes' death is disputed, and Chares' claim that he was imprisoned and later died of obesity and a disease of lice sounds suspiciously like *apologia*.[63] Having crushed resistance on two fronts, Alexander now prepared to move on to India.

CONQUEST OF THE PUNJAB

CHAPTER SEVEN

WHEN ALEXANDER SET OUT FOR INDIA IN THE SPRING OF 327, it was to secure the eastern fringes of the empire – Gandhara[1] and the Indus lands had been under Achaemenid rule since the time of Darius I, although Persian authority had weakened somewhat – not to seek the ends of the earth or greater glory beyond. As elsewhere, there were dynasts who were content to recognize the overlordship of Alexander, and even to accept Macedonian garrison troops, if it meant stealing a march on their rivals. It is therefore wrong to speak of the Macedonian conquest of India, though some enemies were clearly conquered. Instead it was a matter of restoring the authority of the empire over the eastern satrapies and establishing buffer zones. But India was a land of mystery and enchantment to the Greeks and the Romans, and it was easy to forget that Alexander had not, in fact, advanced beyond the boundaries of the Persian Empire.

The weakening of Persian authority in the Indian satrapies no doubt accounts for the fact that it was here that the Macedonians encountered the most determined resistance. In Bactria and Sogdiana, the opposition had come from the nobles who had close ties with Darius and from the local dynasts who felt secure in the mountain fortresses. But their opposition was motivated primarily by their distrust of Alexander and they were easily won over by the expedient of political marriage. The Aspasians and Assacenians, by contrast, had enjoyed a greater degree of independence on the fringes of a weaker empire and fought to preserve this.[2] In the northwest the most recalcitrant tribes were those of the Swat, Bajaur, and Buner regions, who relied upon the security of the hills and allied themselves with Abisares, the enemy of the rulers of Taxila. By contrast, the Peshawar lands and the kingdom of Taxila offered less protection against invasion. But they also controlled important trade routes and the overarching authority of an empire must have promised economic opportunities.

The relative weakness of Persian control over the Indian satrapies can also be measured by the extent of Indian participation in Darius' final contest with Alexander. Although Arrian (3.8.3) says that Darius' forces were augmented by "the Indians who lived next to the Bactrians," these are in fact part of the Bactrian contingent led by Bessus; similarly there were "mountain Indians" attached to the force of Arachosians under Barsaentes. To these are added only fifteen elephants from the Indians "this side of the Indus" (that is, Gandhara). When Alexander establishes administrators in the provinces of "India" there is no mention of the satraps who ruled before, only references to dynasts and petty kings. Hence, it appears that although the Persians still exercised some authority over the Indians through the presence of the neighboring satraps, Achaemenid power in these regions had diminished considerably since the time of Darius I.[3]

THE BAJAUR AND SWAT CAMPAIGNS

When Alexander recrossed the Hindu Kush in late spring 327, he returned first to Alexandria-in-the-Caucasus, where he deposed Neiloxenus, whom he had left behind as *hyparchos*. What his shortcomings were is not stated, but it has been suggested that he may have failed to make sufficient preparations for the Indian campaign.[4] Arrian, however, remarks that he had shown poor leadership, and it may be that Alexander deposed him in response to complaints from either the native settlers or the Macedonian invalids who had been left there.[5] From here he moved to Nicaea, the second city he had established among the Parapamisadae, and sent Perdiccas and Hephaestion ahead to the Indus with a force of perhaps 7,000–8,000 men.[6] Their mission had been preceded by diplomatic contacts, and little opposition was expected, except perhaps at Peucelaotis – which, in fact, turned out to be the case. Alexander and the remainder of the army moved against the recalcitrant tribes of the mountainous regions, who trusted in the remoteness of their settlements. The Macedonians had, however, become adept at this type of warfare. They made short work of the Aspasians, in the Kunar or Chitral valley, a campaign in which Ptolemy son of Lagus finally emerged as a commander of the first rank. Despite his fame as one of Alexander's leading generals, he was in fact a late bloomer and, even when he did begin to play a regular role in military affairs, we cannot be sure how much of his reputation is based on his own *History*.[7] Moving ahead with the mobile forces, Alexander stormed the enemy's positions and then left the work of consolidation to Craterus, who trailed behind.

More serious was the threat from the Assacenians, who prepared to resist with a substantial army, but after the death of their leader took refuge in the city of Massaga in the Katgala pass. Here the mother, or perhaps the widow, of the dynast Assacenus held out against the Macedonian forces. When she came to terms with the invader, she received favorable treatment because, according to rumor, she was intimate with Alexander. Although her story is told by other sources as well, only Curtius, Justin, and the *Metz Epitome* – all of which may have derived their information ultimately from Timagenes of Alexandria – name her: Cleophis. Her liaison with Alexander, her reputation as "the royal whore" (*scortum regium*), her own name, and the birth of a son named for his father, Alexander, all call to mind Cleopatra VII of Egypt.[8] Resistance in the area continued nevertheless and, after taking Ora (Ude-gram) and Bazira (Bir-kot), the Macedonian army was confronted by Aphrices (apparently another relative of Assacenus) in the Buner region. He was killed by his own men, but many natives had fled to the realm of Abisares or taken refuge on the rock known as Aornus

(Pir-sar), on the banks of the Indus.[9] This too Alexander captured with a combination of daring and engineering; for he felled trees and moved boulders to form a ramp that facilitated the army's approach to the enemy on the heights. Cut off and overpowered by the enemy, many of the defenders fell to their deaths as they tried to descend the very cliffs in which they had placed their hopes of salvation.

Alexander rejoined Hephaestion and Perdiccas at Peucelaotis (Pushkalavati: modern Charsadda). Here the local dynast Astis was defeated and killed; his replacement was Sangaeus, who had the support of Taxiles, the ruler of the land beyond the Indus who had determined to throw in his lot with Alexander. Leaving a garrison in the city, Alexander crossed the Indus on the boat-bridge prepared by Perdiccas and Hephaestion and advanced to Taxila, in the vicinity of modern Islamabad. En route he was met by Taxiles' son, Omphis, who made formal submission. Father and son welcomed Macedonian support against their powerful neighbors: Abisares to the north, Porus to the east. To these rulers Alexander sent envoys demanding submission, though he knew full well that he was doing little more than establishing a pretext for the coming campaign. Abisares declined to come to Alexander, excusing himself on the grounds of ill health, but it is clear that he was preparing to assist Porus. It appears that Abisares had already planned to join Porus in a campaign against the Sudracae to the south, but Alexander's ambassador Nicocles (presumably the Cypriote *hetairos*) had at least prevented the uniting of the enemies' forces. There may nevertheless have been some truth to Abisares' claim of illness: when Alexander left India he was informed of the death of Abisares and approved his son as successor.[10] Porus, for his part, was less evasive, marching out with his troops to oppose the Macedonians on the banks of the Hydaspes (Jhelum) River.

THE BATTLE OF THE HYDASPES

The battle at the Hydaspes is perhaps one of Alexander's most famous, particularly since it illustrates the practice of what military historians call "convergence" or in simpler terms "deception."[11] The strategy was relatively straightforward, with Alexander outflanking the enemy in order to effect a river crossing, but what deserves special attention is Alexander's use of the terrain and the elements to accomplish his purpose. Porus was aware of Alexander's coming – indeed, he had refused demands to submit and was awaiting military aid from Abisares – and he occupied the eastern banks of the Hydaspes at the point of the main crossing near Haranpur (roughly 110 miles from Taxila).

At the main crossing point, the river was rising as the monsoon rains set in, and the elephants positioned on the banks increased the difficulty of a frontal attack, especially for the horses, which were unaccustomed to such animals and easily frightened.[12] Alexander stationed Craterus with the bulk of the army, including the phalanx battalions of Alcetas and Polyperchon, directly opposite Porus. Farther upstream he positioned another detachment of the army under the command of Meleager, Attalus, and Gorgias; their force comprised three phalanx battalions and a large number of Greek mercenaries.[13] The king himself made frequent feints upstream, always closely shadowed by a contingent of Indians on the opposite bank. When he learned of an island in the bend of the Indus, some seventeen miles upstream (in the vicinity of modern Jalalpur), he determined to lead his troops there and attempt a crossing, using the forces under Craterus to fix the enemy's position near Haranpur. He was aided in this deception by the heavy rains and thunder of the monsoon season, which obscured both the sight and sound of his encircling march. The island served to screen his crossing, but it was also misleading; for the men, upon reaching the island, mistakenly thought they had reached the other side of the river. Nevertheless, the crossing was effected with sufficient speed and surprise so that the forces sent by Porus to prevent a crossing upstream were caught off guard. After a brief skirmish, they withdrew to Porus, who was now forced to turn his forces to deal with Alexander. Porus' own move in that direction was the signal for Craterus to bring his army across.

In the Hydaspes battle, Porus is thought to have commanded some 30,000 infantry but only 4,000 mounted troops, compared with perhaps 15,000–20,000 infantry and more than 5,000 cavalry in Alexander's force,[14] once it had been strengthened by contingents under Meleager,

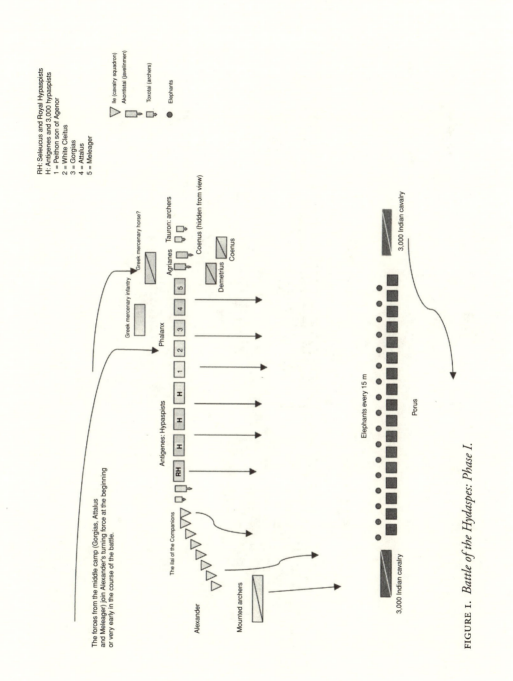

FIGURE 1. *Battle of the Hydaspes: Phase I.*

117

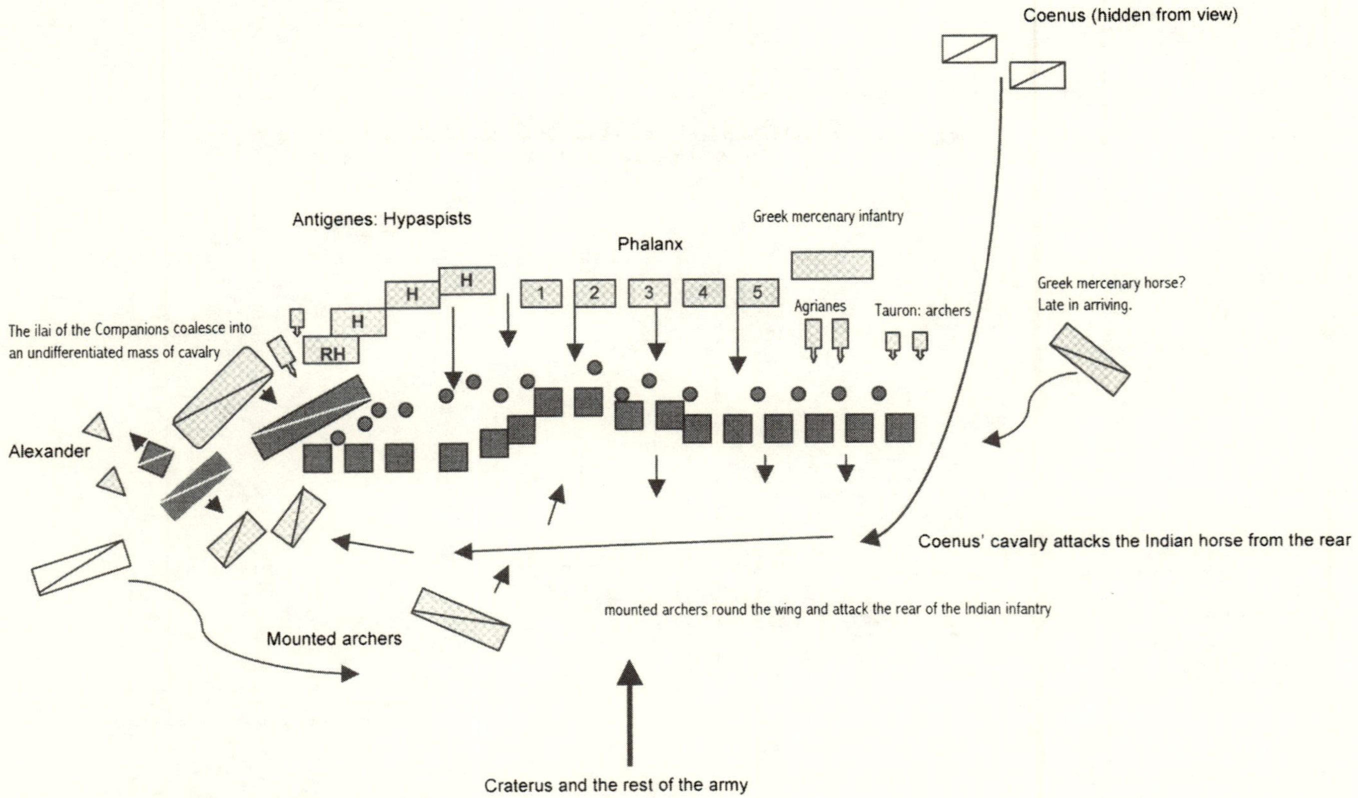
Coenus (hidden from view)
Antigenes: Hypaspists
Greek mercenary infantry
Phalanx
1
2
3
4
5
H
H
H
RH
Greek mercenary horse?
Late in arriving.
Agrianes
Tauron: archers
The ilai of the Companions coalesce into
an undifferentiated mass of cavalry
Alexander
Coenus' cavalry attacks the Indian horse from the rear
mounted archers round the wing and attack the rear of the Indian infantry
Mounted archers
Craterus and the rest of the army

FIGURE 2. *Battle of the Hydaspes: Phase II.*

Attalus, and Gorgias. Since Porus was deficient in horsemen, he hoped to offset this disadvantage by stationing his elephants, of which he had 200, at regular intervals amongst the front line of his infantry. But Alexander, reading the Indian's intentions, held back his own phalanx and proceeded to attack Porus' forces on the flanks with his cavalry. Although the ancient descriptions of the battle are far from clear, it appears that Alexander massed his cavalry on his right wing, keeping the hipparchy of Coenus hidden from view on the left. When Porus transferred the cavalry on his own right to the left, where he was vastly outnumbered, Coenus' horsemen rode behind the Indian ranks and attacked their cavalry from the rear. The fact that Coenus did not attack the now exposed right flank of Porus' infantry suggests that Alexander's purpose was to annihilate the Indian cavalry, in the belief that he would then have the infantry entirely at his mercy.

The reconstruction of the events that played out in the center must be based in large part on conjecture. Porus' infantry, anchored by the elephants, cannot have formed a particularly mobile battle group, especially on the muddy plain, which had already caused the charioteers such hardships. Alexander's decision to hem them in and delay contact with his own infantry units may be due to the fact that the bulk of the infantry, phalangites, and mercenaries would still have been coming up under the leadership of Meleager and his colleagues. The ancient sources do not remark upon their arrival, for it was generally the case that the historians directed their attentions to Alexander's own actions. But the Macedonian victory is scarcely credible without their participation. Since Porus placed his elephants in front to the infantry line at intervals of roughly 15 meters, the Indian line must have extended well beyond the Macedonian left, even if Porus' forces were deployed in depth (see Appendix Two). It is more likely that the boats used to transport Alexander's encircling force now sailed downriver to pick up the second Macedonian contingent. By the time of their crossing, Porus' guard under Spitaces had been defeated and routed, and their landing must have been unopposed. Perhaps they were extending and firming up the Macedonian center at the same time as the horsemen launched their attack on the Indian left. If the Greek mercenary cavalry arrived at this time, they may have taken up a position on the Macedonian left, which since the departure of Coenus and Demetrius was denuded of cavalry and protected only by archers and Agrianes.

In the confrontation of the two infantry lines, the elephants were thrown into disarray by the effective use of javelins and bristling sarissas, which more than negated the fearsome power of the pachyderms. The beasts, crazed by their wounds, soon proved as dangerous to their own forces as to the enemy. Pinned down by the Macedonian infantry and pressed on all sides by the victorious cavalry, Porus' troops were defeated before Craterus and his divisions could join the battle.

In one of the best-known stories intended to illustrate Alexander's magnanimity, the heavily wounded and defeated Porus is asked by the Macedonian conqueror how he would like to be treated. He responds with the words "Like a king." And Alexander, we are told, is happy to acquiesce, not only allowing him to retain his kingdom but adding to it. Despite the story's purpose, Alexander was moved by something other than greatness of spirit. He did not have a distinguished record of treating noble adversaries with respect. The Tyrians suffered no less a fate than the Thebans; Batis, the defender of Gaza, was brutally killed and mutilated; and Ariamazes, who trusted to the natural defenses of the Rock of Sogdiana, was crucified, his followers sold into slavery. Porus, we may assume, would have suffered similar indignities had Alexander not needed a strong kingdom on the borders of his empire. The treatment of Porus and the strengthening of his kingdom are clear signs of Alexander's intentions.[15]

THE HYPHASIS "MUTINY"

He lived for war, loved its hardships and adventures even more than victory itself, and the more impossible the odds against him, the more eagerly he accepted them. Wrapped in an impenetrable reserve, his faith in himself was boundless, and his power of self-deception unlimited— nothing seemed to him to be beyond his reach. The numerical superiority of his enemy; the strength of his position; the weariness of his own troops; their lack of armament and supplies; foundering roads, mud, rain, frost

and scorching sun appeared to him but obstacles set in his path by
Providence to test his genius. Nothing perturbed him, every danger and
hazard beckoned him on.

These words could easily be taken by those who have become accus-
tomed to the hero worship of modern scholarship as a description
of Alexander the Great. They are, in fact, the opening remarks of
Major-General J. F. C. Fuller's characterization of Charles XII of Sweden (1682–1718).[16] Much of what Fuller says is true of both men, but
Alexander averted disaster precisely because he did put limits on his own
ambitions.

Alexander's actions after the defeat of Porus and the founding of the
cities of Bucephala and Nicaea have been the subject of considerable
debate. The traditional view, which sees Alexander as a man obsessed
with marching to the ends of the earth and the eastern ocean, simply
assumes that his continuing eastward across the Punjab was a natural
consequence of the victory over Porus. He would drive on until he
reached the Hyphasis (Beas) River, only to be forced to turn back by
his own troops, who rejected his pleas that they should advance to the
Ganges. This view, however, has little to commend it, and in fact the
ancient evidence argues strongly against it. It is important to remember here what we have stressed all along, that the Alexander historians
reported three types of things: what Alexander did (though this is not
always reported accurately); what Alexander wanted the world to believe
(i.e., propaganda which originated with the king and his court); and
later propaganda – what we might call the legend of Alexander. All
three elements are present in the historical account and they can easily
be separated.

Military historian David Lonsdale has commented: "When we shift
our attention to India, it is more difficult to identify Alexander's operational art. This is mainly due to the fact that Alexander had lost some of
his strategic focus. Aside from searching for an ocean frontier, the campaign did not appear to have clear and definable objectives. Without
clear strategic objectives, operational art had no hook to hang on."[17]

In fact, nothing could be farther from the truth, and it is only modern scholars' preconceptions about Alexander's desire to push into the unknown that have blinded them to what was a highly sensible, and well-executed, strategy. Porus' kingdom was clearly intended to form a buffer zone on the fringe of the empire. The extent of Achaemenid control in Tataguš had always been limited, and Alexander was content to acknowledge Porus as a vassal in the hope of protecting the stability of Taxila and Gandhara. Also, Porus' realm formed a link on the eastern banks of the Indus with the satrapy of Hinduš or Sindh, which Alexander had yet to secure.

Alexander had allowed Porus to keep his kingdom – significantly there is no mention of a satrap, a *strategos*, or a garrison – and he had sought to establish friendly relations between Porus and Taxiles. The founding of two cities on either bank of the Hydaspes is also typical of Alexander's frontier policy, and there is little doubt that Bucephala and Nicaea were intended to control the limits of his empire. Furthermore, since the area in the north of Porus' kingdom was heavily wooded, Alexander left troops and laborers behind to construct a vast fleet, with which he planned to make a descent of the Indus river system. He also offered sacrifices to the sun god, Helios – thank-offerings for the success he had already achieved in India. But since it was the monsoon season and his men could not be kept idle under the most depressing and debilitating conditions, he conducted further campaigns in the Punjab, foraging for the supplies he would need to maintain the army (and, presumably, for the Indus expedition) and subduing the neighboring tribes. These were, significantly, annexed to Porus' kingdom, and the garrisons planted there comprised Porus' own troops. In effect, Alexander had renounced all claims to conquest east of the Hydaspes.

The king's behavior at the Hyphasis was utterly fraudulent[18] – not merely the establishment of a camp of superhuman proportions, intended to deceive posterity, but the actual drama that was played out by Alexander and the army. The historians are unanimous in their claims that Alexander announced his intention to proceed beyond the Hyphasis and subdue the Gangetic kingdom of the Nandas, but that the army refused to follow him and thus handed him his only defeat. Bosworth suggests that the information acquired by Alexander about the extent of India surprised but did not deter him. He had formerly "believed the eastern Ocean close at hand."[19] Hence, he planned to march to the Ocean and then return to the Hydaspes. But, when he learned of the vast lands of the Gangetic plain, he was fired by the desire for further conquest: "For him it was an inspiring challenge, but for his troops it came as the last straw, a promise of misery without end, and their refusal was absolute."[20] The attraction of this theory is that it conforms with Alexander's attested ability to improvise in the light of new developments. Such ability is essential on the battlefield but less so for the formulation of grand strategy. Indeed, to deviate from a well-formulated plan on the basis of a whim is unsound; nor is it in keeping with Alexander's previous actions when he reached the edges of the Persian Empire. Elsewhere, he had not pushed mindlessly into the unknown, and there is no reason to assume that he wished to do so now. Was his longing to unravel the mysteries of India and his obsession with the eastern Ocean any greater than his interest in other regions? Only in the minds of modern writers.

There is, furthermore, the question of leadership to be considered. First there is the curious fact that an experienced commander presented in full detail the strength and superior numbers of the enemy to a group of demoralized men. In effect, he confirmed the very rumors that were causing them distress, in a speech that was hardly inspiring or motivational. Second, although one of the chief arguments presented by the soldiers' spokesman, Coenus, was the poor condition of the men's military equipment, Alexander never indicated that new armor for 25,000 men was on its way, along with substantial reinforcements.[21] He neither mentioned them nor indicated that he was prepared to await their arrival. Instead, these were waiting for him when he led the army back to the Hydaspes to begin the journey downriver. The Hyphasis, more than any other event in Alexander's career, displays a complete failure of leadership in that the king asked his men to do something that was dangerous in the extreme and of questionable value to the success of his campaign. He did nothing to make his proposal palatable to his men, whose personal safety and suffering he utterly disregarded. In fact, his approach was such that the only reasonable conclusion is that he wanted to incite the men to mutiny. And this can only mean that he had no serious intention of proceeding but wanted to place the blame for turning back on the shoulders of his men. [22]

This brings us back to Lonsdale's comment (above) that Alexander had no "clear strategic objectives." The king made these objectives more than clear when he began the construction of the Hydaspes fleet. He had consistently advanced to borders of the Persian Empire and confirmed them by strengthening their defenses and conducting symbolic sacrifice to the gods – very often his globe-trotting ancestor, Heracles, and Athena, goddess of victory (Minerva Victoria). He had avoided prolonged conflict with the Getae north of the Danube and the Scythians beyond the Iaxartes; nor was he tempted to venture into the lands of the Ethiopians or conduct an expedition against the Amazons. In fact, he rejected the offer of the Chorasmian king to join in a campaign against the Amazons on the grounds that he had to give his attention to the task at hand. So, too, an advance beyond the Hyphasis would have been a counterproductive diversion. Nor, indeed, would it have made sense for Alexander to strengthen the position of Porus, whom he would have had to leave, unfettered, astride his lines of communication. The altars set up on the Hyphasis, along with the camp designed to create the impression of the Macedonian *Übermensch*, marked also the limits of Porus' buffer state. Alexander's concern was with what remained of Persia's erstwhile empire, the Indus lands to the south.

Whether the redirection of the expedition had, in fact, been predetermined or forced upon Alexander by the recalcitrance of his men, the "abandonment" of the eastern progress must have had left a lingering impression of failure. Even if the troops were manipulated into opposing what they believed were the king's real intentions, they nevertheless bore the burden of guilt. They had selfishly considered only their own well-being, and in the process deprived the king of eternal glory. This setback, or rather the appearance of such, was countered by the later minting of commemorative coin issues (the so-called Porus

Decadrachm) showing Alexander on horseback attacking Porus, who sits defiantly atop his elephant. It shows, in fact, a duel (*monomachia*) that never occurred, but it symbolizes, effectively, the great struggle to secure the East. The message seems clear enough, though the dating of the coins is disputed. [23]

THE OCEAN AND
THE WEST

CHAPTER EIGHT

T HE MARCH FROM THE HYPHASIS (BEAS) TO THE HYDASPES (Jhelum) marked the beginning of the long road home. This is not to say that there were no more battles to be fought or hardships to be endured, but it was clear to all that Alexander had established the Indus river system as the eastern limit of his empire. Thus he reasserted the claims of the Achaemenid kings, if only for a short while. Little did he know that the collapse of the Nanda dynasty was imminent and the Mauryan kingdom of Chandragupta (Sandrocottus) was destined to subjugate the Punjab and the Indus lands to the south. At the time, it seemed prudent to secure Porus' realm against the threat of hostile neighbors, namely the Sudracae and Mallians, but in the long run Alexander's actions may have weakened the Punjab in the face of new enemies to the east.

All newly acquired territories east of the Hydaspes were given to Porus. Alexander received Abisares into alliance and assigned to him control of Hazara, where Arsaces remained as satrap; furthermore, he had broken the resistance of others who opposed Porus – the so-called Cowardly Porus and the Cathaeans – and now directed his energies against the tribes to the south. Porus retained the rank of king and enjoyed expanded territories and fewer restrictions on his power than Taxiles, who remained under the watchful eye of Philip son of Machatas. "Friendship" between the two rulers was secured by a political marriage, but the settlement imposed by Alexander must have disappointed Taxiles' expectations.

DESCENT OF THE INDUS

In September 326, the Macedonian forces returned from their campaign in the eastern Punjab to Nicaea and Bucephala on the Hydaspes. The new settlements had been ravaged by the monsoon, but the fleet-building program begun in the month after Alexander's victory over Porus was in full swing. In addition to the ships that had been prepared in his absence, Alexander built others, until the grand total of vessels — warships, troop and horse transports, supply ships, and native craft — had swollen to nearly 2,000.[1] Reinforcements, equipment, and medical supplies from the west raised the morale of the troops, and the expedition was launched with great fanfare and supplication of the gods. Thus began a systematic conquest of the Indus region, as the armada moved impressively downstream, flanked on either side by the heavy infantry and elephants. The path to the Ocean would take them past the confluences of the great tributaries of the Indus and through the lands of Porus' traditional enemies, the Sudracae. These peoples had paid tribute to the Achaemenid kings through the satrap of Arachosia.[2] To the south lay the Sibi, Aggalasseis, and Adrestae; and even these were linked by remote traditions – at least as far as the Greeks understood them – with Heracles. Beyond was the land of Sindh (Hinduš) and the delta region of Patalene. The army marched, divided by the river, for logistical reasons, for maximum military effect, and to keep apart commanders who had now turned to feuding.

Alexander's two most trusted officers and friends, Hephaestion and Craterus, had come to blows in the days that followed the Hydaspes battle, and their personal rivalry had spread to their respective troops. Such friction between officers is common enough in armies, but Hephaestion had a special talent for making enemies. He was abrasive and quarrel-some, no doubt because his friendship with Alexander allowed him to offend with impunity. But many of the *hetairoi* attributed his promotion to higher offices to Alexander's personal favor rather than merit. The king did nothing to dispel such notions by publicly calling Hephaes-tion "a fool and a madman, if he did not realize that without Alexander he was nothing."[3] Nevertheless, in any dispute, Hephaestion had the advantage of being able to plead his case with Alexander in private, and although Craterus had the respect of the soldiers and officers alike, his opponent had the king's ear. From this point on, we see the decline of Craterus' authority. The forces were divided as follows: Alexander, with the hypaspists, Agrianes, archers, and the *agema* of the cavalry, sailed with the fleet; Craterus, with a share of the infantry and cavalry, marched along the western bank of the river; Hephaestion, with the larger and more powerful contingent, as well as some 200 elephants, descended along the eastern bank. Before the army reached the Indus Delta, Craterus would be sent westward through Drangiana with the heavy infantry, many of whom were scheduled to be demobilized.

THE MALLIAN CAMPAIGN

The Sudracae (also wrongly called the "Oxydracae") and the Mallians were inveterate foes of Porus. An earlier expedition conducted in con-junction with Abisares had accomplished little. Alexander's army, which was at least twice as large as the one with which he had crossed into Asia, may have given them pause, but they nevertheless were able to mobilize substantial forces of their own.[4] Furthermore, they ended their internal political quarrels to present a united front to the enemy. It was in the attack on the town of the Mallians[5] that Alexander once again recklessly exposed himself to danger. He had done so many times dur-ing his career, but this time it almost cost him his life. Leading the troops who were scaling the walls, he found himself inside the Mallian stronghold with only a few personal guards. The other infantrymen, who had been slower to advance, now rushed to his aid. In their haste, however, they overloaded the ladders, which broke under their weight. Before sufficient numbers could arrive, Alexander had been wounded in the chest with an Indian arrow, as some of his defenders lay dead beside him and Peucestas, though also wounded, protected him with his hoplite shield; some say it was the sacred shield of Athena, which had been taken from the temple in Troy at the beginning of the campaign.[6]

The king was carried to safety, but the sources disagree about who treated the wound: some said Critobulus (a physician who had once removed the arrow from Philip II's eye at Methone); others claim that the task was given to Perdiccas, the man who was to play a major, but short-lived, role in the age of the Successors. As in virtually every case where Alexander was wounded by the enemy, the conquered paid a price in blood, as the Macedonians consoled themselves with wanton slaughter.

Some have suggested that the soldiers were war-weary and reluctant to engage in further battle and that they exposed their king to danger through their sluggishness. If this is true, the lapse was a very short one, and no recriminations were ever made – except by modern scholars. Certainly, later on, when the fleet continued its descent downriver, a rumor that Alexander had died, and the suspicion that their officers were withholding the truth from them, caused a near riot of the troops. The king was placed on the deck of the ship, where he could be seen by the men, who looked for any wave or nod as a sign of life and approval.[7] The royal hypaspist, Peucestas, later received an exceptional promotion to the rank of Somatophylax. This elite group was limited to seven men, but Peucestas was enrolled, temporarily, as an exceptional eighth member.[8]

In the time that Alexander was recuperating, an incident occurred that casts an interesting light on the tensions between Greeks and Macedonians as well as between warriors and professional athletes.[9] A quarrel arose in the camp when a Macedonian infantryman named Corrhagus accused the boxer (or pancratiast) Dioxippus of remaining in the safety of the camp, oiling his body, while "real men" risked their lives in battle. The argument grew more heated and ended with a challenge to single combat. Corrhagus, armed in the Macedonian style, was met by Dioxippus, naked and carrying a wooden club. The resemblance to Heracles must have been evident to all who watched. Strong and agile, he evaded the Macedonian, broke his sarissa with his club and threw him to the ground. Alexander ordered him to release Corrhagus, but the humiliation was felt by the king no less than by Corrhagus and his companions. The incident brought to the surface the latent hostilities between the Greeks and their Macedonian masters,[10] and it is significant that it is not reported by Arrian (and thus may not have been in Ptolemy's work); Cleitarchus, who was undoubtedly responsible for preserving the tale, may have heard it from discharged Greek soldiers who had been in the camp at the time.

The Dioxippus affair was one of many examples of friction within the Greco-Macedonian army. Nearchus (who was a naturalized Makedon but of Cretan origin) and Eumenes from Cardia were regarded with suspicion in the days that followed Alexander's death, and doubtless during his lifetime as well – though Nearchus, at least, had the advantage of being a close personal friend of the king. Plutarch alleges that, at the time of the Cleitus affair, Alexander remarked to some visiting Greeks that in the midst of the quarreling Macedonians they must have seemed like demigods amongst wild beasts.[11] If there is any truth to the story, Alexander's remark can have done nothing to reduce the tension between the two camps. Similarly, Callisthenes was said to have spoken favorably about the Greeks and in a derogatory fashion about the Macedonians;[12] even if it was nothing more than a rhetorical exercise, it failed to win him any friends. The Panhellenic crusade was by now long in the past.

The remainder of the Indus campaign seemed, by comparison with the conquest of the Punjab and the Mallians, little more than a formality. Local dynasts surrendered at the news of Alexander's approach, though some, like Musicanus, oscillated in their loyalty to the conqueror and paid the extreme penalty; the Brahmins, who incited his defection, were slaughtered in great numbers.[13] Likewise, Oxicanus and Porticanus – if they were, in fact, different individuals – rebelled, only to be arrested by contingents sent out by Alexander. One other dynast, Sambus, a neighbor and rival of Musicanus, first fled and then surrendered. From Musicanus' kingdom, Alexander controlled the route leading from Alor to Kandahar (Alexandria-in-Arachosia), along which he sent Craterus and the bulk of the heavy infantry, those unfit for military service, and the elephants westward to mop up resistance in Drangiana.[14] The king himself advanced to Patala and sailed down both arms of the Indus to the Ocean. Peithon son of Agenor was left behind as satrap of Sindh, but it must have been clear to Alexander that the administration of the satrapy would prove difficult at best.[15]

VIA DOLOROSA: THE GEDROSIAN DISASTER

Patala and the Indus Delta had been well supplied with ship-sheds and facilities for the fleet, which was scheduled to sail, once the winds permitted, from the river mouth to the Persian Gulf. Although the naval mission would be one of exploration, the route between India and Hormuz had been used long before the arrival of the Macedonians, and the voyage of the fleet offered one more means of bringing home a contingent of the expeditionary force and the spoils of conquest. [16] Security and supply were nevertheless matters of acute concern, and Alexander's march through the Makran wastelands, known in antiquity as Gedrosia, was made primarily in support of the fleet. Some writers, ancient and modern, have dismissed the march as pure folly, the result of the king's urge (*pothos*) to emulate his predecessors, the legendary Assyrian queen, Semiramis, and Cyrus the Great.[17] Others have suggested that Alexander subjected his men to the hardships of the Gedrosia as punishment for their failure to follow him to the ends of the earth (i.e., the Hyphasis mutiny).[18] In fact, the success of Nearchus' expedition depended on the coordinated activities of a portion of the army, remaining in contact with the coast, ensuring water and supplies, and suppressing hostile tribes. Even when Arrian claims that the king was inspired by emulation, he notes the importance of supplying the fleet.[19]

In retrospect, it is easy to fault Alexander's apparent "error in judgment" or hubristic venture – if that is what it was. Armies have come to ruin in the course of retreat, when no route offered safety or succor and only the instinct to survive preserved the most determined. So it was with Antony's ill-fated Parthian campaign, or Napoleon's miserable retreat from Russia. Other expeditions perished in extravagant quests through ignorance of geography or the nature of the enemy. Then again, there are spectacular marches that accomplish the unexpected and generate victory through sheer audacity, such as T. E. Lawrence's dash to Aqaba or Bolívar's crossing of the Andes in 1819. The latter cost *El Libertador* two-thirds of his force and has been interpreted variously as an incomparable feat of daring and as the action of a madman.[20] But no such factors animated Alexander and, although he may have misjudged the difficulties or have been misled by his informants, he cannot be blamed for recklessness. To separate the needs of the fleet, indeed the very purpose of the naval campaign, from the overland march makes no sense whatsoever. Nor did he himself shirk the personal hardships of this vital campaign.

Lewis V. Cummings, whose familiarity with much of the terrain encountered by Alexander accounts in part for the republication of his biography of the conqueror during the "Alexandermania" of 2004, remarks:

> In view of the then existing caravan route, of which Alexander could have not remained ignorant, he can be accused only of willful disregard for his army or an incredible disbelief in the difficulties of the seashore route he chose. Of course he desired to maintain contact with the fleet; there were other and more logical plans by which, if followed, the disastrous march would have been rendered unnecessary.

Cummings does not say what these "more logical plans" might have been, and it appears that Alexander was, like so many other commanders, at the mercy of fortune.

He had sent the bulk of the heavy infantry and the troops unfit for military service (*apomachoi*) – in short, the very troops who had defied him at the Hyphasis (and the ones some writers have suggested he was intent upon punishing) – along the less rigorous route to Carmania. This would have taken Craterus through the Mulla Pass, rather than the Bolan, which at that time was not in use; furthermore, the former is open year round.[21] Nevertheless, even this route can scarcely be called *easy*, at least that portion leading north from Kalat. The nineteenth-century adventurer Josiah Harlan observed that the area around Quetta "consists of mountains divided by small unproductive valleys, with barely vegetation sufficient to sustain the pastoral population, which is sparse and savage. The quantity of water is only capable of sustaining small bodies of men and animals. . . . "[22] Ancient conditions cannot have differed much from those of the nineteenth century.

In his passage through the lands of the Oreitae and the desert beyond, Alexander assigned the tasks of supply and fortification to Hephaestion and the more strictly military ones to Leonnatus and Ptolemy. The more mobile columns hampered the inhabitants' abilities to endanger the fleet – though most communities fled at the approach of the Macedonians – and secured supplies and booty. But the great hardships came in the region between Rhambacia in the land of the Oreitae and the borders of Gedrosia, a punishing march of some sixty days.[23] Although the human loss was great, those who suffered most were camp followers.[24] The simple fact is that the Macedonian army had to follow the southern route in sufficient numbers to be of use to the fleet and secure it against enemies. The preparations that were made, and the precautions taken (such as marching during the night), were based on the best available information and estimates. Even the king's discovery of water in the shale-covered regions of the coast owed more to native information than divine providence.[25] Some conditions could, indeed, be mitigated by appropriate action. But Alexander, like any other commander, could not foresee natural disasters. That which overtook the camp as a result of a rainstorm sounds remarkably like the flash flood, described so vividly by Otto of Freising, which all but destroyed the German camp during the march to the Holy Land in 1148.[26] Similarly, we might compare the Russian campaign of Charles XII of Sweden in 1708–9, which ended in disaster at Poltava: here careful attention to supplying the army was rendered useless by poor communications and the coldest winter on record.[27] Countless parallels could be adduced. It is sufficient to note that Alexander's experience in the Gedrosian wasteland was neither unique nor attributable to whim or megalomania.

In part, the catastrophe can be blamed on the neighboring satraps, who ignored (or did not react quickly enough to) Alexander's demands for provisions. But, when the king later executed certain of the neighboring satraps, meting out what has been regarded as excessive punishment, it is more likely that they were guilty of disobedience or derelict in some other exercise of their office than that they were mere scapegoats.[28] The administrative shakeup had begun long before Alexander left the Indus and would continue in the coming weeks, but for the time it was counterbalanced by a slackening of discipline in the army in consideration of the hardships the soldiers had undergone. The army is said to have progressed through Carmania, mindless of military considerations ("you could see no shield, no helmet, no sarissa": Plut. *Alex.* 67.4), and given over to drinking and debauchery; Alexander and his closest companions led the way on a specially constructed wagon drawn by eight horses. The famous "Bacchic revel" in Carmania has been rejected by the majority of scholars, many of whom felt that it exaggerated Alexander's alleged fondness for drink and represented a low point in his military career. As such, it has been conveniently dismissed as fiction, the work of hostile sources, many of them influenced by the fate of Callisthenes. The details of this bacchanalia and the extent of the debauchery are doubtless overdone by the sources, but there is no good reason for rejecting the story either as bad history or as poor generalship on Alexander's part. The king, now that he had returned to territories that were securely under Macedonian control, gave his troops much-needed and greatly deserved R&R. The crisis was behind him.[29] Large armies often moved at a snail's pace, and it is doubtful that the partying troops covered much ground in what was essentially friendly territory; but some movement would have been desirable for sanitary reasons, if nothing else. Nevertheless, the sources' failure to mention troops on regular guard duty should not be taken to mean that there were none. At Salmous, the army witnessed the Indian fleet putting into harbor, thus signaling another round of festivities and rejoicing.

As the army moved westward, the full extent of the administrative malfeasance became clear to Alexander: some officials were punished for their failure to supply the army, but the majority of those arrested had been guilty of various crimes and even rebellion. In some cases, they had actually been moved to rebellion by a guilty conscience and by the presence of mercenary armies to support their cause. The king responded by demanding the dispersal of satrapal mercenary armies. But to consider the satraps' activities part of a coordinated effort is misleading. There had been misrule on a large scale – although not all officials who disappeared from record or were removed from office were victims of a purge – and the extent of the punishment was commensurate.[30] It would be unfair to put the actions of Alexander's officials in the same category as the atrocities committed by the conquistadors in the New World, but Alexander was certainly more effective (by his personal intervention) than the Spanish crown was in its attempts to curb the abuses in Peru. The venerable historian of the conquest, William H. Prescott, rightly comments: "had the sovereign [sc. Charles V] been there in person to superintend his conquests, he could never have suffered so large a portion of his vassals to be wantonly sacrificed to the cupidity and cruelty of the handful of adventurers who subdued them." To label Alexander's punishment of a group of thugs, embezzlers, and extortionists a "reign of terror" perverts all notions of justice and morality.[31]

It was probably at this point in his journey that Alexander received news of the defection of his friend, the Imperial Treasurer, Harpalus. Initial reports, brought by the actors Cissus and Ephialtes, was treated with incredulity – indeed, Alexander was prepared to put them in irons on the charge of spreading false rumors – but the presence of Cleander, Sitalces, Agathon, and Heracon confirmed the news and made known the full extent of the abuses. As *strategoi* associated with the deviant treasurer, Cleander and the others were also found guilty of neglect of duty and crimes against the native inhabitants. Alexander executed them, along with some 600 soldiers who had helped to carry out the abuses. Heracon was acquitted at this time, only to be brought up on new charges by other victims and sentenced to death. The charges, which included rape, murder, sacrilege, and intimidation, amounted to war crimes, and Alexander's actions ought to be applauded; too many countries have turned a blind eye to similar activities – witness the atrocities of Tiger Force in Vietnam, which have been swept under the table. Instead, Alexander's measures are seen by many modern scholars as further evidence of his brutality.[32]

In fact, the "victims" of Alexander's alleged purge are a mixed cast of satraps, military men, and Persian rebels. The generals (Cleander, Heracon, Agathon, and Sitalces) all belonged to the same administrative area as Harpalus, whose misconduct cannot be denied or dismissed as a trumped-up charge. As far as the satraps are concerned, the claim that Apollophanes was deposed appears to have been an error on Arrian's part; he died in battle before Alexander reached Pura, where Arrian claims he issued the order of deposition. Tyriaspes' removal from office in 326 occurred too early to be regarded as part of this process. Orxines (a descendant of one of the Seven), Astaspes, Abulites, and his son Oxathres all belonged to the Persian nobility, which had a long history of resisting central authority. Alexander may simply have been less tolerant and less forgiving than his Achaemenid predecessors.

Alexander's position *vis-à-vis* the Persian aristocracy invites comparison with that of William the Conqueror between 1066 and 1086 (the date of *Domesday Book*), though admittedly William had a more legitimate claim to the throne of the conquered.[33] Historian R. Allen Brown observes:

> That in the beginning king William had intended to establish a genuine Anglo-Norman state is proved by his patronage of and patience with the atheling Edgar, earls Edwin and Morcar, Waltheof and Copsi, and those other members of the pre-Conquest nobility of England who submitted to him and made their peace after Hastings. . . . [34]

In the event, rebellion originated with both the old Anglo-Scandinavian aristocracy and some of the new Norman lords; twenty years after the conquest, the landholdings of the native aristocracy amounted to only about five percent of the total. With the failure to bring about an accommodation of the victors and the vanquished, the Norman (like the Macedonian) army was regarded as an occupation force, with Norman castles functioning like Alexander's citadel garrisons.[35]

The case for a "reign of terror" falters in other respects as well. The presence of Stasanor, Atropates, Peucestas, Philoxenus, and Menander in Babylon in 323 does not mean that they too were earmarked for elimination and saved only by Alexander's premature death. Nor is it a foregone conclusion that Antipater would have come to harm, though admittedly he was reluctant to obey the king's instructions.[36] He was, after all, in his seventy-sixth year when Alexander summoned him to Asia.

What incensed Alexander the most, however, was a crime against royal dignity. The tomb of Cyrus the Great in Pasargadae, which he had visited in 330, was now found to have been plundered by robbers. And he executed one of the perpetrators, Polymachus, even though he was a prominent Macedonian from Pella. Here in Persia Alexander was eager to emphasize his role as the legitimate ruler, following the Achaemenid practice of distributing gold coins to the women; on the other hand, he found it necessary to execute Orxines, who claimed descent from the Seven, on a charge of treason. Hostile accounts depicted Orxines as the victim of the eunuch Bagoas, who exercised an undue influence over Alexander. There is, of course, no need to question Bagoas' existence, but the fact that the story of his personal attack on Orxines is unique to Q. Curtius Rufus may be *color romanus* and an attempt to compare Alexander with a corrupt emperor of the early Empire.[37]

Mass Marriages in Susa (324)

In Susa, Alexander conducted another controversial experiment. He ordered more than ninety of his *hetairoi* to take as wives the daughters of prominent Persian nobles. He himself married Stateira, the daughter of Darius who had once been his prisoner, as well as Parysatis, a daughter of Artaxerxes III Ochus, thus linking himself with two branches of the Persian royal house; to Hephaestion he gave Stateira's sister, Drypetis. The program – for such it was – has been presented, unconvincingly, as an attempt to create interracial harmony, as a policy of fusion.[38] But it was surely more than a symbolic gesture. Instead, it appears that Alexander sought to give the new empire a Macedonian aristocratic core, which at the same time had links with the Persian nobility. Like the marriages of the conquistadors to Indian women in New Spain and Peru, the unions that were solemnized at Susa may have involved rights to land, income, and labor.[39] It will be remembered that when Alexander left Macedonia in dire financial straits he encouraged his *hetairoi* to share his expectations:

> But although he set out with such meager and narrow resources, he would not set foot upon his ship until he had enquired into the circumstances of

his companions (*hetairoi*) and allotted to one a farm, to another a village, and to another the revenue of some hamlet or harbor. And when at last nearly all of the crown property had been expended or allotted, Perdiccas said to him: "But for thyself, O king, what are thou leaving?" And when the king answered, "My hopes," "In these then," said Perdiccas, "we also will share who make the expedition with thee." Then he declined the possessions which had been allotted to him, and some of the other friends of Alexander did likewise.[40]

Many of Alexander's *hetairoi* were thus content to sacrifice their properties at home in the expectation of the wealth and lands that conquest brings.

We may, however, look beyond the encomienda system and consider how Spaniards accepted Indian women from the Totonacs (subject, of course, to their conversion to Christianity and with new names conferred upon baptism) for political or military advantage. Bernal Díaz comments that they regarded these women – with the notable exception of one described as "muy fea" – as quite attractive, "considering that they were Indians."[41] The advantages of such marriages were clear, and the actions of the bridegrooms not always cynical. The racial sensibilities of the Spaniards were, at any rate, different from those of most other Europeans as a result of the lengthy experience of *convivencia* and, in some respects, the Macedonians, who had intermarried with Thracians and Illyrians, were more open to such interracial unions than their Greek neighbors to the south. For the Macedonians such marriages were made easier because there were no social or religious conventions concerning monogamy – at least, not amongst the aristocracy.[42] At any rate, we should not rule out the socioeconomic implications of the aristocratic mass marriages.

It has long been regarded as axiomatic that the Macedonian nobles repudiated their Persian brides immediately after Alexander's death. But, in fact, we know of only one such case, and even then the bridegroom, Craterus, was careful to find a worthy husband, Dionysius of Pontic Heraclea, for Amastris, the niece of Darius III.[43] This he did when he agreed to marry Phila, the daughter of Antipater, and he may have been anxious that Amastris not fall into the hands of a political rival who might exploit her family connections. Seleucus, who later became satrap of Babylonia, derived great political advantage from his wife, the daughter of Spitamenes.[44] Hence, we may assume that the mixed unions were designed to create a future pool of commanders and administrators who would be palatable to the conquered peoples and not regarded as foreign oppressors. Arrian, speaking of the later complaints of the Macedonian soldiers at Opis, says that they objected to Alexander's adoption of Persian dress "and the marriages which were conducted according to Persian custom were not to the liking of many of them, and *there were even some of the bridegrooms* who were not happy" [emphasis added].[45] Arrian is clearly referring to the marriages of the *hetairoi* to prominent Persians, and the other side of the argument is that most of these *hetairoi* did not object. Most important was the fact that the ceremony at Susa extended the practice which Alexander himself had begun in Sogdiana – and now continued by marrying the daughters of Darius III and Artaxerxes Ochus to the Macedonian nobility.

Had Alexander and his heirs lived to rule the new empire, the composition of the aristocracy and the distribution of their lands would have spoken volumes about the purpose of the Susan marriages. A leading historian of ancient Persia, Maria Brosius, observes: "The ambiguous attitudes which characterise Alexander's politics towards Persia and the Persians may assist us in understanding why he failed in his ambition to be recognised as king of a new Macedonian-Persian Empire."[46] But Alexander's attitudes merely seem ambiguous because he did not live long enough for the impact of his policy to be felt. And, even if these policies were undone by Alexander's death and the chaos which ensued, we may find an analogy also in Napoleon's marshalate. Historian Frank McLynn argues that the emperor "now sought to emulate the great Macedonian conqueror by creating a new nobility, partly by fusion with the notables and the returned émigrés, partly by intermarriage between his family and other European potentates. . . ."[47]

More difficult to understand is Alexander's purpose in legalizing the unions of some 10,000 Macedonian soldiers and their common-law wives, many of whom had been captives of war or camp followers. It is tempting to see this measure as an inducement to the soldiers to remain in Asia,[48] as regular soldiers or militia or garrison troops. But the number of veterans dismissed at Opis shortly afterwards was also 10,000 and among these were the roughly 3,000 Silver Shields (*argyraspides*), the majority of whom were accompanied by barbarian womenfolk and half-breed children. This does not mean, of course, that the 10,000 soldiers who were dismissed were the same ones whose common-law marriages were legalized, but there must have been some overlap, as the case of the Silver Shields shows.

In Susa, in the spring of 324, foreign troops were added to the Macedonian army in unprecedented numbers. First were the so-called Descendants (*Epigonoi*), thirty thousand young barbarians trained and armed in Macedonian fashion; Alexander ordered the formation of this unit as early as 330. A thousand Persians were formed into a special court infantry guard, and cavalrymen from the best horsemen in Asia – the Bactrians, Arachosians, Areians, Drangians, and the like – were enrolled in cavalry; one particular elite group known as the Euacae were integrated in the Companion Cavalry, as were the sons of prominent Persian satraps and generals. These formed (along with some existing – presumably Macedonian – cavalrymen) a new hipparchy (Arr. 7.6.3), which may have been the one led successively by Hephaestion, Perdiccas, and Seleucus, and formed the basis for Hephaestion's rank as Chiliarch. The exact timing of this Persianizing of the cavalry is uncertain. Barbarian units had served in Alexander's army in Bactria and India, but a full-scale integration probably did not occur until 324. It was the process of "integration" that was the cause of greatest resentment: Arrian notes that the men objected to the fact that the Persians "were given Macedonian lances (*dorata*) instead of the barbarian thonged javelins."[49]

It was believed (and there may be some truth to the idea) that Alexander had assembled the *Epigonoi* as a counterbalance (*antitagma*) to the Macedonians, upon whom the king had found it increasingly difficult to rely. But they were not the only foreign troops added to the ranks: Peucestas, the satrap of Persis and an admirer of barbarian customs and dress, brought some 20,000 slingers and archers from his province. Furthermore, one must keep in mind that Craterus' mission to relieve Antipater in Macedonia was to be followed by the latter's bringing of fresh troops from the homeland. In the event, these plans were disrupted by the king's death and the outbreak of the Lamian War. In the desperate years of the Successors and, later, in the eastern Hellenistic kingdoms more use was made, perforce, of native troops armed and trained in the Macedonian style – and even termed "Macedonians." Nevertheless, Alexander's plans clearly did not involve a wholesale replacement of Macedonians with barbarian troops.

The year 324 was thus a transitional year for Alexander and his empire. The consequences of his measures can be seen, to some extent, in the history of the Successors, but it is less certain how affairs might have played out – indeed, whether the changes and new policies would have provoked an inevitable crisis – if the king had lived on.

THE LONG ROAD FROM SUSA TO BABYLON

CHAPTER NINE

I N 331/30, IN THE FLUSH OF VICTORY AT GAUGAMELA AND IN pursuit of the ultimate prize, Alexander had marched directly from Babylon to Susa. Now, more than six years later, he did not return directly but moved instead to Opis and, ultimately, Ecbatana, which he had passed through quickly in his pursuit of Darius III. But the year 324/3 was to be a long and painful journey from Susa to Babylon. Like the Achaemenid rulers who had preceded him, Alexander now went on procession, fleeing the stifling heat of Susa for the cooler climes of Ecbatana, and sharing the burden and expense of maintaining the royal court amongst the capitals of the empire. To this end, he had deprived himself of the pleasures of Persepolis, but the needs of Alexander's court may have represented a reduction from Achaemenid times.

The king himself returned to the Persian Gulf and sailed with Nearchus to the mouth of the Tigris, and up that river to the town of Opis. Here he was joined by the remainder of the army, which had been led by Hephaestion. Here, too, he announced the demobilization of the veterans – particularly those who were physically unfit – but offered incentives to those capable men who chose to remain. Dismissal was a bitter pill for the men, no matter how much they longed for

142

home. Dismissal, that is to say, under circumstances that caused them to question the entire purpose of their labors. What exactly had been accomplished on the battlefields of the Granicus, Issus, and Gaugamela, if victory meant that the men would see their king dressed in Persian style, turning his back on his Macedonian heritage, producing heirs of mixed blood, and integrating the conquered into the military and administration? Was it for this that they had marched to the ends of the earth and back? The slogans of Panhellenism may have resonated more with the Greek allies and mercenaries, but the Macedonians too had taken to heart the message of revenge and conquest, and to them it meant the subordination of the vanquished and the tangible benefits accruing to the victors.[1] Hence, they opposed Alexander openly and vehemently. This was not the stubborn secession that had halted (at least, officially) the eastward advance at the Hyphasis. This was mutiny, as the men heaped scorn upon the very man they had earlier revered as if he were a god. Now, they complained, he was deluding himself by claiming Amun as his father and disowning Philip.

Alexander for his part defied the mutineers, ordering his hypaspists to seize the ringleaders, thirteen in number, and denouncing the ingratitude of the common soldier. He would campaign without them, he threatened – indeed, replacements were already at hand in the form of the 30,000 *Epigonoi* or "Descendants," Persians trained and armed in the Macedonian fashion. Those who had fomented the discord were shackled and thrown into the Tigris, in a punishment that reflected Near Eastern practice.[2] Ultimately, it was rejection, or more significantly replacement, that induced the Macedonian soldiery to beg the king's forgiveness. Their resentment had turned to dejection, and they complained that Alexander had abandoned his Macedonian Companions (*hetairoi*) and made the Persians his kinsmen (*syngeneis*). Once again, Alexander had shown himself a master of mass psychology, and he accepted the submission of the troops. Concord (*homonoia*) was celebrated with a banquet that stressed the harmony between the two groups but nevertheless underscored the priority of the Macedonians, who were seated around the king, with the Persians in a secondary role. Not a blueprint for the "Unity of Mankind" but rather an accommodation of the conquerors and the conquered, whose differing status remained visible to all.[3]

The troops discharged at Opis amounted to some 10,000 infantry and 1,500 cavalry, the former group including the 3,000 Silver Shields. Most suffered the ill effects of advancing old age and years of hard campaigning, beginning in the reign of Philip II. Even their leader, Craterus, who may have been only in his forties, was so ill that Alexander found it necessary to appoint Polyperchon as second in command and successor in case Craterus died during the march. Indeed, the slow progress made by the returning veterans must be explained in terms of the condition of the troops (as well as what must have been a substantial baggage train) and that of the western empire.

Although the demobilization of Alexander's veterans is understandable in itself, it is important to see the departure of Craterus' forces – for they did still constitute a military entity – in the context of the events of 324. Alexander's boyhood friend and Imperial Treasurer, Harpalus, had been guilty of gross mismanagement, if not actual criminal activity,[4] during the king's absence in India. His was not a spotless record at any rate; for he had already fled from the Macedonian camp before the battle of Issus, apparently absconding with some of the money in his care.[5] Later he was pardoned and reinstated, on account of his previous services and his connections with the Elimiote royal house. But the responsibilities entrusted to him were too heavy for a man of weak moral fiber. In the years that followed his establishment as treasurer, first in Ecbatana and then in Babylon, he used large sums of public money for his own personal projects, some frivolous, others grandiose. The details need not concern us here, entertaining as they are. Most are reported by scandalmongers and writers with a rhetorical flair and little regard for strict truth. But the fact that Harpalus' affairs were lampooned in the works of New Comedy, and indeed in the Macedonian camp itself, suggests that there was an element of truth to them.[6] Certainly, Harpalus' conscience was sufficiently burdened so that he decided to flee from Babylon to Athens, where he hoped to buy protection against the king he had offended. Whether his arrival on the Attic coast helped to precipitate or briefly suspended a rebellion in Greece, it is clear that Alexander made the matter his highest concern and sent Philoxenus from Ionia to demand his extradition. In the event, after distributing some funds to Athenian politicians and triggering one of the most sensational political scandals Athens had ever witnessed, Harpalus fled to Crete, only to murdered by one of his own men.[7]

Harpalus had arrived in Greece very soon after the terms of Alexander's Exiles' Decree became known. Hence, the Athenians in particular were already in a state of alarm. This decree (discussed below) went hand in hand with Alexander's realignment of power at home. Provoked by complaints and rumors from his mother, Olympias, Alexander had decided to install Craterus as his viceroy in Macedonia, giving him also the responsibility of imposing the terms of the Exiles' Decree on the Greek states. The new policy was euphemistically referred to as protecting Greek freedom. Antipater, for his part, was to bring reinforcements to Alexander in Babylon. This changing of the guard can hardly have failed to concern Antipater, who must have reflected upon the fates of Philotas, Parmenion, and his own son-in-law, Alexander Lyncestes. Perhaps he had no need to fear for his personal safety. Perhaps. But his political career, and with it the aspirations of his family members and adherents, was in the process of being terminated. The presence of his son, Cassander, in Babylon in 323 suggests that the father was intent upon delaying his departure from Macedonia, and the rough treatment accorded Cassander – if the story is true[8] – shows that the king was in no mood to negotiate.

The situation in Cilicia had, however, bought time for Antipater, though it doubtless put a strain on Craterus' political loyalties. The satrapy had been without a ruler for several months; for Balacrus son of Nicanor, a former Somatophylax of the king and the husband of Antipater's daughter, Phila, had been killed in a campaign against the neighboring Pisidians. Soon afterwards, Harpalus had arrived in Tarsus, fleeing the king and his army, and almost certainly pilfering the treasury there.[9] Craterus' first task had been to restore order in the satrapy, and to this end he may have installed the Silver Shields as garrison troops, at least temporarily. Events would conspire to take them from the very threshold of Macedonia to ignominy and destruction. But that is another story.[10]

THE EXILES' DECREE AND "GREEK FREEDOM"

In summer 324, Nicanor of Stagira, the son-in-law and adopted son of Aristotle, proclaimed at the Olympic Games the so-called Exiles' Decree, a brief version of which is preserved by Diodorus:

> King Alexander to the exiles from the Greek cities. Though we have not been responsible for your exile, we shall nevertheless assume responsibility for your return to your various homelands, except in the case of those with curses on their heads. We have given Antipater written instructions in this matter; he is to use force in the case of cities refusing to accept the recall (Diod. 18.8.4)[11].

This proclamation – the main thrust of which must have been known to the Greeks beforehand[12] – could only have a disruptive effect on the Greek cities; for those who were being allowed to return had been exiled for political reasons. The returning exiles would destabilize their respective states and renew debate about the legality of their banishment and the confiscation of their property. Nor was Alexander, even as *hegemon* of the League of Corinth, entitled to make such a declaration, which infringed upon local autonomy. Why then did he overstep his authority and introduce measures that would raise the standard of revolt?

There are several explanations, though none is entirely satisfactory. First one must consider the individuals who are central to the problem: Alexander and the exiles themselves. Many political exiles had found employment as mercenaries, particularly in Alexander's campaigns. Those who were not left behind as garrison troops were demobilized and sent back to the Greek peninsula, and their numbers were augmented by those who had served in satrapal armies and were now dismissed on Alexander's orders.[13] Some of those who had been disbanded had turned to brigandage in Asia, though eventually most drifted back to the Greek homeland. Here, along with other exiles, their numbers had swollen to the tens of thousands, a dangerous multitude that could be used against Macedon if the occasion arose. Restoration amounted to a form of payment for services rendered, and it would guarantee the loyalty of these men to Alexander's cause.[14] But the king's primary concern may have been simply to rid himself of potential troublemakers, and he may have misjudged the impact of his policy on the Greek states.[15] Political restoration did not guarantee income, and many of the exiles knew no occupation other than military service. Hence their loyalties shifted from one paymaster to another.

Second, there is the other group directly affected by the decree: the leaders of the affected states and their political adherents. Although the ancient sources single out Athens and Aetolia, those cities in the greatest danger must have been the ones in which oligarchic rule had been imposed. And, if this is the case, Alexander may well have wished to expel oligarchies which had been established in his absence by Antipater. Since Alexander was now embarking upon what would be a struggle with his viceroy in Europe, he may have wished to remove some of the underpinnings of Antipater's power.

Third, we must consider the possibility that Alexander, now that he had finished his Persian campaign, was deliberately trying to foment rebellion in Greece in order to create a pretext for military interference.[16] When he had left Europe in 334, his relations with the Greeks were somewhat precarious. Now he was in a position to deal with those states – especially Athens and Aetolia – whose antics he had been forced to overlook in the early years of his reign. The promotion of Greek freedom now became the pretext for breaking what little independent spirit remained after Chaeronea and Agis' war. Craterus's return with 10,000 veterans was thus scheduled to coincide with this plan; that trusted officer was to replace Antipater as overseer of Europe and guarantor of the "freedom of the Greeks." Should Antipater fail to cooperate, he would be aligning himself with the enemies of freedom.[17]

It is perhaps in the context of the Exiles' Decree that Alexander's request for divine honors can be best understood. There was, of course, no formal demand or *order* that came from the king, as many scholars have pointed out, but there can be little doubt that some, at least, of the Greek states were encouraged to recognize Alexander's divinity. Nor should we believe, as some do, that Alexander was under any delusions about his "divinity." Aelian, a Greek writer of the second/third century AD, rejected and ridiculed Alexander's pretensions to divinity in at least three different passages of his *Varia Historia*.[18] For a pagan writer in an age when emperors were routinely deified this may seem odd, but it can perhaps be explained by Aelian's experience of the reign of Caracalla (211–17), a notorious Alexander imitator, and the excesses of Elagabalus (218–22). But even Alexander's contemporaries were divided on the issue of his divinity. Many of his officers were offended when he accepted the high priest's declaration that he was "Son of Amun,"[19] the Egyptian god whom the Greeks equated with Zeus, and the common soldier was bitter about his concomitant rejection of Philip; flatterers went to great lengths to demonstrate that Alexander had surpassed the achievements of Heracles and Dionysus, and that he was ready to take his place in the pantheon; others published anecdotes showing that the king treated such flattery with cynicism. He was alleged to have dismissed as nonsense Dioxippus' remark – others attributed it to Anaxarchus – that ichor flowed from Alexander's wound.

The simple fact is that deification had political advantages, and these the king was eager to exploit. He had paved the way for divine honors by establishing, with the approval of Amun, the hero cult of Hephaestion; his own divinity was a logical next step. And, just as it makes no sense to speak of "self-delusion" and "logical next steps" in the same breath, so Alexander's request for divinity must be understood as a political move, and a negotiating ploy of sorts. Maybe he thought he could exercise greater power as a god than as *hegemon* of the League. On the other hand, states that acknowledged his divinity might expect favors in return.

The road through the Zagros would have taken the king past Bisitun (Behistun), where the trilingual inscription of Darius I had been carved into the side of the cliff,[20] and beyond that to the Nesean plain of Media, famed in antiquity for its horses. Alexander is said to have found the stock of horses severely depleted: only 50,000 remained of numbers that had reputedly approached 150,000. In Media, too, the satrap Atropates – by this time, the father-in-law of the general, Perdiccas – was alleged to have met the king's army with a hundred mounted women warriors, though this story appears to be a rationalization of the myth of an earlier meeting in Hyrcania between Alexander and the Amazon queen.[21]

At Ecbatana, in the autumn of 324, Alexander celebrated athletic and artistic competitions, and it was while he was attending one of these events that his dearest friend, Hephaestion, who had been suffering from a fever, died. The king was inconsolable. Many of the stories alleging that Alexander imitated Achilles are later fabrications, but there is no reason to doubt the sincerity of the king's emotional outbursts. Whether there was a homoerotic element to the relationship is difficult to determine, and modern interpretations of the friendship are influenced by the changing attitudes of modern generations as much as by an understanding of contemporary mores. Insofar as it affected the king's policies, it matters little whether there was a sexual component to the intense friendship. The simple fact remains that Alexander was mentally and physically devastated by his friend's death, and that certain extravagant reactions to it did have some political impact.[22] After an extended period of grief, the king entrusted Hephaestion's corpse to Perdiccas, with orders to convey it to Babylon, where the construction of an ostentatious funeral monument had been planned. For his part, Alexander occupied himself with a forty-day campaign against the Cossaeans – often depicted as a case of Alexander venting his hostilities through military action[23] – before returning to Babylon at a leisurely pace.

ALEXANDER IN BABYLON

Alexander returned to Babylon in 323 a troubled man, and the task of consolidating the empire proved more difficult and less rewarding than its conquest. Although it cannot be proved, it appears likely that Alexander proposed to make Babylon the administrative center of his empire.[24] Here he received ambassadors from other nations, but whether they came from as far afield as Carthage and Italy is debatable.[25] He had earlier demanded from the Greeks divine honors, a move presaged by the hero-cult of Hephaestion, but the ambassadors who arrived in Babylon came bearing golden crowns, recognizing him as the ruler of

Asia, not as a god. The latter point was still being debated at home, where there must have been considerable sympathy for the Spartan view that "if Alexander wanted to be a god, let him be one."

Although he now had time to devote himself to the business of governing, Alexander nevertheless turned his mind to new conquests. Reconnaissance missions were sent to the Caspian Sea and the Arabian coast, the latter in preparation for a proposed campaign against the Arabs; and ships were to be built in Phoenicia.[26] Finally, it was alleged that Alexander planned an expedition against North Africa as well. Some of the king's grandiose objectives have been called into question, but what we do know is that he was keen to return to the field at a time when administrative matters remained unresolved. The fact that Alexander, in the previous year, had dismissed the numerous mercenaries, who could easily have been employed in further conquests, suggests that the renewal of campaigning was an afterthought. The intricacies of governing the empire may have bored him; certainly he was more interested in acquisition than consolidation. But even here it may be wrong to look for personal motives: the circumstances in which Alexander found himself in 324/3 were not unlike those confronting Philip after Chaeronea (338). Political unions, forged by military conquest, required an enemy in order to externalize that very force before it turned against itself. Not much later, without effective leadership and an external enemy, the armies of Alexander's successors unleashed internecine war. Similarly, the successors of Muhammad and the Mongols of Genghis Khan found it necessary to choose between internal and external strife, and they maintained their power as long as they opted for expansion. Conquest spawned further aggression, the myth of the "common enemy" masking internal differences and postponing their resolution. Of course, the Roman Empire demonstrated that this policy too had its limits, but for the Diadochoi, the decision to cancel Alexander's so-called Final Plans was a fatal mistake, even if the resulting death of the empire was a slow one.

DEATH OF ALEXANDER
On 11 June, 323,[27] Alexander died of an ailment, the nature of which has never been established to everyone's satisfaction, though not for a lack of

scholarly theories. The *Royal Journal* describes the course of the illness, which has been identified by scholars as, among other things, malaria, typhus, and even West Nile virus.[28] The onset was sudden, and the fact that it followed a drinking party and was characterized by high fever and a rapid deterioration of the king's condition, including a creeping paralysis, lent credence to the view that he was the victim of poisoning. This explanation, which circulated soon after Alexander's death, has persuaded some modern scholars, but the source of the poisoning story is a rather complex political pamphlet, crafted in the camp of one of the Successors with a view to discrediting Antigonus the One-Eyed and the family of Antipater. Often dismissed as a literary exercise – though it is clearly too sophisticated and topical to have been written without political purpose – the exact date of its composition is uncertain.[29]

Whether he died of natural causes or was the victim of a plot by his own generals, Alexander's death highlighted his greatest failing as a leader – his refusal to address the question of succession. Not only had he given no thought to producing an heir before leaving Macedonia, though Parmenion and Antipater urged him to do so, but even at the end of his life he continued to evade the issue.[30] That he bequeathed his empire "to the strongest" makes for a good story and typifies the recklessness with which he approached the entire campaign, but it serves also to justify the actions of those generals who either actively dismantled the realm or did little to defend its integrity and the birthright of the living members of the Argead house. The marshals in Babylon were presented with a thankless choice between an illegitimate (half-barbarian) son, now residing in Pergamum, a mentally deficient half-brother of the dead king, and the as-yet-unborn child of Rhoxane. Even if an acceptable choice could be made, the new ruler would require a regent, and here too Alexander must be blamed for the political turmoil. In the years after the elimination of Philotas and Parmenion, the king had been careful to balance the powers of his younger generals, thus failing to establish a clear hierarchy of command.[31] Those, such as Perdiccas, who tried to step into Alexander's shoes were confounded by the machinations of the other marshals and their respective adherents, who viewed them with suspicion and coveted greater power for themselves. Others, such as Craterus, had the support of the troops but lacked the vision to become true statesmen. And others again, such as Leonnatus, had a greater measure of their late king's brilliance but little of his good fortune.[32] The world, it seems, could not bear another Alexander. Ultimately, his legacy was carved up not by the brilliant younger marshals but by lesser men, many of whom were to enjoy wealth and power beyond their wildest dreams.[33] But the struggle for domination saw the conquerors' swords stained with Macedonian blood and the fragmentation of the hard-won empire. Weakened and debased, its constituent parts were drawn slowly into the rival embraces of Rome in the west and the resurgent "Persia" of the Parthian horsemen.

ALEXANDER'S OFFICERS

APPENDIX ONE

The numbers [in brackets] that follow certain names are those used in Heckel 2006a.

General Commanders
Parmenion son of Philotas
Attalus [1] (Justin 9.5.8; Diod. 16.91.2)
Amyntas, son of Arrhabaeus? (Justin 9.5.8)

Somatophylakes (Members of the Seven-Man Bodyguard)
Lysimachus son of Agathocles (Arr. 6.28.4)
Aristonous son of Peisaeus (Arr. 6.28.4)
Peithon son of Crateuas (Arr. 6.28.4)
Arybbas [2] [died 332/1] (Arr. 3.5.5)
Leonnatus son of Anteas (Arr. 6.28.4)
Balacrus son of Nicanor [replaced in 333/2]
Menes son of Dionysius [replaced in 331]
Perdiccas son of Orontes (Arr. 6.28.4)
Hephaestion son of Amyntor [died 324] (Arr. 6.28.4)

Ptolemy son of Lagus (Arr. 6.28.4)
Peucestas son of Alexander [an honorary appointment 324] (Arr. 6.28.4)

Cavalry Commanders
1) *Hipparchs of the Companions*
Philotas son of Parmenion
"Black" Cleitus [2], son of Dropides (Arr. 3.27.4)
Hephaestion son of Amyntor (Arr. 3.27.4)
Demetrius son of Althaemenes (Arr. 4.27.5)
Coenus son of Polemocrates
Perdiccas son of Orontes
Craterus son of Alexander
"White" Cleitus [3] (Arr. 5.22.6; 6.6.4)
Eumenes son of Hieronymus (Plut. *Eum.* 1.5)

2) *Ilarchs*
"Black" Cleitus (*ile basilike*)
Amyntas son of Arrhabaeus (*prodromoi*)
Protomachus (*prodromoi*)
Ariston [3] (Paeonians) (Arr. 1.14.1; 2.9.2)
Ariston [1] (Arr. 3.11.8)
Demetrius son of Althaemenes (Arr. 3.11.8)
Glaucias (Arr. 3.11.8)
Hegelochus son of Hippostratus (Arr. 3.11.8)
Heracleides son of Antiochus (Arr. 3.11.8)
Meleager (Arr. 3.11.8; Curt. 4.13.27)
Pantordanus son of Cleander (Arr. 2.9.3; 3.11.8)
Peroedas son of Menestheus (Arr. 2.9.3; 3.11.8)
Socrates son of Sathon (Arr. 1.14.1)
Sopolis son of Hermodorus (Arr. 3.11.8)
Lysanias?

3) *Thessalian Cavalry*
Calas son of Harpalus (Diod. 17.17.4)
Alexander [4] son of Aëropus (Arr. 1.25.2)
Philip son of Menelaus (Arr. 3.11.10)
Polydamas (Pharsalian horse: Arr. 3.11.10)

4) *Allied and Mercenary Cavalry*
Erigyius son of Larichus
Caranus (Coeranus) (Arr. 3.12.4)
Menidas (Arr. 3.12.2-4)
Agathon son of Tyrimmas (Arr. 1.14.3; 3.12.4)
Anaxippus (Arr. 3.25.2, 5)
Andromachus son of Hieron (Arr. 3.12.5)
Epocillus son of Polyeides (Arr. 3.19.6)

Infantry Commanders
1) *Commanders of Hypaspists (archihypaspistai)*
Nicanor son of Parmenion (Arr. 3.25.4)
Neoptolemus (Plut. *Eum.* 1.6)

2) *Commanders of Royal Hypaspists*
Admetus (Arr. 2.23.2, 23.4-5)
Hephaestion son of Amyntor? (Diod. 17.61.3)
Seleucus son of Antiochus (Arr. 5.13.4)

3) *Chiliarchs and Pentakosiarchs of the Hypaspists*
Adaeus (Arr. 1.21.4)
Timander (Arr. 1.21.4)
Atarrhias (Curt. 5.2.5)
Antigenes (Curt. 5.2.5)
Hellanicus (Curt. 5.2.5)
Amyntas [6] (Curt. 5.2.5)
Amyntas [7] Lyncestes (Curt. 5.2.5)
Antigonus [3] (Curt. 5.2.5)
Theodotus (Curt. 5.2.5)
Philotas (Curt. 5.2.5)
Antiochus [2] (Arr. 4.30.5-6)

4) *Commanders of Pezhetairoi (asthetairoi)*
Philip son of Balacrus
Ptolemy son of Seleucus (died 333)
Polyperchon son of Simmias
Amyntas son of Andromenes (died 330)

Simmias son of Andromenes (a temporary at Gaugamela 331)
Attalus son of Andromenes
Perdiccas son of Orontes
Alcetas son of Orontes
Meleager son of Neoptolemus
Coenus son of Polemocrates
Peithon [son of Agenor? son of Antigenes?]
Craterus son of Alexander
Gorgias (Arr. 4.22.7)
"White" Cleitus [3] (Arr. 4.22.7)

5) *Commanders of Archers (toxarchai)*
Ombrion [Brison?] (Arr. 3.5.6, 12.2)
Eurybotas (Arr. 1.8.4)
Antiochus [1] (Arr. 3.5.6)
Clearchus (Arr. 1.22.7)
Tauron son of Machatas (Arr. 5.14.1)

6) *Commanders of Greek Mercenaries*
Menander (Arr. 3.6.7-8)
Cleander son of Polemocrates (Arr. 3.6.7-8)
Heracon
Andronicus son of Agerrus (Arr. 3.24.5)
Menedemus (Arr. 4.3.7)

7) *Commanders of Thracians and Other Allies*
Attalus [2] (Arr. 2.9.2) Agrianes
Ptolemy (Arr. 4.7.2; Curt. 7.10.11) Thracians
Eudamus (Curt. 10.1.21) Thracians
Sitalces (Arr. 1.28.4) Odrysian javelin-men
Balacrus son of Amyntas (Arr.1.29.3)
Caranus (Arr. 3.5.5-6)

8) *Commanders of Other Infantry*
Philip son of Machatas (Arr. 4.24.10)
Balacrus (Arr. 4.4.6)

Nearchus son of Androtimus
Philotas (Arr. 3.29.7)

Fleet Commanders and Helmsmen
Menoetius (Arr. 1.12.1)
Nearchus son of Androtimus (Arr. *Indica*)
Onesicritus (Arr. 4.5.6, 20.9; Strabo 15.1.28)
Hegelochus son of Hippostratus (Curt. 3.1.19; Arr. 3.2.6)
Amphoterus son of Alexander (Curt. 3.1.19; Arr. 2.2.3)
Nicanor [2] (Arr.1.18.4-5)
Proteas (Arr. 2.2.4-5)
Heracleides son Argaeus (Arr. 7.16.1)
Archias (Arr. 7.20.7)
Androsthenes (Arr. 7.20.7)
Hieron of Soli (Arr. 7.20.7)

Phrourarchoi
Archelaus [1] Bactrian Aornus (Arr. 3.29.1)
Archelaus [2] Tyre (Diod. 18.37.4)
Attinas Bactria/Sogdiana (Arr. 4.16.4-5)
[Eu]dramenes Agrianian town
Nicanor [6]? Parapamisadae (Arr. 4.22.4)
Nicarchides [1] Persepolis (Curt. 5.6.11)
Pantaleon Memphis (Arr. 3.5.3)
Pausanias [1] Sardis (Arr. 1.17.7)
Peucolaus [1] Bactria/Sogdiana (Curt. 7.10.10)
Philip [13] Peucelaotis (Arr. 4.28.6)
Philotas [1] Thebes (Diod. 17.8.7)
Philotas [8] Tyre (Curt. 4.5.9)
Polemon [1] Pelusium (Arr. 3.5.3)
Xenophilus Susa (Curt. 5.2.16)

NUMBERS OF TROOPS

APPENDIX TWO

ALEXANDER'S ARMY AT THE BEGINNING
OF THE EXPEDITION (334)

Even the lost primary historians disagreed on the exact number of troops in Alexander's army: According to Anaximenes of Lampsacus (*FGrH* 72 F29), there were 43,000 infantry and 5,500 cavalry; Ptolemy son of Lagus (*FGrH* 138 F4) gives 30,000 infantry and 5,000 cavalry; and Aristobulus of Cassandreia (*FGrH* 139 F4) 30,000 foot and 4,000 horse. The only writer who breaks down the figures into contingents is Diodorus (17.17.3-4), whose numbers may come directly from Cleitarchus: the 32,000 infantry are broken down into 12,000 Macedonians, 7,000 allies, 5,000 mercenaries, 7,000 Odrysians, Triballians, and Illyrians, and 1,000 Agrianes and archers; of cavalry there were 1,800 Macedonians, an equal number of Thessalians, 600 allies, and 900 Thracians and Paeonians (that is, 5,100, though Diodorus wrongly gives a total of 4,500). Plut. *Alex.* 15.1 gives 43,000 infantry and 5,000 cavalry; Front. *Strat.* 4.2.4 simply gives a round figure of 40,000 for Alexander's army. The lower figures for the army as a whole may not include those forces which had been in Asia since the spring of 336; Polyaenus 5.44.4 speaks of 10,000 men with Parmenion and Attalus.

PERSIAN NUMBERS AT THE GRANICUS RIVER (334)

Diodorus estimates the Persian forces at 10,000 cavalry and 100,000 infantry. Justin (11.6.11), probably the least reliable extant source, says that the Persian army numbered 600,000, but the Latin *sescenta milia* can mean simply "many thousands," somewhat like the English hyperbole "millions." Plut. *Alex.* 16.15 says that the Persian dead totaled 25,000 cavalry and 20,000 infantry, which shows that his figures were also higher than Arrian's 20,000 cavalry and 20,000 infantry.

PERSIAN NUMBERS AT ISSUS (333)

Arr. 2.8.8 says that Darius' army comprised 600,000 men, which agrees with Plut. *Alex.* 18.6 and the anonymous papyrus fragment (*POxy.* 1798 §44 = *FGrH* 148). The common source in this case may be Callisthenes. Callisthenes gave the number of Greek mercenaries as 30,000 (*FGrH* 124 F 35; Arr. 2.8.6; Curt. 3.9.2), but this would equal the total number of Greek and Macedonian infantry in Alexander's army. The true figure must have been around 10,000 (see Parke 1933: 184). This number may derive from Charidemus' alleged request for 100,000 troops, of whom one-third should be Greeks (Diod. 17.30.3). Curt. 3.2.4–9 gives 250,000 infantry and 62,200 cavalry; Diod. 17.31.2 and Justin 11.9.1 have 400,000 infantry and 100,000 cavalry. The totals of 500–600,000 could well be tenfold exaggerations. Arrian's 30,000 Greek mercenaries and 60,000 Kardakes (2.8.5–6) would find no room on the battle line; for they were placed directly opposite the Macedonian *pezhetairoi* and hypaspists, who totaled 12,000. Indeed, the Macedonian force filled the entire space between the sea and the hills, with the allied infantry held in reserve.

THE FORCES AT GAUGAMELA (331)

Diod. 17.39.4 says that after Issus, Darius assembled a new army of 800,000 and 200,000 cavalry, along with a force of scythe-chariots. Justin 11.12.5 reports half that number (400,000 infantry and 100,000 cavalry); Plutarch (*Alex.* 31.1) agrees with Diodorus, saying there were one million troops in all. Arr. 3.8.6 claims 1,000,000 infantry, 40,000 cavalry, and 200 scythe-chariots. Only Curtius reports conservative figures: 200,000 infantry and 45,000 cavalry. For the Macedonian army Arr. 3.12.5 gives 40,000 infantry and 7,000 cavalry.

The Polytimetus Ambush (329 BC)

One version of the story, presumably from Ptolemy, numbers the Macedonian forces as 60 Companions, 800 mercenary cavalry, and 1,500 infantry. A few were captured alive but later killed (Arr. 4.5.2-9). Aristobulus, however, reports that 40 cavalry and 300 infantrymen escaped the slaughter (Arr. 4.6.2). Curt. 7.6.24 speaks of a force of 3,000 infantry and 800 cavalry, naming only Menedemus as commander; the casualties amounted to 2,000 infantry and 300 cavalry (Curt. 7.7.29).

Macedonian and Indian Numbers at the Hydaspes River (326)

Arr. 5.14.1 says that Alexander crossed the Hydaspes some 17 miles north of Porus' position with 6,000 infantry and 5,000 cavalry, the latter consisting of the hipparchies of Hephaestion, Perdiccas, Demetrius, and Coenus and the Bactrians and Sogdianians, as well as the Dahae horse-archers (*hippotoxotai*). But, of the infantry, he says Alexander brought with him the battalions of Coenus [Peithon son of Agenor] and Cleitus, as well as the hypaspists, the Agrianes, and the archers. Now the two phalanx battalions and all the hypaspists together would have totaled 6,000, and perhaps Arrian refers only to heavy infantry. The archers and the Agrianes would have totaled at least 1,000 and perhaps 1,500 in all (Fuller 1960: 187, following Tarn, supposes there were 1,000 Agrianes, 1,000 javelin-men, and 2,000 archers). At any rate, there cannot have been many other Macedonian troops available, since the remaining phalanx battalions are accounted for – Gorgias, Meleager, and Attalus remained at the halfway point between Alexander and Craterus, who had the battalions of Polyperchon and Alcetas – and the named infantry commanders at the Hydaspes battle, in addition to Cleitus, are Seleucus (who commanded the royal hypaspists), Antigenes (hypaspists), and Tauron (archers). Hence, the total forces at Alexander's disposal were not more than 12,500 before he was joined by the commanders of the "middle camp" (these included at least 4,500 *pezhetairoi* and an unspecified number of mercenaries, both infantry and cavalry). Craterus' troops, which included some 5,000 Indians led by Taxiles and the other hyparchs (Arr. 5.8.5, 11.3), came up after the issue had been decided. But this suggests that the total Macedonian forces at the Hydaspes, which amounted to all the troops in India except the garrison left with Philip son of Machatas in Taxila (Arr. 5.8.3), could not have been more than 60,000 or about half of the number estimated by many scholars.

Craterus' forces were unable to cross the river until Porus had turned to deal with Alexander. Hence his troops, when they did come up, would have been involved only in mopping-up operations. On the other hand, Gorgias, Attalus, and Meleager, with their three phalanx battalions and the Greek mercenary infantry and cavalry, could cross (presumably on the boats that had been used by Alexander's men and then floated downstream) as soon as the guarding force under Spitaces had been driven off. These men were thus able to participate in the battle either from the very beginning or at least in the very early stages.

Porus' numbers are even more disputed. According to Arr. 5.15.4 he had 30,000 infantry, about 4,000 cavalry, 300 chariots, and 200 elephants; this agrees with Curt. 8.13.6 in every case except for the number of elephants, which Curtius gives as 85. Diod. 17.87.2 mentions 50,000 infantry, about 3,000 cavalry, 1,000 chariots, and 130 elephants; Plut. *Alex.* 62.2 20,000 infantry and 2,000 horse (but Plutarch's account is otherwise confused). Polyaenus says the elephants were spaced 50 ft (roughly 15 m) apart. Hence the infantry frontage of Porus' line would have been anywhere from 1.25 (85 elephants) to 3.0 km (200 elephants). Each interval would have contained about 16 men, perhaps 8 or 16 men deep, depending on the number of elephants in the line. A realistic figure for the Indian infantry is probably in the range of 25,000.

Aristobulus (*FGrH* 139 F43 = Arr. 5.14.3) says that Porus sent one of his sons with 60 chariots to challenge the circumventing force. Ptolemy (*FGrH* 138 F20 = Arr. 5.14.6), however, says Porus' son had 2,000 cavalry and 120 chariots. Four hundred cavalrymen, including Porus' son, were killed and all the chariots, which had bogged down in the mud, were captured. Hence, Porus' actual cavalry force in the battle with Alexander is thought to have totaled 3,600.

Arr. 5.18.2–3 gives the casualties as 20,000 Indian infantry and 3,000 cavalry killed; all chariots were lost; and two of Porus' sons perished fighting with Spitaces. All surviving elephants were captured, but Arrian does not say how many these were. Diod. 17.89.1 says 12,000 Indians were killed (cf. *Metz Epit.* 61: 12,000 men and 80 elephants). On the Macedonian side 80 infantrymen, 10 mounted archers, 25 Companions, and two hundred troops of other sorts (presumably light infantry or mercenaries) were killed. But Diod. 17.89.3 sets the Macedonian dead at 280 cavalry and more than 700 infantry (*Metz Epit.* 61: 900 infantry, 300 cavalry).

The Indus Fleet

Arrian gives two conflicting sets of figures: *Ind.* 19.7, based on Nearchus (*FGrH* 133 F1), speaks of 800 ships in all, including transports and supply ships; but in *Anab.* 6.2.4, where he follows Ptolemy (*FGrH* 138 F24), Arrian speaks of 80 *triakontoroi* and nearly 2,000 vessels in all. The disparity can perhaps be explained by the fact that Ptolemy includes the Indian vessels ("which had long been sailing the river"), whereas 800 may represent the total of newly built ships. Certainly all the horse transports were new, since the Indians had never seen horses on ships before (Arr. 6.3.4). Curt. 9.3.22 gives the number of ships as 1,000; Diod. 17.95.5: 200 galleys and 800 transports; *Metz Epit.* 70: 800 biremes, 300 transports.

The Return to the West

Craterus returned to the west via Arachosia and Drangiana, taking with him the battalions of Attalus and Meleager (3,000 men) and that of Antigenes, which I take to mean the 3,000 *argyraspides*. To these were added "some archers" (500?) and those ready to be discharged from military service, including Companions (Arr. 6.17.3). Craterus' troops may have included his own former battalion, now commanded by Gorgias (1,500). In all, the Greco-Macedonian core of Craterus' army (which must have been accompanied by an unspecified number of native troops) cannot have numbered much more than 10,000. Justin 12.10.1 speaks of Polyperchon leading the forces "to Babylonia," but this is probably an error for Craterus (cf. Justin 13.8.5, 7; 15.1.1), and we need not suppose that Polyperchon's battalion accompanied Craterus.

No source gives a breakdown of Alexander's forces. It can be assumed, however, that he retained the Agrianes (Arr. 6.17.4), all 3,000 of the hypaspists, four hipparchies and the *agema* of the Companions (4,000–4,500?), the battalions of Alcetas, White Cleitus, Peithon, and Polyperchon (6,000), and the remainder of the archers (though some of these went with Nearchus' fleet) and javelin-men. Plut. *Alex.* 66.4–5 claims that not even a quarter of Alexander's fighting men came through the Gedrosian march alive; he gives the original number as 120,000 infantry and 15,000 cavalry. These numbers have no foundation in fact, and Bosworth 1988a: 142 is probably correct to estimate that the minimum number of Alexander's forces at the beginning of the march must have been about 30,000, of which a little over half were Macedonians. Although there is no space in this volume to analyze reinforcements and casualty/attrition figures, I do not accept the calculations of Engels 1978: 111 and Table 6 (87,000 infantry, cavalry, 52,000 noncombatants). It is clear from the troops assigned to Leonnatus, who fought against 8,000 infantry and 400 cavalry of the Oreitae (Curt. 9.10.19), that the force which made the Gedrosian march included Greek mercenaries, both cavalry and infantry (Arr. 6.22.3). Though we must allow for an element of *apologia* in Arrian's account, the stress in his version is on the loss of pack animals (6.24.4, 25.1-2) and camp followers (6.25.5). How many fighting men sailed with the fleet is uncertain, but the bulk of these must have been lightly armed troops (cf. Arr. *Ind.* 28.3–8).

THE ADMINISTRATION
OF THE EMPIRE

APPENDIX THREE

❋ ❋ ❋

Satrapy	Persian satrap	Alexander's first appointee	Subsequent office holders
Hellespontine Phrygia	Arsites	Calas son of Harpalus (334)	Demarchus (327?)
Lydia	Spithridates	Asander son of Philotas (334)	Menander (331)
Caria	Orontopates	Ada (334/3)	Philoxenos (326); Asander son of Agathon (323)
Lycia	?	Nearchus	Antigonus?
Phrygia	Atizyes	Antigonus (333)	
Cappadocia	Mithrobuzanes/ Ariaces	Sabictas (333)	
Cilicia	Arsames	Balacrus (333/2)	Philotas (324/3)
Syria	Mazaeus	Menon (332)	Asclepiodorus (331); Laomedon (323)
Egypt	Sauaces	Cleomenes?	Ptolemy (323)
Babylonia	Bupares	Mazaeus (330)	Stamenes [Ditamenes] (328)
Armenia	Orontes	Mithrenes	Orontes
Susiana	Abulites	Abulites (331/0)	Oropius; Coenus? (324/3)
Persia	Ariobarzanes	Phrasaortes (330)	Orxines (326); Peucestas (324)

Satrapy	Persian satrap	Alexander's first appointee	Subsequent office holders
Carmania	Astaspes	Astaspes	Tlepolemus (325/4)
Media	Atropates	Oxydates (330)	Atropates (327)
Parthia	Phrataphernes	Amminapes (330)	Phrataphernes (330)
Areia	Satibarzanes	Satibarzanes (330)	Arsaces (330/29); Stasanor (329)
Tapurians	Autophradates	Autophradates	Phrataphernes (327)
Arachosia	Barsaentes	Menon (330)	
Parapamisadae	?	Proexes (329)	Oxyartes (326)
Bactria	Bessus	Artabazus (329)	Cleitus (328); Amyntas (328); Philip (326)
Gandhara	?	Nicanor	
Taxila	? Taxiles	Philip (326)	Taxiles (324)
Sindh	?	Peithon (325)	
Gedrosia	?	Apollophanes (325)	Thoas (325); Sibyrtius (324)

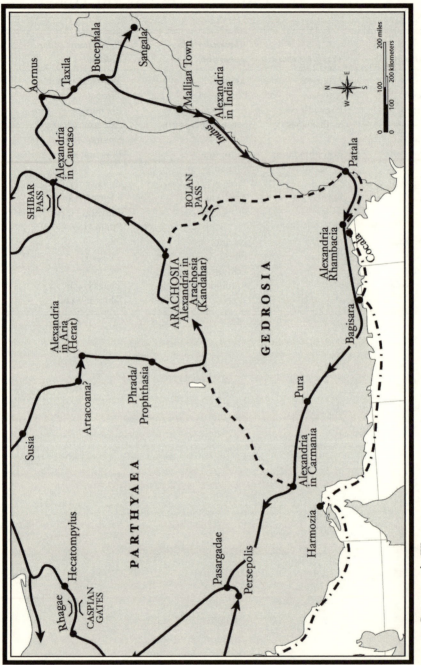

The following labels appear on the map:

Aornus
Taxila
Bucephala
Sangala?
Mallian Town
Alexandria in India
Indus
Patala
Alexandria in Caucaso
SHIBAR PASS
BOLAN PASS
ARACHOSIA
Alexandria in Arachosia (Kandahar)
GEDROSIA
Alexandria Rhambacia
Coccala

Bagisara
Alexandria in Aria (Herat)
Artacoana?
Phrada/Prophthasia
Pura
Susia
Alexandria in Carmania
PARTHYAEA
Hecatompylus
Harmozia
Rhagae
CASPIAN GATES
Pasargadae
Persepolis

200 miles
100
200 kilometers
100
N
E
S
W

MAP 9. *Return to the West.*

166

GLOSSARY

Achaemenidae Descendants of Achaemenes. The Persian royal house.

agema The elite corps within a military body (e.g., the *agema* of the hypaspists). In the later years of the campaign the cavalry also had an *agema*, though this appears to have replaced the *ile basilike*.

antitagma A unit (*tagma* = *taxis*) set up as a counterweight to another.

apologia A defense. Sometimes a "whitewashing."

apomachoi Those unfit for military service as a result of illness, injury, or old age.

apotropaic sacrifice Sacrifice conducted to ward off (literally "turn away") evil or misfortune.

archihypaspistes Commander of the regular hypaspists.

archon A political leader or a military commander.

Argeadae (also "Argeads"). Descendants of Argaeus. The Macedonian royal house.

argyraspides The Silver Shields. Three thousand former hypaspists.

aristeia Excellence. A display of manly virtue.

asthetairoi Perhaps "closest companions" (others have suggested "best companions" or "townsmen companions"). The term applies to a portion of the *pezhetairoi*, but its significance and origin is obscure. See Bosworth 1973.

ataktoi Literally, "those without discipline." Units made up of mutinous troops or men who resist authority.

bailliage Regency or the exercise of power in the king's absence.

bireme (from the Latin *biremis*). A ship with two banks of oars on each side. See also s.v. "trireme."

chiliarch (i.e., *chiliarchos*). Commander of a thousand. The Persian chief official known as *hazarapatish*.

chiliarches (pl. *chiliarchai*) Commander of a thousand men.

condottieri (sing. *condottiero*; also *condottiere*). Leaders or mercenary captains.

douloi Slaves. To the Greek mind, subjects of the Persian King.

Epigonoi Successors or descendants. Particularly the barbarian troops recruited and trained to replace the discharged Macedonian veterans.

en échelon Deployed at an angle, with one wing in advance and the other "refused."

Euacae Elite Persian cavalrymen enrolled in the Macedonian cavalry in 324.

euertgeai (sing. *euergetes*). Benefactors. Those recognized and honored for their past services.

gazophylax "Treasurer" or "guardian of the treasure."

hegemon A leader. In military contexts, a general; in a political context, a commander-in-chief or director of foreign policy.

hetairoi "Companions." The name is used of the aristocrats who formed Alexander's military entourage and served as his counsellors. The term is also used of the Macedonian cavalry, the "Companion Cavalry."

hippakontistai Mounted javelin-men.

hipparch A cavalry commander (in Greek either *hipparchos* or *hipparches*).

hippeis Cavalrymen.

hippotoxotai Mounted archers.

hyparchos A lieutenant. Often used interchangeably with satrap.

hypaspistes (pl. *hypaspistai*, literally "shieldbearers"). A member of the 3,000-man infantry guard of the Macedonian king.

ilarches (pl. *ilarchai*). Commander of a cavalry squadron.

ile (pl. *ilai*). A squadron of cavalry, perhaps about 200–250 men strong.

ile basilike The Royal Squadron, which fought in the immediate vicinity of the king.

hypaspistes basilikos (pl. *hypaspistai basilikoi*). Royal hypaspist.

Kardakes Persian troops. They numbered 60,000 at Issus, but the nature of their armament and recruitment is uncertain. Some writers regard them as light infantry (e.g., Fuller 1960: 160; Lonsdale 2004: 102), but Arr. 2.8.6 says they were hoplites. They appear to have been a body of elite troops drawn from all over the empire rather than on a regional basis. See Briant 1999. Although they may have been the inspiration for Alexander's 30,000 *epigonoi*, it is wrong to see them as an extension of the *paides basilikoi*.

koine eirene "Common Peace." A peace settlement (e.g., the Peace of Antalcidas or "King's Peace" of 387/6 BC) that guaranteed local autonomy.

kopis Cleaver. A slightly curved sword used for striking downwards, and thus a favorite of cavalrymen.

Medism Collaboration with the Persians, particularly in the time of the Persian Wars of the early fifth century BC.

misthophoroi Mercenaries (*misthos* = pay).

monomachia A duel. Single combat.

paides basilikoi Pages. Young men of the nobility brought up at the court of the king.

pentakosiarches (pl. *pentakosiarchai*). Commander of 500 men.

pezhetairoi (also *pezetairoi*, literally "foot companions"). Alexander's sarissa-bearing heavy infantry.

philoi Friends. Often used in place of *hetairoi*.

pothos An urge or longing.

polis (pl. *poleis*). A city-state.

phrourarchos (pl. *phrourarchoi*). A garrison commander (commandant).

primus inter pares First among equals.

prodromoi Those who ride in front (i.e., scouts; cf. *skopoi*)

proskynesis The Persian practice of obeisance. It could range from blowing a kiss to groveling before the Great King.

proxenos A foreigner honored by a state; he tends to be an official representative of his own state.

psiloi Lightly armed infantrymen.

Quellenforschung Source criticism.

satrap A provincial governor.

satrapy A province of the Persian Empire.

sarissa (also *sarisa*). The Macedonian pike, which measured fifteen to eighteen feet in the time of Alexander.

skopoi Those who spy. Scouts.

somatophylakes Literally, "bodyguards." The name is used of the hypaspists, perhaps always referring to the royal hypaspists.

Somatophylakes Written in this form throughout the text, the term applies to Alexander's seven-man Bodyguard.

strategos (pl. *strategoi*). A general. Also a military overseer in a city or province.

taxiarches (also *taxiarchos*). Commander of a *taxis*.

taxis (Pl. *taxeis*). A unit (the size can vary). It is often used by Arrian to refer to the phalanx battalions, which numbered 1,500 men each.

toxotai Archers.

triakontoroi (singular: *triakontoros*) A thirty-oared ship.

trireme A warship with three banks of oars (Greek: *trieres*).

Verschmelzungspolitik Policy of Fusion.

xenoi Mercenaries.

xyston The cavalryman's thrusting spear. This may be what is sometimes referred to as the cavalry *sarissa*. It was probably half the length of the longest infantry *sarissa*.

ABBREVIATIONS

✳ ✳ ✳

SOURCES

Ael. *VH*	Aelian, *Varia Historia*
Arr.	Arrian, *Anabasis* (*History of Alexander*)
Arr. *Ind.*	Arrian, *Indica*
Arr. *Succ.*	Arrian, *Ta met' Alexandron* (*History of the Successors*)
Athen.	Athenaeus, *Deipnosophistae*
Curt.	Quintus Curtius Rufus, *Historiae Alexandri Magni*
Diod.	Diodorus of Sicily, *Bibliotheca*
Etym. Magn.	*Etymologicum Magnum*
FGrH	F. Jacoby, *Die Fragmente der griechischen Historiker*
Frontinus	Frontinus, *Stratagems*
Hdt.	Herodotus, *The Histories*
IG	*Inscriptiones Graecae*
Isoc. *Paneg.*	Isocrates, *Panegyricus*
Justin	Marcus Junianius Justinus, *Epitome of the Philippic History of Pompeius Trogus*
Liber de Morte	*The Last Days and Testament of Alexander the Great* (appended to the *Metz Epitome*)
Metz Epit.	The *Metz Epitome*
Nepos, *Con.*	Cornelius Nepos, *Life of Conon*
Nepos, *Eum.*	Cornelius Nepos, *Life of Eumenes*
Ord. Vit.	Ordericus Vitalis, *Historia Ecclesiastica*
Paus.	Pausanias, *Description of Greece*
Plb.	Polybius
Plut. *Ages.*	Plutarch, *Life of Agesilaus*
Plut. *Alex.*	Plutarch, *Life of Alexander*
Plut. *Artox.*	Plutarch, *Life of Artoxerxes*
Plut. *Demosth.*	Plutarch, *Life of Demosthenes*
Plut. *Eum.*	Plutarch, *Life of Eumenes*
Plut. *Mor.*	Plutarch, *Moralia*
Plut. *Phoc.*	Plutarch, *Life of Phocion*
Polyaenus	Polyaenus, *Stratagems of War*

Strabo	Strabo, *Geography*
Thuc.	Thucydides, *The Peloponnesian War*
Trogus	Pompeius Trogus, *Philippic History*
Val. Max.	Valerius Maximus
Xen. *Anab.*	Xenophon, *Anabasis*
Xen. *Cyr.*	Xenophon, *Cyropaedia* (*Education of Cyrus*)
Xen. *Hell.*	Xenophon, *Hellenica*

SCHOLARLY JOURNALS AND REFERENCE WORKS

AC	*Acta Classica*
AHB	*The Ancient History Bulletin*
AJAH	*American Journal of Ancient History*
AJP	*American Journal of Philology*
CMH²	*The New Cambridge Medieval History*
CP	*Classical Philology*
CQ	*Classical Quarterly*
G&R	*Greece and Rome*
GRBS	*Greek, Roman and Byzantine Studies*
HSCP	*Harvard Studies in Classical Philology*
JHS	*Journal of Hellenic Studies*
LCM	*Liverpool Classical Monthly*
NEJM	*New England Journal of Medicine*
OLP	*Orientalia Lovaniensia Periodica*
PP	*La Parola del Passato*
RFIC	*Rivista di Filologia e Istruzione Classica*
RhM	*Rheinisches Museum für Philologie*
SO	*Symbolae Osloenses*
TAPA	*Transactions of the American Philological Association*
YCS	*Yale Classical Studies*
ZÄS	*Zeitschrift für Ägyptische Sprache und Altertumskunde*
ZPE	*Zeitschrift für Papyrologie und Epigraphik*

NOTES

PREFACE

1. Montgomery 1968: 19.
2. See, for example, Brunt 1965: 208: "It is not likely indeed that Alexander was guided at any time in his life by purely rational calculations. Devoted to the reading of Homer, he conceived himself as a second Achilles. . . . " I had intended to include my own views on Alexander and Achilles in an appendix, but decided that a detailed discussion of sources problems would be out of place in this book.
3. Murison 1972: 414. The author goes on to quote Keil 1924: 19: "Dieser Alexander kann doch wohl nicht der wirkliche Alexander sein!"
4. Cawkwell 2005: 199.
5. Fredricksmeyer 2003: 8.
6. Zinsser 1996: 5–6.
7. Nor am I oblivious to the pitfalls of comparison. The appropriateness of the analogy quickly vanishes when the events used for comparison are given a different interpretation by the scholars in that field: e.g., the now discredited – though not necessarily disproven – view that many of the First Crusaders were second sons in search of lands in the East, which I employ to illustrate the expectations of Alexander's *hetairoi*. Tyerman 2004: 140 is right to reject this as a general rule, but I suspect that Tyerman underestimates the opportunities for wealth and (what is more important) power in the new Latin kingdoms. My comments on the Crusades are based not only on modern scholarly discussions but on a reading of the sources as well; the same is true of my understanding of the *conquistadores*. For the Norman conquest, although I have consulted the work of Orderic Vitalis, I have relied primarily on the works of the distinguished historians R. Allen Brown, Marjorie Chibnall, C. Warren Hollister, and David C. Douglas, and I hope that I have not unwittingly misrepresented their views or taken some of their remarks out of context.
8. See, for example, the questions posed in Coulborn 1965, a study of "feudalism" in world history.
9. Prescott 1998: 28.

CHAPTER ONE: INTRODUCTION

1. Cargill 1977 has questioned the evidence of the *Nabonidus Chronicle*; but Bacchylides, whose account is older than that of Herodotus, appears to support the view that Croesus was put to death. At least, this is how I interpret Croesus' translation to the land of the Hyperboreans.
2. The Common Peace purported to guarantee the local autonomy of all the signatories, though in fact it was a mechanism for "divide and conquer," since it prevented the formation of alliances or political unities (e.g., the *isopoliteia* of Argos and Corinth or the Boeotian League). Thus, the dominant state in Greece could impose its will with the financial backing of the Persian King. Any "rogue state" was thus isolated and could easily be overwhelmed by military force and the economic clout of Persia. See Ryder 1965.
3. There has, of course, been an explosion of "postcolonial" studies, but one might single out Kiernan 1995 (originally published in 1969) as a useful introduction; see also Washbrook 1999.

CHAPTER TWO: HOW DO WE KNOW? SOURCES FOR ALEXANDER THE GREAT

1. The fragments of the lost historians take the form of citations (though these are listed separately as *testimonia*), quotations, and paraphrases. There are occasional papyrus fragments, but these tend to be from otherwise unknown, anonymous historians. See Jacoby, *FGrH*; Robinson 1953; Auberger 2001; cf. Pearson 1960.
2. For example, the Alexander Mosaic (modeled on the painting by Philoxenus of Eretria, from the early age of the Successors) and the Alexander Sarcophagus. For discussions of such sources see Stewart 1993.
3. For example, Chares is generally regarded as the most reliable primary source for the Cleitus affair.
4. Badian 1975: 47: "The reputation of Nearchus, the Cretan from Amphipolis, shines like a good deed in the admittedly naughty world of Alexander historians."

5. The political pamphlet on *The Last Days and Testament of Alexander*, published in the time shortly after the king's death (see Merkelbach 1977; Heckel 1988; Bosworth 2000), mentions earlier allegations of poisoning by Onesicritus (*Liber de Morte* 97). Onesicritus and Nearchus belonged to opposing political camps in the age of the Successors; the former is found with Lysimachus, the latter with Antigonus.

6. Whether this was a deliberate attempt to refute or correct Cleitarchus is uncertain. Arr. 6.11.7–8 shows that Ptolemy recorded details about his own involvement in the campaign that differed from those given by Cleitarchus (Curt. 9.5.21), but since the latter gave information that flattered the king of Egypt, Ptolemy did not, as far as we can tell, openly criticize him.

7. Constantine Porphyrogenitus on Horace, *Ars Poetica* 5.357, calls him *poeta pessimus*.

8. The historical narrative that forms the backbone of Plutarch's *Life of Alexander* is clearly based on Cleitarchus. To this group of works we add also the anonymous *Metz Epitome*, on which see Baynham 1995.

9. For Diodorus' method see Sachs 1990; Hammond 1983: 12–85 argues for a mix of Cleitarchus and Diyllus. Although the opening sentence of his conclusion is certainly correct ("Any historian who studies this book of Diodorus has to separate the grain from the chaff."), the remainder is methodologically flawed and unconvincing: "As we have seen, the passages ascribed to Diyllus as source rest on the best evidence available down to and including Ptolemy's account. On the other hand, most of the passages deriving from Cleitarchus are partly or entirely fictional . . . " (1983: 85).

10. For Justin and Trogus see Yardley & Heckel 1997: 1–41; for Trogus' history see Seel 1972; Alonso-Nuñez 1992.

11. Tarn 1948: 2.125.

12. See Baynham 1998a for his life and work; two volumes of commentary have been published by Atkinson 1980, 1994; and an *index verborum*, Therasse 1976.

13. Plut. *Alex.* 1.3.

14. See Stadter 1980 for his life and writings. The most important work on Arrian is that of A. B. Bosworth. See the first two volumes of his commentary on Arrian (Bosworth 1980a, 1995), as well as Bosworth 1988b.

15. In addition to the *Anabasis*, Arrian wrote numerous other historical works, including *Events after Alexander, Parthica, Indica, Tactica*, and a work on the circumnavigation of the Black Sea.

16. See Lane Fox 1997; Davies 1998 (for an English translation); Tabacco 2000.

17. Trogus' work has, of course, not survived in its original form, but the elements and methods of composition are attributable to him (or his source) rather than to his epitomator, Justin, except where Justin himself introduces new errors in the course of abbreviating or summarizing.

18. Was he, like Dudo of Saint-Quentin, writing on behalf of Duke Richard II of Normandy, creating official history, but a falsification nevertheless? See, e.g., Chibnall 2000: 16–20, who cites also a certain Widukind as claiming that the Saxons were descended from soldiers in Alexander's army!

19. For example, the text of Cornelius Nepos' *Life of Eumenes* (5.1) reports that Perdiccas was assassinated by Seleucus and Antigonus. The latter was certainly not present at the time of the murder, but other witnesses (e.g., Arr. *Succ.* 1.35) tell us that Antigenes was one of those who put Perdiccas to death. Whether the name Antigenes was changed to the better-known Antigonus through author's mistake, scribal error, or editor's correction, we cannot say. But since Antigonus has an alibi, Antigenes' guilt appears to be established.

CHAPTER THREE: THE MACEDONIAN BACKGROUND

1. Casson 1926: 5 describes the Peneus River as the "dividing line between 'European' and 'Mediterranean' Greece."

2. Cf. Borza 1990: 27.

3. Kienast 1973 believes that many of these were adopted by Philip II in imitation of Persian usage, but they appear to antedate Philip and, if they are in fact borrowings from Persia, may belong to the period soon after 513.

4. See, however, Hall 2002: 154–6.

5. For Macedonia in the time of Archelaus see Thomas (2006) 39–40.

6. Philip's status in the years 359–7 is hotly debated. Satyrus' claim (cf. also Justin 7.5.6–10) that he ruled twenty-two years lends credence to the view that he was temporarily regent. For full discussions see Tronson 1984: 120–21; Griffith 1979: 208–9, 702–4; Borza 1990: 200–201.

7. Badian 1963: 244: "the complicated history of his matrimonial affairs mirrors the progress of his political expansion."

8. Athen. 13.557b–d, translated by J. C. Yardley, in Heckel & Yardley 2004: 20. For Philip's marriages see Carney 2000: 51–81 and Ogden 1999: 17–27.

9. Fuller 1954: 29.

10. Diod. 17.86.1.

11. Polyaenus 4.2.2, remarking that Philip's infantry had "retreated" to the higher ground (i.e., near the acropolis).

12. For casualty figures see Diod. 17.86.5–6. The size of the Greek army is not given. Diod. 17.85.6 says that Philip, with his 32,000 men, had the numerical advantage; but Justin 9.3.9 says the opposite. It is probably safe to assume that the forces were fairly evenly matched but that the Macedonians had a larger and better cavalry force.

13. Many modern scholars have, indeed, seen political implications in these domestic disputes, but the evidence is not compelling.

14. See the clever observation, preserved in Plut. *Alex.* 3.4, that Olympias feared Hera's wrath.

15. Plut. *Alex.* 9.4.

16. See Carney 2006: 25.

17. This is surely the campaign against "Pleurias," mentioned by Diod. 16.93.8–9. I see no reason for conflating this with the Pleuratus campaign of 344/3, although Diodorus may be referring to a second campaign against the same Illyrian king.

18. The view that Cleopatra had borne two children, a daughter Europa and a son named Caranus, was rightly rejected by Tarn 1948: 2.260–62; cf. Heckel 1979, but Caranus is regularly revived, on no good evidence (indeed, only on the basis of a very bad source that transforms Caranus from a hypothetical rival into a historical figure: Justin 9.7.3, 11.2.3; cf. 12.6.14).

19. Justin 8.6.5–8 claims that Philip had homosexual relations with his young brother-in-law, Alexander I of Epirus, and made him "a catamite first, and then a king" (Justin 8.6.8, tr. J. C. Yardley). Alexander the Great's rejection of boys may have been a reaction to his father's behavior (cf. Plut. *Alex.* 22.1–2). For pederasty at the Macedonian court see Berve 1926: 1.10–11, who accepts Dicaearchus' statement that Alexander was *ekmanos philopais* ("mad about boys"). I would hesitate to identify many of the king's youthful attendants as "Lustknaben," as Berve does.

20. The sister of Philotas who married Coenus son of Polemocrates was probably Attalus' widow (see Heckel 2006a: 276 **F22, F34**).

21. For example, Marsden 1964: 69 suggests various combinations of 300 (*ile basilike*) and 210, 231, 253, 276, depending on the actual number of Companions at Gaugamela. We must remember, however, that unit sizes are nominal and usually not up to full strength.

22. The first thing that the word *sarissa* conjures up in the mind of the modern reader is length. But, in fact, the *sarrisophoroi* were probably so called because of the type of weapon they used (i.e., because of its function as a thrusting spear) rather than because it was in its proportions similar to the weapon used by the phalangite.

23. *FGrH* 115 F 348; cf. Dem. 2.17; Anaximenes *ap.* Harpocration = *FGrH* 72 F 4; *Etym. Magn.* 699.50–51; cf. Erskine 1989; Griffith 1979: 75–9.

24. Hypaspist commanders distinguished themselves at Halicarnassus (Atarrhias, Hellanicus), Tyre (Admetus), Gaza (Neoptolemus), and the Mallian town (Habreas). Although Admetus and Neoptolemus probably belonged to the royal hypaspists at this time, Neoptolemus certainly later served as *archihypaspistes*. The two units were recruited from different age groups and social classes. For the activities of hypaspists in the campaign against the 'autonomous' Thracians, see Heckel 2005. Smaller units of hypaspists acted as military police: see, for example, the arrest of Philotas (Curt. 6.8.19–22) or of the mutineers at Opis (Arr. 7.8.3).

25. The activities of the *argyraspides* between 326 and 321 are poorly documented and a number of proposals have been put forward. My own views are spelled out in Heckel 1982 and 1992: 307–19; cf. also Anson 1981. Anson and I both reject arguments of Lock 1977, who proposes that the Silver Shields were

not formed as a unit until the settlement of Triparadeisus (321 or 320 BC). Antigenes, the hypaspist commander, who is later attested as the leader of the *argyraspides*, returned from India with the forces under the command of Craterus. Alexander nevertheless had with him the entire corps of hypaspists. I suspect that these were the men who replaced the Silver Shields.

26. Goldsworthy 2003: 23
27. The descent of the Molossian royal house from Neoptolemus son of Achilles was commemorated in Euripides' *Andromache*, and the Athenians would have known of Alexander's mythical descent also from the honors heaped upon his great-uncle, Arybbas, and his descendants (*IG* ii² 225 = *SIG*³ 228; cf. Rhodes & Osborne 2003: no. 70).
28. The Macedonian infantry also destroyed some of the crops, using their sarissas at the level like scythes.
29. There is some debate concerning whether Alexander used Thermopylae (Hamilton 1969: 29; Hammond 1997: 44) or the Asopus Pass (Bosworth 1988a: 32; Brunt 1976: 32 n.1).
30. Plut. *Alex.* 11.7–8; Hamilton 1969: 30; for Philotas as *phrourarchos* see Diod. 17.8.7.
31. It has been suggested that Arrian's source, Ptolemy, deliberately cast the blame for the attack on Thebes on his later enemy, Perdiccas (Errington 1969: 236–7). Even if this is true, the decision to destroy the city could not have been taken without Alexander's approval. Perdiccas, who was nearly killed in the engagement, certainly suffered no check to his career. If anything, he emerged as one of Alexander's most trusted commanders.
32. Diod. 17.14.1; Plut. *Alex.* 11.12; Ael. *VH* 13.7.
33. See Justin 11.3.6–11, with Yardley & Heckel 1997: 92–6. For example, see Arr. 2.15.2 for Alexander's treatment of the captured Theban ambassadors, Dionysodorus and Thessaliscus.

Chapter Four: The Persian Enemy

1. Though not in the direct line from Cyrus, Darius I and his descendants did trace their ancestry to Achaemenes, though, admittedly, Darius II and his wife (and half-sister) Parysatis were the children of Artaxerxes I and Babylonian concubines.
2. Arr. 2.7.8–9 claims that Alexander made reference to the Ten Thousand in his pre-battle speech at Issus. For Cunaxa and its aftermath see Waterfield 2006; Lane Fox 2004; and, on the eternal fame of the Ten Thousand, Rood 2004.
3. The myth of Persian decadence has recently been debunked: see Sancisi-Weerdenburg 1987; Briant 2002.
4. Xen. *Anab.* 1.5.9.
5. Xen. *Anab.* 1.7.6–7.
6. Olmstead 1948: 263.
7. See Lewis 1977: 83–107.
8. Xen. *Hell.* 1.5.8–9. Cf. Diod. 13. 37. 4–5; Thuc. 8. 46. 1–2.
9. Plut. *Ages.* 15.8. The reference is to the daric, a coin stamped with a Persian archer, and the gold that Timocrates the Rhodian was alleged to have distributed to the enemies of Sparta in Greece.
10. This is one of the central themes of Isocrates' *Panegyricus*. For the origins of Spartan betrayal of the Greeks in Asia see Thucydides, Book 8, along with Lewis 1977.
11. It appears that Medism was, at any rate, a reprehensible activity connected with the Persian War (comparable, in modern terms, to collaboration with the Nazis) and not a reference to dealings with Persia in a later period. Although the Athenians of the "Cold War" between Persia and Athens in the fifth century deliberately created a picture of the barbarian as someone to be, at the same time, feared and despised (Hall 1989), the reality of Greek–Persian relations was completely different (cf. Miller 1997).
12. Diod. 17.9.5. Whether the Thebans actually made such a proclamation is debatable. A great deal of thought and literary craft went into the justification of the destruction of Thebes, which depicted Alexander's use of calculated terror as condign punishment of Greece's most notorious Medizers. Cf. Justin 11.3.10, with Yardley & Heckel 1997: 95–6.
13. Isoc. *Paneg.* 122. See particularly the excellent discussion by Flower 2000; see also Seibert 1998. For the development of the hostile view of Persian in the Athenian Empire, see Hall 1989; for Hellenicity, ethnicity, and culture, Hall 2002.

14. Xenophon, *Hellenica* 1.6.7. Cf. Cawkwell 2005: 163: "All this Panhellenist claptrap was congenial to Xenophon."
15. See Heckel & Yardley 2004: 9 (passage 2[e]).
16. The power and status of Assyrian eunuchs is discussed by Grayson 1993; cf. Tougher 2004, for the early Middle Ages. It was an Egyptian eunuch who was sent by the Pharaoh Amasis in pursuit of the mercenary leader Phanes in 526/5 (Hdt. 3.4.2), and Ctesias of Cnidus mentions a number of prominent eunuchs at the Achaemenid court. Oman 1924: 1.32 says that Narses "in spite of his training as a mere court-chamberlain, showed military talents not inferior to Belisarius' own." This is a misunderstanding of Narses' role.
17. The intrigues at the Persian court are described by Diod. 17.5.3–6; Justin 10.3; Strabo 15.3.24 C736; cf. Val. Max. 9.2 ext. 7; Curt. 10.5.23. Darius was 50 at the time of his death in 330 (Arr. 3.22.6). For his heroism against the Cadusians see Diod. 17.6.1; Justin 10.3.3.
18. For discussion of his rebellion and reign see Burstein 2000.

Chapter Five: Conquest of the Achaemenids

1. Plut. *Alex.* 15.2, *Mor.* 327d-e; Arr. 7.9.6; Curt. 10.2.24.
2. For the origins of the wars between east and west see Hdt 1.1. Agesilaus' sacrifice at Aulis was disrupted by the Boeotian cavalry. He never forgave the insult. For Agesilaus' Panhellenism see Cawkwell 1976 and 2005: 163.
3. See Perrin 1895.
4. See Heckel 1997: 196: "the coastal population recognized the Panhellenic Crusade as the thin veil of Macedonian imperialism." Cf. Faraguna 2003: 113.
5. Plut. *Alex.* 15.2, *Mor.* 327e: his war chest amounted to 70 talents; Curt. 10.2.24 says 60. For his financial woes see also Arr. 7.9.6; Plut. *Mor.* 327d. See also Engels 1978: 27–30. Brosius 2003: 173 remarks that Alexander's "ambition to fight a war against Persia was so immense that even his lack of finances did not stop him." It is more likely, however, that Alexander's lack of resources was a motivating (or necessitating) factor (see Austin 1993: 206).
6. In fact, the number of Greek mercenaries may not have exceeded four or five thousand, and it is likely that Alexander's army on this occasion outnumbered that of the Persians.
7. Gaebel 2002: 184.
8. The choice of Amyntas may not have been a coincidence. His father had been executed for complicity in the murder of Philip. Perhaps he volunteered to lead the attack in an effort to salvage his honor. A cynic might suggest that he was deliberately exposed to danger.
9. For the oaths sworn by members of the League of Corinth see Rhodes and Osborne 2003, no. 76.
10. See, especially, the compelling arguments of Hammond 1980: 74.
11. That the Persian cavalry included contingents of Hyrcanians and Medes (Diod. 17.19.4) is highly doubtful; that Alexander carried a shield is almost certainly wrong; and the reference to "Alexander's renown for daring" (17.20.3) is clearly anachronistic and part of the official propaganda. It was probably his very behavior at the Granicus (and the official account of it) that established his reputation for daring and recklessness (cf. Plut. *Alex.* 16.4).
12. Whether this hero was meant to be Achilles is uncertain. It appears that the correlation of Alexander with Achilles is later than Callisthenes. But he is certainly depicted in Diodorus' account as a hero in the Homeric mold. Compare Diod. 17.20.3 ("He hurled his javelin at Alexander with so mighty an impulse and so powerful a cast that he pierced Alexander's shield and right epomis and drove through the breastplate") with Homer, *Iliad* 3.355-60 ("He spoke, balanced his long-shadowed spear and hurled it. It hit Paris' round shield. The heavy weapon pierced the glittering shield, forced its way through the ornate body-armour and ripped right on trhough the side of Paris' tunic. But Paris had swerved and so avoided dark death").
13. Bosworth 1980a: 122–3 rejects the identification of Demaratus the Corinthian with the *xenos* of Philip II (who had earlier reconciled father and son in the aftermath of the quarrel between Alexander and Attalus: Plut. *Mor.* 179c), noting that Demaratus was too old and, at any rate, "only joined Alexander's entourage at Susa in late 330." Demaratus did indeed die of infirmity in 327, but this was seven years after the Granicus. The age of Alexander and his successors has no shortage of warriors advanced in

years. Plut. *Alex*. 56. 1 says that Demaratus made the journey to Susa in 330. He may, however, have remained in Asia Minor after the first year of the campaign. It makes more sense that the virtually gratuitous reference to Demaratus at the Granicus was a deliberate part of the Panhellenic propaganda.

14. Green 1974: 489–512 offers an intriguing interpretation. There were two battles – one in the late afternoon, which was repulsed, and a second, successful one on the following day – and Alexander's slaughter of the Greek mercenaries was retribution for the defeat they had inflicted upon him in the first engagement. It is more likely, however, that Diodorus, in the course of abbreviating his source, simply reported as fact what had been suggested as a possible course of action.

15. Noted also by Devine 1994: 94, though I would stop short of attributing the nature of Callisthenes' account to "beginner's inexperience." He may not have been an accomplished military writer (as Polybius 12.17 ff. delighted in pointing out to his readers), but his primary aim in the description of the Granicus battle was to glorify Alexander. The positions of the Persian commanders can be determined partially from the combined evidence of Arrian and Diodorus. Mithrobuzanes with the Cappadocians and Pharnaces, presumably leading Pontic levies, must have been located to the right of center. For the casualties see Arr. 1.16.3; Diod. 17.21.3.

16. Xen. *Anab*. 1.4.18, noted by J. Rufus Fears in Badian 1976: 28.

17. A defection of this sort by Apollonides turned the tide of battle against Eumenes at the battle of Orcynia in 319 (Diod. 18.40.5–8; Plut. *Eum*. 9.3; cf. Anson 2004: 128).

18. For his career see Heckel 1992: 352–3 and 2006a: 24 "Amyntas [3]."

19. *FGrH* 139 F7. For the Gordian knot story see Curt. 3.1.11–18; Arr. 2.3.1–8; Justin 11.7.3–16; Plut. *Alex*. 18.1–4; cf. Marsyas of Philippi, *FGrH* 135/6 F4. For Hittite origins see Burke 2002.

20. Hall 1989.

21. In addition to Artabazus and his family (discussed below), both Sisines (Curt. 3.7.11) and Amminapes (Curt. 6.4.25) are alleged to have spent time at Philip's court.

22. See particularly Parke 1933; a more recent but less comprehensive account can be found in Yalichev 1997. For mercenaries in Persian service, see Seibt 1977, and for prominent individuals Hofstetter 1978.

23. This appears to have been standard procedure. Cf. the younger Cyrus' remarks about the families of Xenias and Pasion (Xen. *Anab*. 1.1.4.8).

24. At Mytilene the Persians imposed a garrison under Lycomedes of Rhodes. What became of him is unknown. By the time the Macedonians under Hegelochus arrived to recapture the city, it was in the hands of Chares (cf. Arr. 3.2.6; Curt. 4.5.22).

25. Arr. 1.10.4, 6; Plut. *Phoc*. 17.2; *Demosth*. 23.4.

26. On Bianor see Parke 1933: 132 with n.2 and 199.

27. We may reject Arrian's claim (2.6.2) that Alexander advanced from Mallus to Myriandrus (the place is also called Myriandus) in two days.

28. Thus Engels 1978: 131–4.

29. Plb. 12.17.4 = *FGrH* 124 F35

30. Suggested by Dittberner and reaffirmed by Lane Fox, Hammond, and Devine.

31. Stark 1956: 6. The identification was made by Kromayer 1914: 353, and is accepted also by Bosworth 1988a: 60. For the career and travels of Freya Stark see Geniesse 1999.

32. See the photograph (of the Payas) in Wood 1997: 55. The gap in the Macedonian phalanx was caused by a combination of the terrain and the forward surge of the first two battalions on the right.

33. They numbered 60,000 (30,000 on either side of the mercenaries).

34. Arr. 2.10.7. The ferocity of the Greeks is perhaps a direct result of Alexander's unwise decision to show the mercenaries no quarter after the battle at the Granicus. Arrian does not give complete casualty figures for the Macedonian infantry. All figures given by the extant Alexander historians are ridiculously low.

35. For attempts to supply corrective views see Murison 1972; Seibert 1987; Nylander 1993; Badian 2000b.

36. Hdt. 1.214. Xen. *Cyr*. 8.7 says he died peacefully, but I see no reason for preferring his account to that of Herodotus.

37. Xen. *Anab*. 1.8.22; cf. Arr. 2.8.11.

38. It has been argued, of course, that the Persian strategy at the Granicus was to kill Alexander.

39. Xen. *Cyr*. 4.2.2 says that the Hyrcanians, like all the tribes of Asia, brought their households with them (cf. 4.1.17); 3.3.67 describes a similar practice among the Assyrians.

40. For the oriental practice taking women on military expeditions see Xen. *Cyr.* 3.3.67; 4.1.17, 2.2. The presence of women in the camp may have been intended also to inspire the men to fight (cf. Justin 1.6.13–14, where the women actually reproach the men for their "cowardice"). Nor is battle as a "spectator sport" for men *and women* entirely unknown, as we can see from the first battle of Bull Run (Manasses) in the U.S. Civil War (William Howard Russell, quoted by Commager 1995: 106–9) or the sightseers in the Crimean War, also noted by Russell. See, e.g., Royle 2000: 219: "Indeed, so carefree was the moment that the Russians had allowed a party of Sevastopol's prominent citizens to take a picnic to the battlefield so that they could watch the expected defeat of the allied forces. From a hastily improvised grandstand on the Telegraph Hill they sat in elegant rows, watching the preparations through opera-glasses with glasses of champagne within easy reach." Similar spectatorship occurred at sea in the Baltic campaign of 1854 (Ponting 2004: 45).

41. For details see Curt. 3.13.13–15; cf. Arr. 2.11.10, 15.1. The families of Persian notables also served as hostages to guarantee the good conduct of Darius' leaders (Diod. 17.23.5).

42. The patronymic is not certain, but highly probable. Tennes had betrayed the Sidonians, but he had also played Artaxerxes III false and was executed after the capture of the city.

43. Wilcken 1967: 109. For Philip II and the Atheas campaign see Justin 9.2.10–13; the connection is noted by Hamilton 1985: 21.

44. Lyon *Eracles* 11 (see Edbury 1998: 19). For the importance of Tyre in the eastern Mediterranean see Pryor 1988: 112–34. Saladin had reason to regret having abandoned the siege of the city prematurely. See also Runciman 1951: 3.18: "In the moment of triumph Saladin had made one grave mistake, when he let himself be daunted by the fortifications of Tyre."

45. Arr. 2.16–24; Curt. 4.2–4; Diod. 17.40–46; Plut. *Alex.* 24–25; Polyaenus 4.3.3–4, 13; Justin 11.10.10–14. Fuller 1960: 206-16; Kern 1999: 209-17.

46. Arr. 4.20.1–3 gives a combined total of 224 ships (80 from Phoenicia, 10 from Rhodes and 10 more from Lycia, 120 Cypriotes, 3 from Soli and Mallus, and a Macedonian 50-oared ship); Curt. 4.3.11 mentions only 190 ships.

47. Curt. 4.4.19 says it ended six months after it began, but Arr. 2.24.6 dates the sack of the city to Hecatombaeon (July/August).

48. On the basis of these figures, we may estimate the population of Tyre in 332 to have been a little over 50,000. See also Grainger 1991: 33.

49. Gaza, Ashkelon (Ascalon), Ashdod, Gath, and Ekron were the five cities of the Philistines, a people of obscure origins who formed a contingent of the so-called Sea Peoples of the late Bronze Age. By the time the area was incorporated into the Persian Empire, the Philistines as a group had disappeared or been assimilated. The defending force at Gaza may have been made up primarily of Arabs.

50. For the logistical problems see Engels 1978: 57–9. Engels estimates that Alexander's force would have consumed 6,000,000 gallons of water during the two-month siege.

51. Curt. 4.5.10. For Hephaestion's career see Heckel 1992: 65–90 and 2006a: 133–7; Reames-Zimmerman 1998. For the 20 Athenian ships see Diod. 17.22.5; cf. Hauben 1976: 80–81. These may have remained under the command of Nicanor, whose "Hellenic" fleet had been disbanded at Miletus in 334.

52. Cf. Dodge 1890: 343.

53. Arr. 2.13.2.

54. Cf. Chevalier 1859–60: 2.7, cited by Seibt 1977: 113.

55. 2.11.7.

56. Herodotus' account of the conquest of Egypt by Cambyses derives from hostile sources – his informants were the priests of Sais, located near the Greek city of Naucratis – but, despite its general unreliability, it is still common to find his alleged sacrilege (especially the killing of the Apis calf) reported as fact by modern writers. A similar charge was brought against Artaxerxes III, and Alexander's respect for Egyptian institutions does not prove the charges against his Persian predecessors. Rather it confirms that the hostile propaganda had achieved its purpose. Cambyses' attitudes are best summed up by Kuhrt 1995: 663: he was "moulding himself to fit the role an Egyptian king was traditionally expected to fill – honouring the gods, authorising continued offerings, maintaining their sanctuaries in purity, adopting ceremonial Egyptian titles and names." The story that Cambyses sent an army to attack the Ammonii is also a fiction and perhaps a misrepresentation of an embassy to Siwah. Cf. Allen 2005: 35.

57. Such legends are common enough. Hdt. 3.2.1 says "the Egyptians claim Cambyses as one of their own," adding that he was the son of Cyrus and the daughter of the Pharaoh Apries (Hophra). Hence his return and overthrow of the house of Amasis was just retribution, since the conqueror belonged to the line of Apries.

58. On Chababash see Burstein 2000. Lloyd 2000: 390 believes the uprising began as early as 339/8; cf. Spalinger 1978. For the impact of the affairs in Egypt on the Persian navy see Anson 1989.

59. Similar honors were later granted to Philip III Arrhidaeus. See Mysliwiec 2000: 178. Burstein 1991: 141 observes: "A titulary . . . is evidence not of the coronation of a ruler of Egypt but of the acceptance of his rule by the priests."

60. See Aristobulus, *FGrH* 139 F 47 = Athen. 6.251a (Dioxippus, the pancratiast and flatterer of the king, remarked that "the ichor of the immortal gods" flowed from Alexander's wound, but the king responded that it was "just blood"); cf. Plut. *Alex.* 38.3. Bosworth 1988a: 282 points to Strabo 17.1.43 = Callisthenes, *FGrH* 124 F14a, which, he alleges, shows that the Milesian and Erythraean oracles' recognition of Alexander as son of Zeus arrived in Memphis in spring 331, "too soon for them to be influenced by reports of the actual consultation [at Siwah]." But, if we accept the truth of Callisthenes' (reported) remark, we must also believe that the Milesian oracle predicted the victory at Arbela (Gaugamela), the death of Darius, and upheavals in the Peloponnese. Callisthenes, if he did report such prophecies, did not report this until the king was in Central Asia, possibly in the context of the punishment of the Branchidae.

61. For this reason alone I find it difficult to accept the view of D. Mueller (in Badian 1976: 65) that "Alexander misunderstood what the oracle said to welcome him as the legitimate successor of the Pharaohs as applying to him personally." Dandamaev 1989: 79 appears to consider this an actual military expedition and, indeed, a number of funded archaeological teams have searched in vain for Cambyses' "lost army."

62. Diod. 17.32.1–2.

63. See Heckel 1992: 6–12 and Heckel 2006a: 131–2.

64. Curt. 4.1.10–13, tr. by J. C. Yardley.

65. The 1,000 talents to murder Alexander himself appears to refer to the attempt to bribe Philip of Acarnania (Curt. 3.6.4).

66. This offer followed the news of the death of Darius' wife, Stateira, and it is wrong to date the embassy to Alexander's first sojourn in the vicinity of Tyre, as some scholars have done. The inescapable fact is that Stateira died of what were considered to be complications related to pregnancy or childbirth.

67. The Persians allegedly placed iron spikes on the battlefield where they expected the Macedonian charge to take place. Curt. 4.13.36–7 says that a certain Bion, a Greek mercenary who deserted to Alexander, revealed these to the Macedonians.

68. The damage done by the scythe-chariots was almost certainly greater than Arrian's source(s) cared to admit (see Arr. 3.13.5–6); Diod. 17.58.2–5 and Curt. 4.15.14–17 show that they did not pass harmlessly through the ranks. But in terms of their ability to disrupt the enemy line they proved no more effective here than they had at the battle of Cunaxa (Xen. *Anab.* 1.8.20).

69. Cf. Burn 1973: 118: "Instead of turning to right or left, where they might have done immense damage, this roaring tide of men simply rode straight on." But Marsden 1964: 59–60 believes that this was a very small force, ill equipped to exploit the gap in the Macedonian line, whose actual purpose was to "rescue the Persian royal family" (59).

70. Thus Plut. *Alex.* 33.10 = *FGrH* 124 F36. Callisthenes may be responsible only for the remark that Parmenion resented Alexander's "arrogance and pomp," but even this would hardly have been expressed by Callisthenes before Parmenion's death.

71. Diod. 17.65.5.

72. Abulites had certainly been satrap of Susiane before Alexander's arrival, and it appears that the appointment of his son, Oxathres, as satrap of Parataecene (Arr. 3.19.2; Curt. 5.2.8–9) was the confirmation of an existing office. If Mazaeus held the same rank, it was conferred upon him after the death of Bupares at Gaugamela. He may, however, have surrendered Babylon as the highest-ranking Persian in the city. Until Darius' defeat he was still the titular satrap of Syria. For the favored status of Mazaeus see Heckel 2006b.

73. As official government policy, this is called a tax; directed against central authority, it goes by the name of banditry. Similar tolls were exacted by the Cossaeans (Diod. 19.19), despite Alexander's punitive campaign against them over the winter of 324/3 (Diod. 17.111.4–6; Plut. *Alex.* 72.4; Arr. 7.15.1–3). For their dealings with Antigonus the One-Eyed in 317 see Billows 1990: 92–3.

74. For a discussion of the topography and related military and logistical problems see Speck 2002, who in the late 1970s became the first scholar since Sir Aurel Stein to have conducted a topographical investigation. Michael Wood's less exhaustive survey was published sooner (Wood 1997: 102–8) but conducted much later than Speck's. For historiographical aspects, see Heckel 1980.

75. If there is any truth to Ctesias' story of the torture and death of Clearchus, this is nevertheless an isolated example. Greek hoplites evinced their superiority over barbarian infantry on the battlefield: at Marathon, Plataea, Cunaxa, and elsewhere. This military edge may be ascribed to the same principle enunciated by Kennedy 1988: 20–38 for the rise of the West (i.e., Europe) after 1500. The "political diversity" due to geography and the "competitive interaction" of states resulted in a honing of military technology and skills that were not developed in the monolithic empires of the East.

76. A fifteen-year-old girl, who had not in fact been in Kuwait City at the time of the Iraqi invasion and turned out to be the daughter of a Kuwaiti diplomat in Washington, D.C., reported to the U.S. Congressional Human Rights Caucus on October 10, 1990: "I volunteered at the al-Addan hospital. While I was there, I saw the Iraqi soldiers come into the hospital with guns, and go into the room where . . . babies were in incubators. They took the babies out of the incubators, took the incubators, and left the babies on the cold floor to die" (text is quoted on numerous Web sites, including http://www.mindfully.org/Reform/Nayira-Witness-Incubator-Kuwait6jan92.htm). The deception played no small part in marshalling support for the Gulf War. Similar deception was used to inspire crusading fervor, from Pope Urban II's claim that baptismal fonts were polluted with the blood of Christians forcibly circumcised to the parading of ravaged women in Venice in 1258. As Maier 1994: 117 notes: "the main idea behind a crusade sermon seems to have been to create an interior and external *Feindbild*, that is an image of the enemy within and without."

77. Curt. 5.6.1, tr. by J. C. Yardley.

78. See Diod. 17.70.1 for the exemption of the palaces. Morrison 2001 notes the importance of plunder for the morale of the troops. I would, however, disagree with the view that the pillaging excluded Parmenion's troops. Even if they had not yet arrived, they would have received their share of the booty, almost certainly on the basis of merit and status (cf. Curt. 5.6.20 for the division of spoils amongst the *hetairoi*).

79. The reasons for Alexander's delay – he remained in Persepolis for four months – are not certain. Concern about the situation in Greece provides a plausible explanation; but the road to Ecbatana was also impassable during the Persian winter. Diod. 17.73.1 places the campaign in Persis after the destruction of the palaces, but Curtius' account (5.6.11–19) is probably right in dating it before the conflagration. Arrian does not mention the campaign.

80. Her daughter by Ptolemy, Eirene, married Eunostus of Soli (Athen. 13.576e).

81. Arr. 3.18.11. Predictably, Arrian, who based his history on Ptolemy, says nothing about the destruction of the palace or the (alleged) role of Thaïs. It is hard to imagine that Cleitarchus could have published such a story in Alexandria around 310 B.C. unless there was an element of truth to it and it was not regarded as displeasing to Ptolemy.

82. The political ambiguity of the gesture is illustrated by Plutarch, who in his *Alexander* speaks approvingly of Alexander's conquest of Persia but in the *Agesilaus* (15) writes: "I for one cannot agree with Demaratus of Corinth's assertion that the Greeks who had not seen Alexander sitting on Darius' throne had missed a rare treat; in fact, I think that in all likelihood they might have wept at the realization that Alexander and his Macedonians were simply the heirs of the Greeks of the time who squandered the lives of their commanders on the battlefields of Leuctra, Coronea, Corinth, and Arcadia."

83. There was probably little difference between the political roles of men like Mazaeus, Abulites, and Artabazus and of Afghanistan's Hamid Karzai or Iraq's interim prime minister, Ayad Allawi. Mazaeus, however, enjoyed the trust and respect of Alexander. He appears to have been the intended occupant of the Alexander Sarcophagus (see Heckel 2006b).

84. Briant 2002: 569.

85. For a similar sentiment see Holt 2005: 46: "Since the political conflict between Alexander and Bessus involved a throne in far-off Mesopotamia, it probably mattered little to the Bactrians which man eventually sat upon it, so long as nothing much changed in their own homeland." This is not to say that the lower classes had no interest in royalty or the nobility. Plut. *Artox.* 5.6 describes how the common folk appreciated the fact that Stateira, wife of Artaxerxes II, had the curtains of her carriage (*harmamaxa*) drawn back so that she could be seen. Plutarch calls these people "Persians," but even if they were non-Persian subjects the important thing is that the commoners were attracted to the glamor of the privileged class more than to the individuals themselves. Today, most who profess to have loved Princess Diana would not have given her a second look had she passed them in the streets as a commoner.

86. The so-called Seven, though one of these families was that of Darius I himself. Darius and six other conspirators had murdered the man who ruled after Cambyses, alleging that he was falsely claiming to be Cambyses' brother, Bardiya (Smerdis). Some modern scholars believe that the story of the "false Smerdis" was a fabrication meant to conceal the conspiracy against a legitimate ruler.

Chapter Six: Resistance on Two Fronts

1. Cf. Liddell-Hart 1967: 21. "Alexander's succeeding campaigns, until he reached the borders of India, were militarily a 'mopping up' of the Persian Empire, while politically the consolidation of his own."

2. The designation Artaxerxes IV belongs to Arses (Sachs 1977: 147). For the wearing of the tiara upright see Xen. *Anab.* 2.6.23; Arr. 3.25.3.

3. Arr. 3.22.1: "Alexander sent Darius' body to Persia, ordering that he be buried in the royal tombs, like the other kings before Darius."

4. Arr. 3.21.10 names Satibarzanes and Barsaentes as Darius' killers. It is possible that he meant to write Nabarzanes, but *Metz Epit.* 3 names "Ariobarzanes" as a regicide, which may be the reference to Satibarzanes.

5. Bosworth 1980a: 357 puts Artacoana "somewhere along the Hari Rud in the vicinity of Herat" but does not see Alexandria-in-Areia as a resettlement of the place. Engels 1978: 90-91 believes Artacoana lay to the north and east of Susia (Tus) rather than to the south. See also Atkinson 1994: 206-8.

6. Carney 1983: 260.

7. Their names are given only by Curt. 6.7.15: Peucolaus, Nicanor, Aphobetus, Iolaus, Dioxenus, Archepolis and Amyntas. Later, at the trial of Philotas, a certain Calis (possibly "Calas") admitted to planning the whole affair with Demetrius (Curt. 6.11.37).

8. Badian 1961. This is a plot worthy of Agatha Christie or Mary Renault, but it is not good history. It has, unfortunately, been used to construct an image of Alexander as a paranoid schemer, who, rather than being the victim of conspiracies, actively plotted against his own men (thus Badian 2000a).

9. See Hamilton 1969: 134-5.

10. Curt. 6.7.17-18, noted by Adams 2003: 118.

11. The notion of a constitutionally established Macedonian army assembly (Granier 1931) is no longer accepted, but it is clear that Alexander and later rulers had recourse to the decision of the army in difficult cases, thereby seeming to legalize the process and deflecting blame from the king.

12. Cleander son of Polemocrates was the brother of Coenus, Parmenion's son-in-law. Coenus himself played no small part in the destruction of Philotas.

13. Bosworth 1980a: 373. For the "European Scythians" see Arr. 4.1.1. For the Tanais problem see also Hamilton 1971.

14. Engels 1978: 94–6. Holt 2005: 32–3 argues that Alexander chose the Khawak over the Shibar Pass from Bamian, although the second was lower and easier, to retain the element of surprise. For the adventures of Josiah Harlan in the footsteps of Alexander in the Hindu Kush see MacIntyre 2004: 209-28.

15. Another champion was the Paeonian prince Ariston, who killed Satropates shortly before the battle of Gaugamela (Curt. 4.9.25). Cf. the killing of the Mexican notable by Juan de Salamanca, which effectively turned the tide of the battle of Otumba on 14 July, 1520. The death of the Indian warrior was followed by the loss of the standard, but the psychological effect was decisive. Van Wees 2004: 240 notes that the decline of single combat was tied to the fact that "Classical battle . . . concentrated purely on the honour and glory of the community." But, of course, many conquest societies were organized on an aristocratic, heroic basis. There was not much difference between Homer's heroes and the *hetairoi*

of Macedon, the knights of the Crusades, or the *hidalgo* class that spearheaded the Spanish conquest of the New World.

16. See Bloedow 2002, with interesting modern parallels.

17. See the Gobares (Bagodaras) episode: Diod. 17.93.7; Curt. 7.4.1–19. It is important to add that, although modern scholars tend to lump the Bactriani and Sogdiani together as if they were a unified group, the concerns of those south of the Oxus (Amu-darya), agriculturalists for the main part, were different from those to the north, who tended to be pastoralists and seminomadic, often both culturally and ethnically akin to the Scythians (see Vogelsang 2002: 122).

18. Perhaps something similar to the Mongol cangue, which restrained Temujin (Genghis Khan) during his period of captivity.

19. Milns 1968: 170 says "Alexander . . . stopped the chariot in which he had taken to riding. . . . " Green 1974: 355 notes that the "treatment of Bessus seems to have been mainly dictated by a desire to impress the recalcitrant Iranian nobility" but fails to note the role of the chariot. See Curt. 3.3.15 for the Persian royal chariot.

20. For the different accounts of Bessus' death see Diod. 17.83.9; Plut. *Alex.* 43.6; Arr. 4.7.3. Curt. 7.5.19–26, 7.10.10 conflates the accounts of Cleitarchus and Ptolemy (see Heckel 1994: 70). Bosworth 1980a: 376 rightly notes that Bessus' "usurpation was the reason for the humiliation and mutilation."

21. Unless the campaign described by Arr. 3.30.10–11 is meant. Clearly Arrian knew (or believed) nothing about the story of the Branchidae. The barbarians in this campaign had wounded Alexander with an arrow, breaking his fibula, and only 8,000 of a total 30,000 were said to have escaped with their lives.

22. Curt. 7.5.27–35. Bosworth 1988a: 108 treats the massacre as historical, though he does not accept the identity of the victims as the Branchidae. I would disagree, however, with his conclusion (108 n. 251) that "There is no apparent reason for invention, which certainly cannot be laid at the door of Callisthenes." Cf. Holt 2005: 184: "There is no reason to dismiss the story, although ardent admirers of Alexander (such as W. W. Tarn) would rather it not be true." For the crimes of the Branchidae see Hdt. 6.19, who puts the despoiling of the temple in the reign of Darius I; for the possibility that a variant was reported by Ctesias see Brown 1978: 64–78, esp. 75–8.

23. Curt. 7.5.27.

24. Holt 2005: 81–2 rejects the notion of Spitamenes as a "national leader." But Harlan 2005: 12–13, written in 1842, remarked on the situation in Afghanistan after the first British invasion: "A nation whose principle of existence lies in the disunion and separate interests of its constituent tribes, became united by common oppression into one unanimous community, goaded to madness by the systematic and consecutive tyranny of their invaders."

25. For Alexander's loss of horses see Arr. 3.30.6. Bloedow 1991 suggests that the requisitioning of horses was the primary cause of unrest in the area; Bosworth 1995: 18 rightly dismisses this idea as unlikely. The horse breeders of Sogdiana might have seen this as a "business opportunity."

26. Pharnuches' role is described only by Arrian (4.3.7, 5.3–9, 6.1–2).

27. For the numbers of troops and casualties see Appendix II.

28. Bosworth 1995: 24.

29. Arr. 4.1.5; Curt. 7.6.14–15. See also the discussion in Bosworth 1995: 17–19.

30. Curt. 7.10.11–12: Ptolemy and Menidas brought 4,000 infantry and 1,000 cavalry; Asander another 4,000 infantry and 500 cavalry; and Asclepiodorus arrived with 8,000 Greek infantry and 600 cavalry; cf. Arr. 4.7.2 (without figures).

31. Arr. 4.18.4, 19.4–5 is alone in claiming that Rhoxane, the daughter of Oxyartes, was captured at the Rock of Sogdiana. This is chronologically implausible and contradicted by all other sources: Strabo 11.11.4 C517; C 8.4.23; cf. *Metz Epit.* 28–9. I do not accept the view that she was captured on this occasion and later married to Alexander at the Rock of Chorienes (Sisimithres).

32. Milns 1968: 176.

33. Just as he had refrained from marrying before leaving Macedonia. See Baynham 1998b. For the marriage offer see Arr. 4.15.2–3 (wrongly placing the embassy in Bactra; cf. Bosworth 1995: 101); Curt. 8.1.9. "Ultimately the Sacan proposal may have been the seminal event which led to Alexander's marriage with Roxane and eventually to the mass wedding at Susa" (Bosworth 1995: 104).

34. Holt 1988: 78–9 n. 118; for his heroism see also Holt 2005: 72–3.

35. Tritle 2003; see also Tritle 2000: esp. 56–61; Shay 1994, 2002; Hillman 2004: 31–3, 64–6.
36. Johann Georg Korb (1968: 79). Korb's *Diarium itineris in Moscoviam* was published in Latin in 1698. Massie 1980: 266 reproduces the English translation of Count Mac Donnel (London, 1863; reprinted in 1968). This is a stilted paraphrase, and I have supplied my own translation of the German version of Leingärtner.
37. See Plut. *Antony* 71.
38. Massie 1980: 265.
39. Curt. 8.8.7-8; tr. Yardley 1984: 194.
40. The rebels proceeded to attack the satrap Amyntas but were defeated with heavy casualties (Curt. 8.2.14–17). Nautaca has been identified as modern Shahrisabz (Shakhrisyabz, near the birthplace of Temur or Tamerlane) and Xenippa as in the vicinity of Karshi (Holt 2005: 79-80; Bosworth 1995: 121; cf. Schwarz 1893: 74–5), but the sources suggest otherwise. Sisimithres is said to have been the ruler of the region around Nautaca (Curt. 8.2.19; cf. *Metz Epit.* 19); and Diodorus ("Contents") refers to Alexander's attack on the Nautaces. If the Macedonians had taken control of the city, it is natural to assume that Sisimithres fled to the safety of the mountains. His fortress is described by Strabo as in Bactriana (11.11.4), which by Strabo's own definition is south of the Oxus (11.11.2). Perhaps Strabo's source regarded the Waksch River, which flows into the Amu-darya, as the boundary between Sogdiana and Bactria in the east (perhaps his source mistook it for the Oxus): the Rock of Chorienes (Koh-i-nor) lies beyond the Waksch.
41. Diodorus ("Contents of Book 17") says that Alexander killed 120,000 insurgents in retaliation.
42. For the pardon see Curt. 8.2.18. One of those who surrendered on this occasion may have been Oxyartes, whose family had taken refuge with Sisimithres on Koh-i-nor. I regard it as highly doubtful that Oxartes (Curt. 8.2.25ff.) and Oxyartes (Curt. 8.4.21ff., even if we allow for the MSS error) are different individuals.
43. Curt. 8.2.25 calls him "Oxartes." There is no indication of how it was that this man came to support Alexander.
44. Allen 2005: 147 downplays the significance of the marriage, arguing that "Alexander . . . put something of a cosmetic seal on the subjugation of the north-eastern satrapies . . . by marrying into the local nobility." Since both the names Rhoxane and Oxyartes (Oxyathres) occur in the Achaemenid royal house, Oxyartes may have been more than just a "local noble."
45. Curt. 8.4.30. *Metz Epit.* 30–31 says that other Macedonians took barbarian wives on the same occasion, a story told also by Diodorus but no longer in the surviving manuscripts (see Diod. *Contents*: "How Alexander fell in love with and married Rhoxane, the daughter of Oxyartes, and persuaded many of his friends to marry the daughters of prominent barbarians").
46. It is generally assumed that Chorienes was the "official" name of Sisimithres, perhaps related to the area he ruled (Schwarz 1893: 83–4; Berve 1926: 2.354–5). Bosworth 1981 has argued that the two are separate individuals.
47. Lane Fox 1974: 320 rightly calls it "one of the most misrepresented episodes in [Alexander's] life."
48. Arr. 4.12.1–2. Some have identified this Leonnatus with the son of Antipater from Aegae. I believe that the offender can only have been a man of very high standing, and thus the Somatophylax and son of Anteas. The story is told by Curt. 8.5.22–6.1 of Polyperchon, who was absent at the time. See Heckel 2006a: 148, 227, with notes. The extent of the Persian's abasement is a reflection of his position as a conquered subject, without social and kin relationships with the ruler. This should not imply that Alexander required his Macedonians to perform similar obeisance; indeed, he would soon have established a new hierarchy amongst his prominent Persian subjects.
49. Hdt. 1.134. Although Herodotus uses the word *proskynein* only in the last instance, it is clear that the process of *proskynesis* covered the entire range. It was the last form that was best known and most offensive to the Greeks.
50. This they managed to avoid by trickery or through the intermediary of the Persian hazarapatish (who served as *eisangeleus*). See, for example, Ael. *VH* 1.21 (for Ismenias the Theban); Nepos, *Con.* 3.3.
51. Curt. 8.7.1. For the Hermolaus episode see Heckel & Yardley 2004: 250–56.
52. Curt. 8.7.13.
53. Curt. 8.8.13, tr. by J. C. Yardley.
54. Curt. 8.8.15, tr. by J. C. Yardley.

55. See the concluding comments at 8.8.20–23.

56. Curt. 8.5.5–6, tr. by J. C. Yardley 1984: 187. This is clearly one of Curtius' editorializing passages, as can be seen from the reference to "control over men's . . . tongues." Shortly before (8.4.30), Curtius uses similar language about the marriage to Rhoxane: " . . . but with the suspension of free speech following Clitus' murder, they [sc. Alexander's friends] signified their approval with their facial expressions, the feature of a man most prone to servility."

57. It is wrongly assumed that whenever Arrian omitted unpleasant details these were not found in Ptolemy. In fact, Arrian's *History* was probably more apologetic than those of his sources (see especially Arr. 4.9.1, 12.6–7, 19.6). See Heckel 1994 for examples of contradictory evidence in Curtius ascribable to the use of different sources.

58. Plut. *Alex.* 44.4-6 = *FGrH* 125 F14, tr. B. Perrin.

59. See Arr. 4.12.4–5. Lane Fox 1974: 323 rightly notes that Alexander conducted the experiment "in private with a few selected friends" and that whole affair went remarkably well. But men like Craterus were notably absent. At best this shows that the followers of Alexander were divided on the matter, but that there were nevertheless many who placed Alexander's wishes and the expectation of gain ahead of their own principles. Rogers 2004: 179 contends that Alexander made two attempts at introducing *proskynesis*, but Arrian merely gives two different versions of the same episode; the second, introduced as a *logos*, is that reported by Chares of Mitylene.

60. Xen. *Anab.* 1.9.3–4. For the Macedonian pages and the concept of *somatophylakia* see Heckel 1992: 237–98.

61. See, for example, Barlow 2000: 23–4. The role of aristocratic youths as hostages was not a mere formality. England's King John in June 1212 had twenty-eight of them put to death on account of their Welsh fathers' actions (Warren 1997: 181).

62. Hermolaus was the son of the ilarch Sopolis. His co-conspirators included Antipater, son of the Syrian satrap Asclepiodorus, and Epimenes son of Arsaeus, who was the lover of Charicles, a son of the Lydian satrap Menander. It is interesting to note that both Sopolis and Asclepiodorus had recently been in the camp. The other conspirators were Sostratus son of Amyntas, Philotas son of Carsis, and Anticles son of Theocritus.

63. See Arr. 4.14.3: Ptolemy claimed that he was tortured and hanged; Aristobulus agrees in general terms with Chares, whose version is reported by Plut. *Alex.* 55.9. The apologists' claim was clearly that Callisthenes would have received a fair trial, had he not died in captivity.

CHAPTER SEVEN: CONQUEST OF THE PUNJAB

1. Detailed description of the topography of Gandhara can be found in Stein 1929; McCrindle 1894, though dated, is still useful. For Peucelaotis and Taxila see Wheeler 1976; Marshall 1951; Badian 1987; Karttunen 1990.

2. Indians from Gandhara served in Darius' army at Gaugamela (Curt. 4.9.2; Arr. 3.8.3, 6; Diod. 17.59.4), but no figures are given. Fifteen elephants were sent from India (Arr. 3.8.6), not a large contribution. The Assacenians confronted Alexander with a force that included 30 elephants, and earlier the local hyparchs had submitted and brought the king 25 elephants as a gift.

3. Nevertheless, see Briant 2002: 756–7, and 1027 on the flexibility of Persian administration in the area.

4. Seibert 1985: 145.

5. Arr. 4.22.4.

6. Arr. 4.22.7. The battalions of Gorgias, White Cleitus, and Meleager; half the Companions and all the mercenary cavalry. The Macedonian contingent itself will have numbered close to 6,000.

7. For the early career of Ptolemy see Heckel 1992: 222–7 and 2006a: 235–8; Seibert 1969: 1–26; Ellis 1994: 1–16.

8. Justin 12.7.11; see Yardley & Heckel 1997: 242, with earlier literature.

9. The venues of these sieges have been established by the topographical researches of Stein 1929. The recent attempt of Eggermont 1984 to identify Aornus with Mt Ilam has gained little acceptance; indeed, it ignores the fact that the river (i.e., the Indus) flowed at the foot of the stronghold (cf. Bosworth 1995: 178–80).

10. Curt. 10.1.20–21; cf. Heckel 2006a: 2.

11. Liddell-Hart 1967: 21 calls it "a masterpiece of indirectness." Latimer 2003 has written an entire book about "Deception in War," in which this type of maneuver – concentrating on one point and attacking at another – plays a prominent role.

12. It is perhaps reasonable to ask whether Alexander had made any attempt during his stay with Taxiles to accustom his cavalry horses to elephants. But the fact that the cavalry was used primarily on the flanks, away from the elephants, suggests otherwise or, at least, that attempts to condition the horses had met with limited success in the short time available.

13. Bosworth 1995: 277–8 supposes that Gorgias, Attalus, and Meleager no longer had their *taxies* with them and could not have joined the battle before it began.

14. For troops figures see Appendix II.

15. Bosworth 1988a: 134, by contrast, thinks that after the Hyphasis mutiny "Alexander had practically lost interest in the area," echoing Lane Fox 1974: 375: "Only Porus benefited from the new despair. The 'seven nations and two thousand towns' between the Jhelum and the Beas were added to his kingdom; they had lost their interest now that the march to the east had been cancelled." This argument fails to account for Alexander's turning over territories to Porus *before* he reached the Hyphasis, indeed, before he had crossed the Hydraotes (Arr. 5.21.5).

16. Fuller 1955: 163.

17. Lonsdale 2004: 219.

18. For what follows see Spann 1999; Heckel 2003. Diod. 17.94.3–4 adds that Alexander tried to buy the goodwill of his troops by allowing them to plunder and by promising stipends and bonuses to their wives and children. But Curt. 9.2.10 shows that the acquisition of booty was counterproductive.

19. Bosworth 1996: 79. I believe this is contradicted by Diodorus' statement that "he intended to get to the boundary of India and, when he had subjugated its inhabitants, to sail down the river to the Ocean" (Diod. 17.89.5). This makes no sense if Alexander genuinely believed that the Ocean was just to the east. Furthermore, I would take "India" in this case to mean the Punjab.

20. Bosworth 1996: 80.

21. Diod. 17.95.4 reports the arrival of reinforcements and *matériel* as if it were a coincidence; cf. Curt. 9.3.21. But, if this had in fact been the case – and I find it hard to imagine that Alexander did not know that it was on its way or that he did not plan to use it for the rest of the Indian campaign – it is strange that the moralizing historians did not comment on the irony. Just before reporting the arrival of the equipment, Curtius comments on the death of Coenus: "it was merely for the sake of a few days that Coenus had made his long speech, as if he were the only one who would see Macedonia again" (9.3.20, Yardley tr.).

22. Ironically, Kurke 2004: 32 uses the Hyphasis episode to illustrate what he calls a lesson in leadership. "He [Alexander] turned the army's decision into his decision; therefore, there was no mutiny. However, he was not seen to be backing down, either." Not surprisingly, neither "Beas" nor "Hyphasis" shows up in the index of Bose 2003, a work subtitled "The timeless leadership lessons of history's greatest empire builder."

23. Holt 2003: 133 rightly notes: "the battle between Alexander and Porus has been shown symbolically. There is no reason to worry whether we can find some ancient text that exactly describes this very scene." Holt remarks that "[w]ith cunning, [Alexander] congratulated his men on their bravery in the recent battle" (163), though I am somewhat sceptical of the view that the "elephant medallions have taken us as deep as we may ever get into the mind of Alexander the Great" (165). See also Bosworth 1996: 6–9. Lane Fox 1996 argues that the coins were struck in Susa no later than early 324, and that the inscribed letters BA (or AB; they can be read either way) on the Porus decadrachm and the Greek letter *xi* on the elephant and chariot coins refer to Abulites (satrap of Susiana) and Xenophilus, the *phrourarchos* of the city. I am not sure why Abulites would have chosen Indian images for his coins, when in the context of 324 recognition of Alexander's undisputed rule in the Persian heartland would have been more effective.

CHAPTER EIGHT: THE OCEAN AND THE WEST

1. Arr. 6.2.4 = Ptolemy (*FGrH* 138 F24). For the numbers see Appendix II.

2. Curt. 9.7.14; cf. Briant 2002: 757.

3. Plut. *Alex.* 47.11.

4. Diod. 17.98.1 says the Sudracae had 80,000 infantry, 10,000 cavalry, and 700 chariots; Curt. 9.4.15 90,000 infantry, 10,000 horse, and 900 chariots; Justin 12.9.3 80,000 foot-soldiers and 60,000 horsemen.

5. It has become fashionable to place the Mallian town in the vicinity of Multan (see, for example, Wood 1997: 199–200, cautiously), but the Mallians (Malavas) appear to have lived on the shores of the Hydraotes River (Ravi) above the point where it joined with the Acesines (Chenab); their allies, the Sudracae (Kshudrakas), occupied the territory between the Hydraotes and the Hyphasis. Cf. Smith 1914: 94–6. For the campaign see Bosworth 1996: 133–41.

6. For the shield of Athena see Arr. 6.10.1 (cf. 1.11.8). The other protectors of the king were Abreas (or Habreas), Limnaeus (also called Timaeus), and Leonnatus; the last survived the attack. Cleitarchus and Timagenes alleged that Ptolemy son of Lagus saved the king's life on this occasion and earned the title Soter (Savior).

7. Arr. 6.12–13. Rumor that Alexander had been killed spread to Bactria and Sogdiana, where it prompted an uprising by mercenaries, who planned to return to the west (Curt. 9.7.1–11).

8. Arr. 6.28.4.

9. Cf. Pritchett 1974: 215–17; on Dioxippus see Brown 1977, esp. 88.

10. For the duel between Corrhagus and Dioxippus see Diod. 17.100.1–101.6; Curt. 9.7.16–26; Ael. *VH* 10.22.

11. Plut. *Alex.* 51.4.

12. Plut. *Alex.* 53.3–6.

13. Arr. 6.17.1–2; Cleitarchus, *FGrH* 137 F25, apparently confusing the supporters of Musicanus with those of Sambus (thus Eggermont 1975: 22–4).

14. Arr. 6.17.3 (6.15.5 is a clumsy doublet).

15. Nevertheless, Peithon as satrap of Sindh is attested in the settlements in both Babylon (323) and Triparadeisus (320).

16. See Casson 1974: 60 for the route. There were, no doubt, also trade implications, for the area was rich in spices and aromatic woods.

17. Once again we see the difference between the practicalities of the campaign and the legend that developed. For Alexander's concerns for the fleet see Arr. 6.21.3, 23.1–2, 23.4–6. Cummings 2004: 400 n. 1 comments: "Of course he [sc. Alexander] desired to maintain contact with the fleet; there were other and more logical plans which, if followed, the disastrous march would have been rendered unnecessary." Cummings does not, however, say what such a plan might entail, and makes light of the difficulties of supplying a large fleet. For a useful corrective see Engels 1978: 116–17.

18. I note, by way of example, the sensible observations of Rogers 2004: 233–4 on the subject.

19. Arr. 6.21.3, 23.1–2, 23.4–6, 24.2–3.

20. Langley 1996: 198; cf. Crow 1992: 450, who notes that suffering the hardships of a march can have a unifying effect. For Aqaba see Graves 1928: 191–211.

21. Smith 1914: 102 n.1.

22. Harlan 2005: 7.

23. Arr. 6.24.1; Plut. *Alex.* 66.7.

24. See Appendix II for numbers.

25. Arr. 6.26.4–5.

26. Mierow 1966: 80–81.

27. See Fuller 1955: 169–73, based on the evidence of M. Gustavus Alderfeld. I note that Clausewitz regularly compares Charles XII with Alexander the Great (see esp. Clausewitz 1993: 221, 712; cf. 210).

28. Plut. *Alex.* 66.7, Diod. 17.105.8, and Curt. 9.10.22 (all based on the same primary source, apparently Cleitarchus) claim that the satraps responded by sending supplies in abundance. This can have been only partially true. The failure of Abulites (satrap of Susa) to supply provisions – he sent money instead – must pertain to demands made after Alexander emerged from Gedrosia (Plut. *Alex.* 68.7).

29. Plut. *Alex.* 67.1–6; Diod. 17.106.1; Curt. 9.10.24–29. Cf. Bosworth 1988a: 147: "It was fundamentally a matter of therapy."

30. Recognized by Rogers 2004: 236–8; insufficient attention has been given by scholars to the balanced arguments of Higgins 1980, challenging the theory of Badian 1961 (which is often treated as orthodoxy).

31. Prescott 1999: 528. It is in keeping with the spirit of "conspiracy theory" that all actions by the ruler are motivated by malice and the urge to eliminate rivals. This is even more true of those accounts which are fond of comparing Alexander with Hitler and Stalin, creating in the process a *leyenda negra* concerning

Alexander and the Macedonian conquest (cf. recently Hanson 2001: 89: "Scholars sometimes compare Alexander to Caesar, Hannibal or Napoleon. . . . There are affinities with each; but an even better match would be Adolf Hitler – a sickening comparison that will no doubt shock and disturb most classicists and philhellenes." See also Worthington 1999, reprinted and perhaps more accessible in Worthington 2003: 303–18).

32. For the excesses of Harpalus and the generals see Diod. 17.108.4; Curt. 10.1.3–5. Alexander was particularly hostile to perpetrators of sexual abuse (cf. Plut. *Alex.* 22.1–4). Lane Fox 1974: 411, oddly, finds Harpalus "congenial." For Tiger Force see Sallah & Weiss 2006.

33. Alexander claimed the Achaemenid throne by virtue of conquest, the punishment of the usurper Bessus, and finally marriage to Darius III's daughter, Stateira, as well as to Parysatis, daughter of Artaxerxes III. But William was related by blood to Queen Emma and her son, Edward the Confessor. Claims that the latter had named him as his heir are, however, debatable at best. William nevertheless treated Harold Godwinson as a usurper.

34. Brown 1985: 178.

35. Orderic Vitalis ii.165 ff.; Chibnall, *CMH* IV² 2.199.

36. The fabricated *Last Days and Testament of Alexander* begins with the premise that Antipater (who had been maligned by Alexander's mother, Olympias) sent his son, Cassander, to poison the king in order to avert punishment at his hands.

37. On Bagoas see Badian 1958b. Tarn 1948: ii.319–26 rejected the existence of Bagoas in an appendix on "Alexander's Attitude towards Sex," and his motive was to deny that Alexander had homosexual relations with him. Orxines' guilt need not be doubted, but Curtius' account probably differs from that found in his primary source. For Curtius' reworking of source-material see Heckel 1994.

38. The views of Berve 1938 on *Verschmelzungspolitik* have been challenged, persuasively, by Bosworth 1980a.

39. For the Persian aristocracy and possession of land see Briant 2002: 335; Wiesehöfer 1996: 71–5; Brosius 1996: 123–9.

40. Plut. *Alex.* 15.3–5. B. Perrin tr., Loeb Classical Library.

41. *A la hija de Cuesco, que era un gran cacique, se puso por nombre doña Francisca; ésta era muy hermosa para ser india:* cap. LII. Warren 1997: 34 aptly calls Henry II's conquerors of Ireland "Anglo-Norman *conquistadores*," observing that "they married Irish heiresses and set about establishing principalities for themselves." Although aristocratic Persian brides had dowries (and dower lands), it is less clear what, if any, rights of inheritance the Persian brides of Alexander's *hetairoi* could claim.

42. One might compare, also, the First Crusaders who sold or mortgaged their lands in order to join the expeditions to the Holy Land. Many did indeed return to the West, but a significant number of men from noble families acquired lands in the Latin East. The view that the Crusaders were second sons, with no hope of inheritance at home, who sought estates in the East is out of fashion (see Tyerman 2004: 140). Nevertheless, for a core group the creation of new kingdoms and the possession of conquered lands were adequate compensation for the financial sacrifices made at the beginning of and throughout the expedition (see further Tibble 1989; also France 2005: 53–7).

43. See Heckel 2006a: 21 "Amastris."

44. Just as Henry I, son of William the Conqueror, chose to take a wife, Edith (renamed Matilda), who could trace her descent back to Alfred the Great. There were, of course, not the same interracial aspects, but the political considerations were similar. "King Henry I himself had endeavored to graft the Norman ducal house to that of the Old English kings by marrying a young woman of the West Saxon royal line" (Hollister 2001: 9). Similarly, Gonzalo Pizarro was encouraged by his followers to proclaim himself "king" of Peru and support his claim by marrying the *Coya*, i.e., the legitimate Inca queen. (Prescott 1998: 578, citing Gómara and Garcilaso de la Vega.) He did not, however, follow this advice. To what extent this contributed to his failure we cannot say.

45. Arrr. 7.6.2. Lane Fox 1974: 323 makes a similar observation about the attitude of Alexander's *hetairoi* to the introduction of *proskynesis*.

46. Brosius 2003: 179.

47. McLynn 1998: 310. Allen 2005: 150 notes that the Persian marriages "had the joint benefit of diffusing the exclusivity and integrity of the Persian families surrounding the kingship, clans who might otherwise produce well-born pretenders like Orxines, while linking the foreigners themselves with the same inherited status."

48. Arr. 7.11.8 speaks of those who "wished to leave him" and gives unfitness for military service as only one of the reasons. Hence, attachments to families in Asia and the realization that they would not be welcome in Macedonia must have been a deciding factor for many.

49. Arr. 7.6.5. See the thorough discussion of Brunt 1963.

CHAPTER NINE: THE LONG ROAD FROM SUSA TO BABYLON

1. Their disappointment echoes in the words of the conquerors of Peru who, when informed that new laws restricted their wealth and exploitation of the Indians, lamented: "Is this the fruit . . . of all our toil? Is it for this that we have poured out our blood like water? Now that we are broken down by hardships and sufferings, to be left at the end of our campaigns as poor as at the beginning!" (Prescott 1998: 535).

2. The ordeal of the river was prescribed already in the Code of Hammurabi.

3. Arr. 7.11.8. Cf. Brosius 2003: 193: "The celebration of Greek religious festivals and banquets were an expression of Macedonian domination over the Persian noble class." The notion of "Unity of Mankind," on the other hand, has been so thoroughly discredited that it seems superfluous to refer to the respective views of Tarn 1933 and Badian 1958a (see the readings in Worthington 2003: 193–235).

4. Diod. 17.108.4 speaks of rape and other forms of sexual misconduct, but his most egregious crime was the misappropriation of the king's money.

5. For this episode see Arr. 3.6.7.

6. A play entitled *Agen*, by a certain Python of Catana or Byzantium, is said to have been performed in the Macedonian camp. The comedy touched on the honors accorded by Harpalus to his dead mistress, the courtesan Pythionice, and his treatment of her replacement, Glycera. Other accounts of the treasurer's misdeeds are given by Theopompus and Dicaearchus. For Harpalus' career and crimes see Heckel 1992: 213–21 and 2006a: 129–31. For the impact of his flight on Greek politics and its relationship to the later Lamian War see Jaschinski 1981; Will 1983: 113–27; and Blackwell 1999; for the Harpalus-related cases in the Athenian courts see Worthington 1992, with additional literature.

7. Either by the Spartan Thibron (Diod. 18.19.2; cf. Strabo 17.3.21 C837), who later attempted to win Cyrene for himself, or by a servant named Pausanias (Paus. 2.33.4–5).

8. See Plut. *Alex.* 74.2–6. Alexander is supposed to have resorted to physical violence when Cassander ridiculed Persians doing *proskynesis*, and he refused to accept Cassander's arguments in defence of his father. Such was the impact of his treatment by Alexander that, even after the king's death, the mere sight of his statue induced trembling. These stories must, however, have had their origins in the propaganda wars of the Successors and must be treated with caution.

9. This scenario was proposed already by Higgins 1980: 150. For the death of Balacrus see Diod. 18.22.1. For his marriage to Phila, Heckel 1987; Badian 1988; Bosworth 1994.

10. For the origins and operations of the *argyraspides* see Heckel 1992: 307–19.

11. Heckel & Yardley 2004: 86.

12. It was first announced by Alexander in Susa, and some 20,000 exiles were present in Olympia when the decree was proclaimed there at the very end of July or beginning of August 324.

13. Diod. 17.106.3; cf. 111.1. It is important to make a distinction between "satrapal armies" and garrison troops; clearly Diodorus is speaking of surplus troops who had been used in the suppression of resistance. The garrisons remained where they were, as is clear from the uprising in the Upper Satrapies after Alexander's death.

14. Phillip Harding has suggested (in an unpublished paper delivered in 2002) that the measure may have been similar to that of Roman generals who sought to reward their soldiers (and thus retain their loyalty) through grants of land.

15. This view will, no doubt, strike many as simplistic and there will those who contend that Alexander could not have made such a serious misjudgment. But he may have believed that, despite opposition, he could impose an unpopular measure on the Greek states. One must bear in mind that the Lamian War did not break out until after the king's death and that it cannot be regarded as inevitable.

16. Cf. Zahrnt 2003. Such a view is, however, at odds with Alexander's alleged plans to direct his attentions to North Africa and Arabia.

17. For a good discussion of the relationship between the Exiles' Decree and the Lamian War see Dmitriev 2004. Since, in 318, Polyperchon (in the name of the inept king, Philip III) proclaimed the "Freedom of the Greeks" in order to counter the supporters of Cassander, it may well be that many of the mercenaries

who fought the Lamian War in 323/2 did so because Antipater, once Alexander had died, did *not* enforce the Exiles' Decree in those oligarchic states that formed his support in the south. But, if some of the states that joined the Hellenic alliance in 323 had overthrown their oligarchic rulers, the sources have failed to report this. The question remains, however: why would mercenaries, who were in many cases political exiles, fight for governments that were resisting the implementation of a measure that was to their own benefit?

18. Ael. *VH* 2.19, 5.12, 9.37, collected and translated in Heckel & Yardley 2004: 221–2.

19. See for example Philotas' "conspiracy" in Egypt (Arr. 3.26.1; Plut. *Alex.* 48) and that of Hegelochus (Curt. 6.11.22–9).

20. For the entertaining story of Henry Rawlinson's transcription and decipherment of the Behistun text see Adkins 2004.

21. For the Amazon story, its sources, and its significance, see Baynham 2000.

22. See Reames-Zimmerman 2001.

23. Thus Plut. *Alex.* 72.4. The effects of the campaign cannot have been long-lasting; for when Antigonus visited the region in his campaign against Eumenes, he found them again demanding money for safe passage.

24. The suggestion that he intended to make Alexandria in Egypt his capital is absurd; for the city is almost as remote from the imperial center as Pella. Alexandria would, of course, have assumed a more central position if Alexander had carried out his alleged plans to conquer North Africa (Diod. 18.4.4).

25. Arrian (7.15.6) notes that neither Ptolemy nor Aristobulus mentioned an embassy from the Romans. This appears to be a later embellishment.

26. These may have formed the core of White Cleitus' fleet in 322.

27. For the precise date of his death see Depuydt 1997.

28. See, for example, Oldach et al. 1998; and Marr & Calisher 2003, for West Nile virus.

29. See Heckel 1988 and Bosworth 2000; both studies refer to important earlier literature.

30. At that time, it could be argued, Alexander's decision avoided other political problems: see Baynham 1998b.

31. See Heckel 2002.

32. Details of their roles in the early history of the Diadochoi (with references to ancient and modern literature) can be found in Heckel 1992 and 2006a: s.vv.

33. Particularly appropriate is the observation of Arthur Helps: "It is interesting to notice the way in which great deeds, which are waiting to be done, refuse, as it were, to be done by the men set in authority to do them, and, falling through their hands, remain to be done by men, who, when these deeds were first taken in hand, were in but a subordinate position, and altogether precluded from taking any prominent part with reference to them" (Helps 1869: 35–6).

BIBLIOGRAPHY

THE GREEK AND ROMAN SOURCES IN TRANSLATION

The fragments of the lost historians have been collected in F. Jacoby, *Die Fragmente der griechischen Historiker* (*FGrH*), nos. 117–53 (to which we may add writers such as Theopompus, Diyllus, Duris, Anaximenes, and Idomeneus), and translations can be found in Robinson 1953 (English) and Auberger 2001 (French). See also Pearson 1960. A collection of extant sources, arranged thematically, can be found in Heckel & Yardley 2004; but see also Tania Gergel (ed.), *Alexander the Great. The Brief Life and Towering Exploits of History's Greatest Conqueror as Told by His Original Biographers* (London: Penguin 2004).

Diodorus of Sicily, Book XVII, has been edited with notes by C. Bradford Welles in the Loeb Classical Library no. 422 (Cambridge, MA, 1963); for Curtius Rufus there are the two volumes of the Loeb (nos. 368, 369) by J. C. Rolfe (Cambridge, MA, 1946) and the Penguin translation by J. C. Yardley (Yardley 1984). For Justin see J. C. Yardley (tr.), *Justin. Epitome of the Philippic History of Pompeius Trogus* (Atlanta: Scholar's Press, 1994); cf. Yardley & Heckel 1997. The Loeb edition of Arrian by I. Robson has now been superseded by P. A Brunt's two volumes (Brunt 1976, 1983) and there is a Penguin translation by A. de Sélincourt, *The Campaigns of Alexander* (London: Penguin, 1971). Most easily accessible are the numerous translations of Plutarch's *Life of Alexander*. See particularly I. Scott-Kilvert (tr.), *Plutarch. The Age of Alexander* (London: Penguin, 1973) and Robin Waterfield (tr.), *Plutarch. Greek Lives* (Oxford, 1998).

WORKS CITED

Adams 2003	W. L. Adams, "The Episode of Philotas: An Insight," in W. Heckel and L. A. Tritle (eds.), *Crossroads of History: The Age of Alexander* (Claremont, CA; Regina): 113–26
Adkins 2004	Lesley Adkins, *Empires of the Plain. Henry Rawlinson and the Lost Languages of Babylon* (New York: St Martin's Press)
Allen 2005	Lindsay Allen, *The Persian Empire* (Chicago: University of Chicago Press)
Alonso-Nuñez 1992	José Miguel Alonso-Nuñez, *La Historia Universal de Pompeyo Trogo* (Madrid: Ediclás)
Anson 1981	E. M. Anson, "Alexander's Hypaspists and the Argyraspids," *Historia* 30: 117–20
Anson 1989	E. M. Anson, "The Persian Fleet in 334," *CP* 84: 44–9
Atkinson 1980	J. E. Atkinson, *A Commentary on Q. Curtius Rufus' Historiae Alexandri Magni, Books 3 and 4* (Amsterdam: J. C. Gieben)

Atkinson 1994   J. E. Atkinson, *A Commentary on Q. Curtius Rufus' Historiae Alexandri Magni, Books 5–7.2* (Amsterdam: Hakkert)

Auberger 2001   J. Auberger, *Historiens d'Alexandre* (Paris: Les Belles Lettres)

Austin 1993   Michel Austin, "Alexander and the Macedonian Invasion of Asia: Aspects of the Historiography of War and Empire in Antiquity," in J. Rich and G. Shipley (eds.), *War and Society in the Greek World* (London: Routledge): 197–223

Badian 1958a   E. Badian, "Alexander the Great and the Unity of Mankind," *Historia* 7: 425–44

Badian 1958b   E. Badian, "The Eunuch Bagoas: A Study in Method," *CQ* 8: 144–57.

Badian 1961   E. Badian, "Harpalus," *JHS* 91: 16–43

Badian 1963   E. Badian, "The Death of Philip II," *Phoenix* 17: 244–50

Badian 1975   E. Badian, "Nearchus the Cretan," *YCS* 24: 147–70

Badian 1976   E. Badian, "The Deification of Alexander the Great," in *Center for Hermeneutical Studies in Hellenistic and Modern Culture, Colloquy 21* (Berkeley: Center for Hermeneutical Studies)

Badian 1987   E. Badian, "Alexander at Peucelaotis," *CQ* 37: 117–28

Badian 1988   E. Badian, "Two Postscripts on the Marriage of Phila and Balacrus," *ZPE* 73: 116–18

Badian 2000a   E. Badian, "Conspiracies," in A. B. Bosworth and E. J. Baynham (eds.), *Alexander the Great in Fact and Fiction* (Oxford: Oxford University Press): 50–95

Badian 2000b   E. Badian, "Darius III," *HSCP* 100: 241–68

Barlow 2000   Frank Barlow, *William Rufus* (New Haven: Yale University Press; originally published in London, 1983)

Baynham 1995   E. J. Baynham, "An Introduction to the *Metz Epitome*: Its Traditions and Value," *Antichthon* 29: 60–77

Baynham 1998a   E. J. Baynham, *Alexander the Great. The Unique History of Quintus Curtius Rufus* (Ann Arbor: University of Michigan Press)

Baynham 1998b   E. J. Baynham, "Why Didn't Alexander Marry before Leaving Macedonia?" *RhM* 141: 141–52

Baynham 2000   E. J. Baynham, "A Baleful Birth in Babylon: The Significance of the Prodigy in the *Liber de Morte*–An Investigation of Genre," in A. B. Bosworth and E. J. Baynham (eds.), *Alexander the Great in Fact and Fiction* (Oxford: Oxford University Press): 242–62

Berve 1926   H. Berve, *Das Alexanderreich auf prosopographischer Grundlage*, 2 vols. (Munich: Beck)

Berve 1938   H. Berve, "Die Verschmelzungspolitik Alexanders des Grossen," *Klio* 31: 135–68

Billows 1990 — Richard A. Billows, *Antigonus the One-Eyed and the Creation of the Hellenistic State* (Berkeley: University of California Press)

Blackwell 1999 — Christopher W. Blackwell, *In the Absence of Alexander. Harpalus and the Failure of Macedonian Authority* (New York: Peter Lang)

Bloedow 1991 — E. M. Bloedow, "Alexander the Great and Those Sogdianaean Horses: Prelude to Hellenism in Bactria–Sogdiana," in J. Seibert (ed.), *Hellenistische Studien. Gedenkschrift für Hermann Bengtson* (Munich: Beck): 17–32

Bloedow 2002 — E. M. Bloedow, "On the Crossing of Rivers: Alexander's *diphtherai*," *Klio* 8: 57–75

Borza 1990 — E. N. Borza, *In the Shadow of Olympus: The Emergence of Macedon* (Princeton: Princeton University Press)

Bose 2003 — Partha Bose, *Alexander the Great's Art of Strategy* (New York: Gotham Books)

Bosworth 1973 — A. B. Bosworth, "*ΑΣΘΕΤΑΙΡΟΙ*" *CQ* 23: 245–53

Bosworth 1980a — A. B. Bosworth, *A Historical Commentary on Arrian's* History of Alexander, vol. 1 (Oxford: Clarendon Press)

Bosworth, 1981 — A. B. Bosworth, "A Missing Year in the History of Alexander the Great," *JHS* 101: 17–39

Bosworth 1988a — A. B. Bosworth, *Conquest and Empire. The Reign of Alexander the Great* (Cambridge: Cambridge University Press)

Bosworth 1988b — A. B. Bosworth, *From Arrian to Alexander* (Oxford: Clarendon Press)

Bosworth 1994 — A. B. Bosworth, "A New Macedonian Prince," *CQ* 44: 57–65

Bosworth 1995 — A. B. Bosworth, *A Historical Commentary on Arrian's* History of Alexander, vol. 2 (Oxford: Clarendon Press)

Bosworth 1996 — A. B. Bosworth, *Alexander and the East. The Tragedy of Triumph* (Oxford: Clarendon Press)

Bosworth 2000 — A. B. Bosworth, "Ptolemy and the Will of Alexander," in A. B. Bosworth and E. J. Baynham (eds.), *Alexander the Great in Fact and Fiction* (Oxford: Oxford University Press): 207–41

Briant 1999 — P. Briant, "The Achaemenid Empire," in Kurt Raaflaub and Nathan Rosenstein (eds.), *War and Society in the Ancient and Medieval Worlds* (Cambridge, MA: Harvard University Press): 105–28

Briant 2002 — P. Briant, *From Cyrus to Alexander. A History of the Persian Empire.* Translated from the French (Paris, 1997) by Peter T. Daniels (Winona Lake, IN: Eisenbruns)

Brosius 1996 — Maria Brosius, *Women in Ancient Persia (559–331 BC)* (Oxford: Oxford University Press)

Brosius 2003   Maria Brosius, "Alexander and the Persians," in J. Roisman (ed.),
                Brill's Companion to Alexander the Great (Leiden: E. J. Brill):
                169–93

Brown 1977   T. S. Brown, "Alexander and Greek Athletics, in Fact and in
                Fiction," in K. H. Kinzl (ed.), *Greece and the Eastern
                Mediterranean in Ancient History and Prehistory. Studies Presented
                to Fritz Schachermeyr on the Occasion of His Eightieth Birthday*
                (Berlin: De Gruyter): 76–88

Brown 1978   T. S. Brown, "Aristodicus of Cyme and the Branchidae," *AJP* 99:
                64–78

Brown 1985   R. Allen Brown, *The Normans and the Norman Conquest*
                (Woodbridge: Boydell Press)

Brunt 1963   P. A. Brunt, "Alexander's Macedonian Cavalry," *JHS* 83: 27–46

Brunt 1965   P. A. Brunt, "The Aims of Alexander," *G&R* 12: 205–15

Brunt 1976   P. A. Brunt, *Arrian. History of Alexander and Indica*, vol. 1
                (Cambridge, MA: Heinemann)

Brunt 1983   P. A. Brunt, *Arrian. History of Alexander and Indica*, vol. 2
                (Cambridge, MA: Heinemann)

Burke 2002   Brendan Burke, "Anatolian Origins of the Gordian Knot Legend,"
                GRBS 42: 255–61

Burn 1973   A. R. Burn, *Alexander and the Middle East* (London: Penguin)

Burstein 1991   S. M. Burstein, "Pharaoh Alexander: A Scholarly Myth," *Anc. Soc.*
                22: 139–45

Burstein 2000   S. M. Burstein, "Prelude to Alexander: The Reign of Khababash,"
                AHB 14: 149–54

Cargill 1977   J. Cargill, "The Nabonidus Chronicle and the Fall of Lydia,"
                AJAH 2: 97–116

Carney 1983   E. D. Carney, "Regicide in Macedonia," *PP* 211: 260–72

Carney 2000   E. D. Carney, *Women and Monarchy in Macedonia* (Norman, OK:
                University of Oklahoma Press)

Carney 2006   E. D. Carney, *Olympias, Mother of Alexander the Great* (London:
                Routledge)

Casson 1926   Stanley Casson, *Macedonia, Thrace and Illyria* (Oxford: Oxford
                Univeristy Press)

Casson 1974   Lionel Casson, *Travel in the Ancient World* (London; reprint
                1994)

Cawkwell 1976   G. L. Cawkwell, "Agesilaus and Sparta," *CQ* 26: 62–84

Cawkwell 2005   G. L. Cawkwell, *The Greek Wars* (Oxford: Oxford University Press)

Chibnall 2000   Marjorie Chibnall, *The Normans* (Oxford: Blackwell)

Clausewitz 1993 Carl von Clausewitz, *On War*, edited and translated by Michael
                Howard and Peter Paret (New York: Modern Library)

Commager   Henry Steele Commager, *The Blue and the Gray* (New York;
   1995   reprint of the edition published in Indianapolis, 1950)
Coulborn 1965   Rushton Coulborn (ed.), *Feudalism in History* (Hamden, CT;
                     originally published in Princeton, NJ by Princeton University
                     Press, 1956)
Crow 1992   John A. Crow, *The Epic of Latin America*, fourth edition (Berkeley:
                     University of California Press)
Cummings   Lewis V. Cummings, *Alexander the Great* (New York; originally
   2004   published in 1940)
Dandamaev   M. A. Dandamaev, *A Political History of the Achaemenid Empire.*
   1989   Translated from the Russian by W. J. Vogelsang (Leiden: E. J.
                     Brill)
Depuydt 1997   Leo Depuydt, "The Time of Death of Alexander the Great: 11 June
                     323 B.C. (-322), ca. 4:00–5:00 PM," *Die Welt des Orients* 28:
                     117–35
Devine 1994   A. M. Devine, "Alexander's Propaganda Machine: Callisthenes as
                     the Ultimate Source for Arrian, *Anabasis* 1–3," in I.
                     Worthington (ed.), *Ventures into Greek History* (Oxford: Oxford
                     University Press)
Dmitriev 2004   S. Dmitriev, "Alexander's Exiles Decree," *Klio* 86: 348–81
Dodge 1890   T. A. Dodge, *Alexander. A History of the Origin and Growth of the
                     Art of War from the Earliest Times to the Battle of Ipsus 301 BC,
                     with a Detailed Account of the Campaigns of the Great
                     Macedonian* (Boston; reprint New York: De Capo)
Edbury 1998   Peter W. Edbury, *The Conquest of Jerusalem and the Third Crusade.*
                     Crusade Texts in Translation (Aldershot: Ashgate)
Eggermont   P. H. L. Eggermon, *Alexander's Campaigns in Sind and Baluchistan
   1975   and the Siege of the Brahmin Town of Harmatelia* (Leuven:
                     Leuven University Press)
Eggermont   P. H. L. Eggermont, "Ptolemy the Geographer and the People of
   1984   the Dards," *OLP* 15: 191–200
Ellis 1994   Walter M. Ellis, *Ptolemy of Egypt* (London: Routledge)
Engels 1978   Donald W. Engels, *Alexander the Great and the Logistics of the
                     Macedonian Army* (Berkeley: University of California Press)
Errington 1969   R. M. Errington, "Bias in Ptolemy's History of Alexander," *CQ* 19:
                     233–42
Erskine 1989   A. Erskine, "The *pezevtairoi* of Philip II and Alexander III,"
                     Historia 38: 385–94
Faraguna 2003   Michele Faraguna, "Alexander and the Greeks," in J. Roisman
                     (ed.), *Brill's Companion to Alexander the Great* (Leiden: E. J.
                     Brill): 99–130

Fawcett 2006   Bill Fawcett (ed.), *How to Lose a Battle. Foolish Plans and Great Military Blunders* (New York: Harper)

Flower 2000   Michael Flower, "Alexander the Great and Panhellenism," in A. B. Bosworth and E. J. Baynham (eds.), *Alexander the Great in Fact and Fiction* (Oxford: Oxford University Press): 96–135

France 2005   John France, *The Crusades and the Expansion of Catholic Christendom*, 1000–1714 (London: Routledge)

Fredricksmeyer 2003   E. A. Fredricksmeyer, "Introductory Essay," in W. Heckel and L. A. Tritle (eds.), *Crossroads of History. The Age of Alexander* (Claremont, CA: Regina Books): 1–10

Fuller 1954   Major-General J. F. C. Fuller, *A Military History of the Western World: From the Earliest Times to the Battle of Lepanto, Vol. 1,* (New York: Da Capo)

Fuller 1955   Major-General J. F. C. Fuller, *A Military History of the Western World. Vol. 2. From the Defeat of the Spanish Armada to the Battle of Waterloo* (New York: Da Capo)

Fuller 1960   Major-General J. F. C. Fuller, *The Generalship of Alexander the Great* (New York: Da Capo)

Gaebel 2002   Robert E. Gaebel, *Cavalry Operations in the Ancient Greek World* (Norman, OK: University of Oklahoma Press)

Geniesse 1999   Jane Fletcher Geniesse, *Passionate Nomad. The Life of Freya Stark* (New York: Random House)

Goldsworthy 2003   A. Goldsworthy, *In the Name of Rome. The Men Who Won the Roman Empire* (London: Phoenix)

Grainger 1991   John D. Grainger, *Hellenistic Phoenicia* (Oxford: Oxford University Press)

Granier 1931   F. Granier, *Die makedonische Heersversammlung. Ein Beitrag zum antiken Staatsrecht* (Munich: Beck)

Graves 1928   Robert Graves, *Lawrence and the Arabs* (London)

Grayson 1993   A. K. Grayson, "Eunuchs in Power: Their Role in the Assyrian Bureaucracy," in M. Dietrich and O. Loretz (eds.), *Vom Alten Orient zum Alten Testament* (Neukirchen-Vluyn): 85–98

Green 1974   P. Green, *Alexander of Macedon* (London: Penguin)

Griffith 1979   G. T. Griffith, in N. G. L. Hammond and G. T. Griffith, *A History of Macedonia*, vol. 2 (Oxford: Oxford University Press)

Hall 1989   Edith Hall, *Inventing the Barbarian. Greek Self-Definition through Tragedy* (Oxford: Oxford University Press)

Hall 2002   Jonathan M. Hall, *Hellenicity. Between Ethnicity and Culture* (Chicago: University of Chicago Press)

Hamilton 1969   J. R. Hamilton, *Plutarch*, Alexander: *A Commentary* (Oxford: Clarendon Press)

Hamilton 1971   J. R. Hamilton, "Alexander and the Aral," *CQ* 21: 106–11

Hamilton 1985   J. R. Hamilton, "Alexander and His Ancestors," in Robin Hankey
                 and Douglas Little (eds.), *Essays in Honour of Agathe Thornton*
                 (Dunedin: Department of Classics, University of Otago)

Hammond   N. G. L. Hammond, "The Battle of the Granicus River," *JHS* 100:
1980   73–88

Hammond   N. G. L. Hammond, *Three Historians of Alexander the Great: The
1983   So-Called Vulgate Authors, Diodorus, Justin and Curtius*
                 (Cambridge: Cambridge University Press)

Hammond   N. G. L. Hammond, *The Genius of Alexander the Great* (Chapel
1997   Hill, NC: University of North Carolina Press)

Hanson 2001   Victor Davis Hanson, *Carnage and Culture: Landmark Battles in
                 the Rise of Western Power* (New York: Doubleday)

Harlan 2005   Josiah Harlan, *A Memoir of India and Afghanistan* (reprint of the
                 1842 edition, Philadelphia)

Hauben 1976   H. Hauben, "The Expansion of Macedonian Sea-Power under
                 Alexander the Great," *Anc. Soc.* 7: 79–105

Heckel 1979   W. Heckel, "Philip II, Kleopatra and Karanos," *RFIC* 107: 385–93

Heckel 1980   Waldemar Heckel, "Alexander at the Persian Gates," *Athenaeum*
                 58: 168–74

Heckel 1982   Waldemar Heckel, "The Career of Antigenes," *SO* 57: 57–67

Heckel 1987   Waldemar Heckel, "A Grandson of Antipatros at Delos," *ZPE* 70:
                 161–2

Heckel 1988   Waldemar Heckel, *The Last Days and Testament of Alexander the
                 Great: A Prosopographic Study.* Historia Einzelschriften, Heft 56
                 (Stuttgart: Franz Steiner Verlag)

Heckel 1992   Waldemar Heckel, *The Marshals of Alexander's Empire* (London:
                 Routledge)

Heckel 1994   Waldemar Heckel, "Notes on Q. Curtius Rufus' *History of
                 Alexander*," *AC* 37: 67–78

Heckel 1997   Waldemar Heckel, "Resistance to Alexander the Great," in L. A.
                 Tritle (ed.), *The Greek World in the Fourth Century. From the Fall
                 of the Athenian Empire to the Successors of Alexander* (London:
                 Routledge): 189–227

Heckel 2002   Waldemar Heckel, "The Politics of Distrust: Alexander and his
                 Successors," in D. Ogden (ed.), *The Hellenistic World: New
                 Perspectives* (London: Duckworth): 81–95

Heckel 2003   Waldemar Heckel, "Alexander the Great and the 'Limits of the
                 Civilised World,'" in W. Heckel and L. A. Tritle (eds.),
                 Crossroads of History. The Age of Alexander (Claremont, CA:
                 Regina Books): 147–74

Heckel 2005   Waldemar Heckel, "*Syaspismos*, Sarissas and Wagons," *AC* 48: 189–94

Heckel 2006a   Waldemar Heckel, *Who's Who in the Age of Alexander. Prosopography of Alexander's Empire* (Oxford: Blackwell)

Heckel 2006b   Waldemar Heckel, "Mazaeus, Callisthenes and the Alexander Sarcophagus," *Historia* 55: 385–96

Heckel &   W. Heckel and J. C. Yardley, *Alexander the Great. Historical Sources*
  Yardley 2004   *in Translation* (Oxford: Blackwell)

Helps 1869   Arthur Helps, *The Life of Pizarro with Some Account of His Associates in the Conquest of Peru* (London: Bell and Daldy)

Higgins 1980   W. E. Higgins, "Aspects of Alexander's Imperial Administration: Some Modern Methods and Views Reviewed," *Athenaeum* 48: 129–52

Hillman 2004   James Hillman, *A Terrible Love of War* (New York: Penguin)

Hofstetter 1978 J. Hofstetter, *Die Griechen in Persien. Prosopographie der Griechen im persischen Reich vor Alexander* (Berlin)

Hollister 2001   C. Warren Hollister, *Henry I*, edited and completed by Amanda Clark Frost (New Haven: Yale University Press)

Holt 1988   Frank L. Holt, *Alexander the Great and Bactria* (Leiden: E. J. Brill)

Holt 2003   Frank L. Holt, *Alexander the Great and the Mystery of the Elephant Medallions* (Berkeley: University of California Press)

Holt 2005   Frank L. Holt, *Into the Land of Bones. Alexander the Great in Afghanistan* (Berkeley: University of California Press)

Jaschinski 1981 S. Jaschinski, *Alexander und Griechenland unter dem Eindruck der Flucht des Harpalos*, Dissertation (Bonn)

Karttunen 1990   K. Karttunen, "Taxila: Indian City and a Stronghold of Hellenism," *Arctos* 24: 85–96

Keil 1924   J Keil, "Der Kampf um den Granikosübergang und das strategische Problem der Issosschlacht," *Mitteilungen des Verein Klassischer Philologen in Wien* 1: 15–19

Kennedy 1988   Paul Kennedy, *The Rise and Fall of the Great Powers. Economic Change and Military Conflict from 1500 to 2000* (New York: Harper Collins)

Kern 1999   Paul Bentley Kern, *Ancient Siege Warfare* (Bloomington, IN: Souvenir Press)

Kienast 1973   D. Kienast, *Philipp II. von Makedonien und das Reich der Achaimeniden*, Abhandlungen der Marburger Gelehrten Gesellschaft, Jahrjang 1971, no. 6 (Munich)

Kiernan 1995   Victor Kiernan, *The Lords of Human Kind. European Attitudes to Other Cultures in the Imperial Age* (London: Serif)

Kuhrt 1995   A. Kuhrt, *The Ancient Near East: c. 3000–330 BC.* 2 vols. (London: Routledge)

Kurke 2004   Lance Kurke, *The Wisdom of Alexander the Great* (New York:
                  Amacom)
Lane Fox 1974   Robin Lane Fox, *Alexander the Great. A Biography* (New York:
                  Dial Press)
Lane Fox 1996   Robin Lane Fox, "Text and Image: Alexander the Great, Coins
                  and Elephants," *BICS* 41: 87–108
Lane Fox 2004   Robin Lane Fox (ed.), *The Long March: Xenophon and the Ten
                  Thousand* (New Haven: Yale University Press)
Langley 1996   Lester D. Langley, *The Americas in the Age of Revolution, 1750–1850*
                  (New Haven: Yale University Press)
Latimer 2003   Jon Latimer, *Deception in War* (Woodstock & New York:
                  Overlook)
Leingärtner 1968 Edmund Leingärtner (editor and translator), Johann Georg Korb,
                  Tagebuch der Reise nach Russland (Graz: Akademische Durck-
                  u. Verlagsanstalt)
Lewis 1977   David M. Lewis, *Sparta and Persia* (Leiden: E. J. Brill)
Liddell-Hart   B. H. Liddell-Hart, *Strategy*. Second revised edition (New York:
  1967   Meridian)
Lloyd 2000   A. B. Lloyd, "The Late Period (664–332 BC)," in Ian Shaw (ed.),
                  The Oxford History of Ancient Egypt. Oxford: Oxford
                  University Press: 369–94.
Lock 1977   R. Lock, "The Origins of the Argyraspids," *Historia* 26:
                  373–8
Lonsdale 2004   David J. Lonsdale, *Alexander the Great, Killer of Men: History's
                  Greatest Conqueror and the Macedonian Art of War* (New York:
                  Carroll & Graf)
MacIntyre 2004   Ben MacIntyre, *The Man Who Would Be King. The First American
                  in Afghanistan* (New York: Farrar, Strauss, and Giroux)
Maier 1994   Christoph T. Maier, *Preaching the Crusades. Mendicant Friars and
                  the Cross in the Thirteenth Century* (Cambridge: Cambridge
                  University Press)
Marr & Calisher   J. S. Marr and C. H. Calisher, "Alexander the Great and West
  2003   Nile Virus Encephalitis," *Emerg. Infect. Dis.* 9: 1599–1603
Marsden 1964   E. W. Marsden, *The Campaign of Gaugamela* (Liverpool:
                  Liverpool University Press)
Marshall 1951   J. Marshall, *Taxila* (Cambridge: Cambridge University Press)
Massie 1980   Robert K. Massie, *Peter the Great* (New York: Random House)
McCrindle 1894   J. W. McCrindle, *Ancient India. Its Invasion by Alexander the
                  Great* (London: Methuen)
McLynn 1998   Frank McLynn, *Napoleon. A Biography* (London: Pimlico)
Merkelbach 1977   R. Merkelbach, *Die Quellen des griechischen Alexanderromans*,
                  second ed. (Munich: Beck)

Mierow 1966   Charles Christopher Mierow (transl.), *The Deeds of Frederick Barbarossa, by Otto of Freising and his Continuator, Rahewin* (New York: Norton)

Miller 1997   M. C. Miller, *Athens and Persia in the Fifth Century BC* (Cambridge: Cambridge University Press)

Milns 1968   R. D. Milns, *Alexander the Great* (New York: Pegasus)

Montgomery   Field Marshal Viscount Montgomery, *A Concise History of Warfare*
1968   (London)

Morrison 2001   Gary Morrison, "Alexander, Combat Psychology, and Persepolis," *Antichthon* 35: 30–44

Müller 2003   Sabine Müller, *Maßnahmen der Herrschaftssicherung gegenüber der makedonischen Opposition bei Alexander dem Großen* (Frankfurt a. M.: Peter Lang)

Murison 1972   C. L. Murison, "Darius III and the Battle of Issus," *Historia* 21: 399–423

Mysliwiec 2000   Karol Mysliwiec, *The Twilight of Ancient Egypt: First Millennium B.C.E.*, translated by David Lorton (Ithaca, NY: Cornell University Press)

Nylander 1993   C. Nylander, "Darius the Cowardly King," in J. Carlsens et al. (eds.), *Alexander the Great. Reality and Myth* (Rome: Bretschneider):

Ogden 1999   D. Ogden, *Polygamy, Prostitutes and Death: The Hellenistic Dynasties* (London: Duckworth)

Oldach et al.   D. Oldach et al. "A Mysterious Death," *NEJM* 338: 1764–8
1998

Olmstead 1948   A. T. Olmstead, *History of the Persian Empire* (Chicago: University of Chicago Press)

Oman 1991   C. Oman, *A History of the Art of War in the Middle Ages*, vol. 1 (London: Greenhill; originally published in 1885)

Parke 1933   H. W. Parke, *Greek Mercenary Soldiers from the Earliest Times to the Battle of Ipsus* (Oxford: Oxford University Press)

Pearson 1960   L. Pearson, *The Lost Histories of Alexander the Great* (Philadelphia: American Philological Association)

Perrin 1895   B. Perrin, "Genesis and Growth of an Alexander-Myth," *TAPA* 26: 56–68

Ponting 2004   Clive Ponting, *The Crimean War. The Truth behind the Myth* (London: Pimlico)

Prescott 1998   William H. Prescott, *History of the Conquest of Peru* (New York: Random House)

Pritchett 1974   W. K. Pritchett, *The Greeks States at War*, vol. 2 (Berkeley: University of California Press)

Reames-
Zimmerman
1998

J. Reames-Zimmerman, "An Atypical Affair? Alexander the Great,
Hephaistion Amyntoros and the Nature of their Relationship,"
AHB 13: 81–96

Reames-
Zimmerman
2001

J. Reames-Zimmerman, "The Mourning of Alexander the Great,"
Syllecta Classica 12: 98–145

Renault 1974

Mary Renault, *The Persian Boy* (London: Penguin)

Rhodes &
Osborne
2003

P. J. Rhodes and R. Osborne, *Greek Historical Inscriptions, 400–32
BC* (Oxford: Oxford University Press)

Robinson 1953

C. A. Robinson, Jr., *The History of Alexander the Great.* 2 vols.
(Baltimore: Johns Hopkins University Press; repr. Kraus,
1977)

Rogers 2004

Guy MacLean Rogers, *Alexander. The Ambiguity of Greatness* (New
York: Random House)

Rood 2004

Tim Rood, *The Sea! The Sea! The Shout of the Ten Thousand in the
Modern Imagination* (London: Duckworh)

Royle 2000

Trevor Royle, *Crimea. The Great Crimean War, 1854–1856* (New
York: Palgrave)

Runciman 1951

S. Runciman, *A History of the Crusades.* 3 vols. (Cambridge:
Cambridge University Press)

Ryder 1965

T. T. B. Ryder, *Koine Eirene. General Peace and Local Independence
in Ancient Greece* (Oxford: Oxford University Press)

Sachs 1977

A. Sachs, "Achaemenid Royal Names in Babylonian Astronomical
Texts," *AJAH* 2: 129–47

Sachs 1990

K. Sachs, *Diodorus Siculus and the First Century* (Princeton, NJ:
Princeton University Press)

Sallah & Weiss
2006

M. Salleh and M. Weiss, *Tiger Force. The True Story of Men and
War* (Boston)

Sancisi-
Weerdenburg
1987

H. Sancisi-Weerdenberg, "Decadence in the Empire or Decadence
in the Sources? From Source to Synthesis: Ctesias," *Achaemenid
History* 1 (Leiden): 33–46

Schwarz 1893

F. v. Schwarz, *Alexanders des Grossen Feldzüge in Turkestan*
(Munich)

Seel 1972

O. Seel, *Eine römische Weltgeschichte* (Nurnberg)

Seibert 1969

J. Seibert, *Untersuchungen zur Geschichte Ptolemaios' I.* (Munich:
Beck)

Seibert 1985

J. Seibert, *Die Eroberung des Perserreiches durch Alexander den
Grossen auf kartographischer Grundlage* (Wiesbaden)

Seibert 1987

J. Seibert, "Dareios III," in W. Will (ed.), *Zu Alex. d. Gr.*
(Amsterdam: Hakkert)

Seibert 1998   J. Seibert, "'Panhellenischer' Kreuzzug, Nationalkrieg,
                    Rachefeldzug oder makedonischer Eroberungskrieg?–
                    Überlegungen zu den Ursachen des Krieges gegen Persien," in
                    W. Will (ed.), *Alexander der Grosse. Eine Welteroberung und ihr
                    Hintergrund* (Bonn): 5–58

Seibt 1977   G. Seibt, *Griechische Söldner im Achaimenidenreich* (Bonn)

Shay 1994   Jonathan Shay, *Achilles in Vietnam. Combat Trauma and the
                    Undoing of Character* (New York: Schribner)

Shay 2002   Jonathan Shay, *Odysseus in America. Combat Trauma and the Trials
                    of Homecoming* (New York: Schribner)

Smith 1914   Vincent A. Smith, *The Early History of India from 600 B.C. to the
                    Muhammadan Conquest Including the Invasion of Alexander the
                    Great* (Oxford: Oxford University Press)

Spalinger 1978   A. Spalinger, "The Reign of Chabbash: An Interpretation," *ZÄS*
                    105: 142–54

Spann 1999   Philip O. Spann, "Alexander at the Beas: Fox in a Lion's Skin," in
                    F. Titchener and R. F. Moorton, Jr. (eds.), *The Eye Expanded*
                    (Berkeley: University of California Press): 62–74

Speck 2002   Henry Speck, "Alexander at the Persian Gates: A Study in
                    Historiography and Topography," *AJAH* n.s. 1: 1–234

Stadter 1980   Philip A. Stadter, *Arrian of Nicomedia* (Chapel Hill, NC:
                    University of North Carolina Press)

Stark 1956   Freya Stark, *Alexander's Path from Caria to Cilicia* (New York:
                    Harcourt, Brace and World, Inc.)

Stein 1929   Aurel Stein, *On Alexander's Track to the Indus* (London; reprint
                    Chicago: Ares Press)

Stewart 1993   Andrew Stewart, *Faces of Power. Alexander's Image and Hellenistic
                    Politics* (Berkeley: University of California Press).

Tabacco 2000   Raffaella Tabacco, *Itinerarium Alexandri* (Turin: Leo S.
                    Olschki)

Tarn 1933   W. W. Tarn, "Alexander the Great and the 'Unity of Mankind,'"
                    Proceedings of the British Academy 19: 123–66

Tarn 1948   W. W. Tarn, *Alexander the Great*, 2 vols. (Cambridge: Cambridge
                    University Press)

Therasse 1976   J. Therasse, *Quintus Curtius Rufus Index Verborum. Relevès lexicaux
                    et grammaticaux* (Berlin: Georg Olms)

Thomas 2006   Carol G. Thomas, *Alexander the Great in His World* (Oxford:
                    Blackwell)

Tibble 1989   Steven Tibble, *Monarchy and Lordships in the Latin Kingdom of
                    Jerusalem, 1099–1291* (Oxford: Oxford University Press)

Tougher 2004   S. Tougher, "Social Transformation, Gender Transformation? The
                 Court Eunuch, 300–900," in L. Brubaker and Julia M. H.
                 Smith (eds.), *Gender in the Early Medieval World. East and West,
                 300–900* (Cambridge: Cambridge University Press): 70–82

Tritle 2000   Lawrence A. Tritle, *From Melos to My Lai. War and Survival*
                 (London: Routledge)

Tritle 2003   Lawrence A. Tritle, "Alexander and the Killing of Cleitus the
                 Black," in W. Heckel and L. A. Tritle (eds.), *Crossroads of History.
                 The Age of Alexander* (Claremont, CA: Regina Books): 127–46

Tronson 1984   A. Tronson, "Satyrus the Peripatetic and the Marriages of Philip
                 II," *JHS* 104: 116–26

Tyerman 2004   C. Tyerman, *Fighting for Christendom: Holy War and the Crusades*
                 (Oxford: Oxford University Press)

Van Wees 2004   Hans van Wees, *Greek Warfare. Myths and Realities* (London:
                 Duckworh)

Vogelsang 2002   W. Vogelsang, *The Afghans* (Oxford: Blackwell)

Washbrook   D. A. Washbrook, "Orients and Occidents: Colonial Discourse
  1999   Theory and the Historiography of the British Empire," in
                 Robin W. Winks (ed.), *The Oxford History of the British Empire*,
                 vol. 5: *Historiography* (Oxford: Oxford University Press): 596–611

Warren 1997   W. L. Warren, *King John* (New Haven: Yale University Press;
                 originally published in 1961

Waterfield   Robin Waterfield, *Xenophon's Retreat* (Cambridge, MA: Belknap)
  2006

Wheeler 1976   M. Wheeler, *My Archaeological Mission to India and Pakistan*
                 (London: Thames and Hudson)

Wiesehöfer   Josef Wiesehöfer, *Ancient Persia from 550 BC to 650 AD* (London: I.
  1996   B. Tauris)

Wilcken 1967   U. Wilcken, *Alexander the Great*, translated by G. C. Richards,
                 with an introduction by E. N. Borza (New York: Norton)

Will 1983   W. Will, *Athen und Alexander. Untersuchungen zur Geschichte der
                 Stadt von 338 bis 322 v. Chr.* (Munich)

Wood 1997   Michael Wood, *The Footsteps of Alexander the Great* (Berkeley:
                 University of California Press)

Worthington   I. Worthington, *A Historical Commentary on Dinarchus* (Ann
  1992   Arbor, MI: University of Michigan Press)

Worthington   I. Worthington, "How Great Was Alexander?" *AHB* 13: 39–55
  1999

Worthington   I. Worthington, *Alexander the Great: A Reader* (London:
  2003   Routledge)

Yalichev 1997   Serge Yalichev, *Mercenaries of the Ancient World* (London: Constable)

Yardley 1984   J. C. Yardley (transl.), *Quintus Curtius Rufus. The History of Alexander*, introduction and notes by Waldemar Heckel (Harmondsworth: Penguin)

Yardley &   *Justin: Epitome of the Philippic History of Pompeius Trogus. Books*
Heckel 1997   *11–12: Alexander the Great.* Translated by J. C. Yardley, commentary by Waldemar Heckel (Oxford: Oxford University Press)

Zahrnt 2003   M. Zahrnt, "Versöhnen oder Spalten? Überlegungen zu Alexanders Ehrendekret," *Hermes* 131: 407–32

Zinsser 1996   Hans Zinsser, *Rats, Lice and History* (New York; Barnes and Noble; originally published in 1934)

INDEX

❀ ❀ ❀

Abdalonymus, King of Sidon, 66
Abisares, 113–16, 126, 128
Abreas (Habreas), 187
Abulites, 81, 136, 180–81, 186–87
Abydus, 41
Acesines (Chenab), 187
Achaemenid, 1, 3, 31–32, 35, 65, 85–87, 96, 99, 112–13, 122, 126–27, 136–37, 142
Achaemenid empire, 31
Achaemenid scholars, 32
Achilles, vii, 8, 28, 42, 149, 173, 177
Ada, Queen of Halicarnasus, 51–52
Ada the Younger, 52
Adams, Simon, viii
Admetus, 175
Adrestae, 127
Aegae (Vergina), 24
Aegean, 1, 2, 13, 34, 35, 45, 56, 57, 65, 67
Aegospotami, 35
Aelian, 148
Aeolia, 51
Aëropus, 24
Aetolia, 147
Afghanistan, 183
Agamemnon, 42
Agathocles, 52
Agathon, 78, 135
agema, 25, 128
Agesilaus, 32, 35, 37–38, 40, 42, 177
Aggalasseis, 127
Agis III, 69, 83
Agis' war, 147
Agrianes, 26–28, 61, 120, 128, 158, 160, 163
Ajax, 42
Alcetas, 116, 160, 163
Alcibiades, 35
Alcimachus, 22, 51
Alderfeld, M. Gustavus, 187

Alexander historians, 6, 7, 11, 38, 47, 60, 82, 121, 174
Alexander I (Philhellene), 10, 14, 21, 22
Alexander II, 15
Alexander III (the Great), Lost sources: 6–8; extant sources: 8–10; son of Philip II and Olympias: 15; Chaeronea and events leading to his accession: 17–24; his army: 24–28, 153–65; his campaigns in Europe: 28–30; beginning of his campaign: 41–44; battle of the Granicus River: 45–51; first indications of orientalizing policies: 51–53; learns of the plot of Alexander Lyncestes: 51–54; undoes the Gordian knot: 54–55; defeats Darius III at Issus: 57–65; besieges Tyre and Gaza: 65–71; affairs in Egypt: 71–73; negotiations with Darius: 73–74; defeats Darius at Gaugamela: 75–80; captures the capitals of the Persian empire: 80–84; his reaction to the death of Darius' wife: 84–85; pursuit of Bessus: 87–88, 92–95; conspiracy of Philotas: 88–92; campaigns in Bactria and Sogdiana: 96–100; kills Cleitus at Maracanda: 100–04; marries Rhoxane, daughter of Oxyartes: 104–05; attempts to introduce proskynesis: 106–09; conspiracy of Hermolaus and execution of Callisthenes: 109–11; conquest of the Punjab: 112–25; defeats Porus at the Hydaspes: 115–20; his troops refuse to cross the Hyphasis: 120–25; descent of the Indus: 126–31; near-fatal wounding at the town of the Mallians: 128–29; the Gedrosian march: 131–33; punishment of the satraps (no "Reign of Terror"): 133–37; mass-marriages in Susa: 137–39; introduction of orientals into the army and mutiny at Opis: 139–41; demobilization of veterans: 142–44; learns of Harpalus' crimes and flight: 144–46;

Alexander III (*cont.*)
  issues Exiles' Decree: 146–47; *Alexander's*
  "divinity": 147–48; *death of his best friend,*
  Hephaestion: 149; *Alexander's death*:
  150–52.
Alexander I of Epirus, 23, 175
Alexander Mosaic, 173
Alexander Romance, 71
Alexander Sarcophagus, 174, 181
Alexander the Lyncestian, 24, 53–54 (his
  arrest), 73, 88, 91, 102, 145
Alexandria-Eschate (mod. Khojend), 97–98
Alexandria-in-Areia, 88, 182
Alexandria-in-Arachosia, 92, 130
Alexandria-in-Egypt, 7, 9, 72, 190
Alexandria-in-the-Caucasus, 113
Alexandrou Praxeis, 7
Alfred the Great, 188
Allawi, 181
Alor, 130
Alorus, 15
Amanus, 58
Amasis, 177, 180
Amastris, 138, 188
Amazon queen, 149, 190
Amazons, 124
Amminapes, 178
Amphictyonic League, 17
Amphoterus, brother of Craterus, 53, 67
Amun, 21, 72, 73, 91, 108, 143, 148
Amyntas I, 14
Amyntas III, 22, 14–15
Amyntas IV, 24, 53, 73, 90
Amyntas, member of Dimnus conspiracy,
  182
Amyntas, member of Macedonian garrison
  at Thebes, 29
Amyntas, son of Antiochus, 57, 70, 72–73
Amyntas, son of Arrhabaeus, 39, 46, 51, 54
Amyntas, son of Nicolaus, 104, 184
Anabasis (of Xenophon), 10, 31, 52
Anabasis Alexandrou, 20
Anaxarchus, 110, 148
Anaxippus, 88

Andromache, 176
Andromachus, 78, 98, 102
Andromenes, sons of, 90
Anticles, son of Theocritus, 185
Antigenes, 160, 174
Antigonus the One-Eyed, 55, 151, 174, 181,
  190
Antiochus, 24, 57, 70, 72, 73
Antipater, son of Iolaus, 22, 24–25, 29, 53–54,
  88, 136, 138, 140, 145–47, 151, 189
Antipater, father of Leonnatus, 184
Antipater, son of Asclepiodorus, 185
antitagma, 140
Antony (Marcus Antonius), 104, 131
Aornus, 94, 114, 185
Apame, daughter of Artaxerxes II, 56
Aphrices, 114
Aphobetus, 182
Apis, 39
Apollo, 16, 96
Apollonides, 178
Apollophanes, 136
apotropaic sacrifice, 42
Apries (Hophra), 180
Aqaba, 132, 187
Arachosia, 75, 162
Arachosians, 113, 140
Aral, 92
Araxes, 82
Arbela, 75, 80, 180
Arcadia, 38, 181
Archelaus I, 14, 174
Archepolis, 182
archers, 27, 36, 46, 81, 120, 128, 140
archihypaspistes, 26
archon, 28
archonship, 16
Areia, 88, 92
Areians, 140
Aretes, 78
Argaeus, 15
Argeadae, 14
Argos, 173
Argyraspides, 140, 175, 189

Ariamazes, 100, 104–05, 120
Ariaspians, 92
Ariobarzanes, former satrap of Hellespontine
    Phrygia, 43
Ariobarzanes, satrap of Persis, 81–82
Ariobarzanes, 182
aristeia, 50, 94
Aristobulus, 8, 10, 11, 55, 180, 185, 190
Aristomedes, 57
Ariston, 182
Aristotle, 6, 146
Armenia, 31, 51
Arrhabaeus, 24, 39, 46, 51, 53–54, 57, 73
Arrhidaeus (Philip III), 15, 52, 180
Arrian, 8, 10–11
Arsames, 50
Arses (= Artaxerxes IV), 38–39, 182
Arsites, 45, 50
Artabazus, 45, 56, 57, 92, 100–01, 104, 178, 181
Artacoana, 88, 182
Artasata (*see* Darius III), 38
Artaxerxes I, 176
Artaxerxes II, 31, 34–35, 38, 45, 56, 182
Artaxerxes III Ochus, 34, 38, 45, 65, 71, 137,
    179
Artaxerxes IV (= Arses), 38–39, 182
Artaxerxes V (= Bessus), 87
Artemis, temple of (Ephesus), 43
Asander, 183
Ascalon (Ashkelon), 179
Asclepiodorus, satrap of Syria, 183, 185
Ashdod, 179
Asia, 2, 3, 23–24, 36, 39, 40, 42–43, 45, 51–54,
    56–57, 66, 74, 81, 84–88, 92, 94, 98, 100,
    104, 128, 136, 140, 146, 150, 189
Asia Minor, 2, 3, 24, 39–40, 43, 45, 53–54,
    56–57, 66, 74, 98
Aspasians, 113–14
Assacenians, 113–14, 185
Assacenus, 114
Assyrians, 178
Astaspes, 136
Astis, 115
Atarrhias, 175

Atheas, 66, 179
Athena, 42, 124, 129, 187
Athenaeus of Naucratis, 20
Athenian Empire, 3, 36, 55
Athenians, 2, 9, 17, 28, 35–37, 51, 145, 176
Athens, 10, 14, 17, 22, 35, 37, 144–45, 147
Atizyes, 53
Atropates, 136, 148
Attalus, son of Andromenes, 116, 119,
    160–62, 186
Attalus, uncle of Cleopatra, enemy of
    Alexander III, 16, 20–24, 39, 56, 73, 158
Attica, 17
Attinas, 99
Audata, 15
Aulis, 42, 177
Autariatae, 28
autonomous Thracians, 28
Axius, 13
Azemilcus, king of Tyre, 66, 68

Babylon, 31, 75, 81, 83, 136, 142, 144–45, 149,
    151, 180, 189
Babylonia, 55, 139
Bacchae, 14
Bactra (Zariaspa), 94, 99, 102, 109, 183
Bactria, 75, 87, 92, 95, 99–101, 112, 140, 187
Bactrians, 78, 94, 96, 113, 140, 160, 182–83
Badian, Ernst, 90
Bagoas, 38–39, 98, 137
Bagoas the Elder, 38
Bagodaras (Gobares), 183
Bahçe Pass, 58
Bajaur, 113
Balacrus, son of Nicanor, 145, 189
Bamian, 182
Bardiya, 182
Bardylis, 15
Barsaentes, 113, 182
Barsine (daughter of Artabazus, mistress of
    Alexander), 45, 56, 65, *see also* 85
Batis, 69, 120
Bazira (Bir-Kot), 114
Beas (*see also* Hyphasis), 121, 126, 186

Begram, 92
Behistun inscription of Darius I, 190
Belisarius, 177
Bessus, 75, 78, 87–88, 92, 94–95, 97, 99, 101, 105, 113, 182–83
Bianor, 57, 178
Bion, 180
Black Sea, 16–17, 31
Bodyguard, 51, 90
Boeotia, 17, 29
Boeotian League, 173
Bolan Pass, 132
Bolívar, 132
Bosworth, A. B., 58, 123
Brahmins, 130
Branchidae, 95–96, 104, 183
Briant, Pierre, 85
British Empire, 4
Bronze Age, 179
Brosius, Maria, 139
Brown, R. Allen, 136
Bubaces, 14
Bucephala, 121–22, 127
Bucephalas, vii
Bull Run (Manasses), 179
Bumelus, 75
Buner, 113–14
Bupares, 180

Cadmeia, 29
Cadusian(s), 177
Caesar, 188
Calas, 43, 45, 54, 90
Calis, 90, 182
Callicratidas, 37
Callisthenes of Olynthus (historian), 6–7, 43, 49–50, 52, 60, 80, 82, 96, 109–11, 130, 134, 177–78, 180, 183, 185
Cambyses, 71–72, 179–80, 182
Cannae, 27
Cappadocia, 55
Cappadocians, 178
Caracalla, 148
Caranus, 78, 92, 98, 102

Caranus, alleged son of Philip II, 175
Caria, 39, 51
Carmania, 132, 134
Carney, Elizabeth, 89
Carthaginians, 67
Caspian, 92, 150
Cassander, 145, 188–89
Castabulum, 58
Catanes, 95
Cathaeans, 126
Caucasus, 92, 113
cavalry, 17, 25–27, 40, 46–48, 58, 60–61, 75, 78, 80, 97, 101–02, 116, 119–20, 128, 140, 144, 158–63, 177
Cebalinus, 89, 90
Celaenae, 55
Cephisus River, 17, 19
Chababash, 39, 72
Chaeronea, 2, 9, 17, 20, 22, 25, 29, 39, 41, 147, 150, 181
Chandragupta (Sandrocottus), 126
Chares, 7, 57, 109, 111, 173, 185
Chares, Athenian, 178
Charicles, 111, 185
Charidemus, 57, 159
Charikar, 92
Charlemagne, 110
Charles V, 135
Charles XII of Sweden, 121, 133, 187
Charsadda, 115
Chenab River, 187
Chiliarch, 38, 140
chiliarchies, 26
Chitral, 114
Choerilus, 8
Chorienes (see also Sisimithres), 105, 183–84
Christie, Agatha, 182
CIA, 3
Cicero, M. Tullius (orator), 7
Cicero, Q. Tullius, 8
Cilicia, 57–58, 66, 81, 145
Cilician Gates, 55
Cleander, son of Polemocrates, 53, 91, 135, 182

Cleitarchus, 7–9, 82–83, 109, 130, 174, 181, 183, 187

Cleitus ("the Black"), 50, 100–05, 107, 110, 130, 173, 185

Cleitus ("the White"), 160, 163, 185, 190

Cleitus, Illyrian chieftain, 29

Cleopatra, sister of Alexander the Great, 15, 22–23

Cleopatra (Eurydice), last wife of Philip II, 16, 20, 22, 175

Cleopatra VII of Egypt, 114

Cleophis, 114

Climax (Mt.), 52

Cnidus, battle of (394 BC), 35

Codomannus (= Darius III), 38

Coenus, son of Polemocrates, 53, 68, 104–05, 119–20, 123, 160, 175, 182, 186

Coeranus, 78

Cold War, 37, 176

color romanus, 11, 137

Common Peace, 3, 173

Companion Cavalry, 25, 52, 101, 140

Companions, 2, 25, 26, 27, 46, 52, 61, 78, 99, 143, 175, 185

condottieri, 56

Conon, Athenian *strategos*, 35

conquistadors, 135, 137

Conrad of Montferrat, 67

Constantius II, 10

Copais (Lake), 29

Cophes son of Artabazus, 100

Copsi, 136

Corinth, 38, 52, 173

Corinthian War, 35

Coronea, 38, 181

Corrhagus, 129–30, 187

Cossaeans, 149, 181

Cothelas, 16

Cowardly Porus, 126

Coya, 188

Craterus, 27, 53, 75, 81, 97, 99, 105, 114, 116, 120, 127–28, 130, 132, 138, 140, 144–45, 147, 151, 161–63, 185

Crete, 27, 145

Crimean War, 179

Critobulus, 129

Crocus Field, 16

Croesus, 2, 173

Crusades, Crusaders, 16, 67, 173, 188

Crusader states (kingdoms), 67, 173

Crusader's cross, 16

Ctesias of Cnidus, 177, 181, 183

Cummings, Lewis V., 132

Cunaxa, 31, 35, 64–65, 176, 180–81

Curiati, 94

Curtius (Quintus Curtius Rufus), 8–9

Cyclades, 57

Cynnane, 15

Cypriotes, 179

Cyprus, 70

Cyrus the Great, 2, 64, 71, 85, 92, 97, 131, 137, 176, 180

Cyrus the Younger, 31–32, 35, 52, 64

Cyzicus, 45

Dahae, 75, 94, 98–99, 160

Damascus, 57, 65, 70

Danube, 13, 28, 97, 124

Darius I, 2, 14, 36, 55, 73, 83, 112, 113, 148, 176, 182

Darius II, 34–35, 71, 176

Darius III, ix, 24, 27; 38–40 (his early reign); 45, 53–54; 57–61, 64 (at Issus), 65–6, 69–80 (negotiations, battle of Gaugamela), 81 (flees to Ecbatana); 83–88 (death); 99, 101, 105; 112–13 (Indian support for Darius); 138, 139, 142, 177, 182–83

Datames, 57

Dataphernes, 95

Datis, 36

David and Goliath, 94

Davis, Jefferson, 34

Deli Çay, 58

Delian League, 3

Demaratus, 38, 50, 52, 177–78

Demetrius (Pheidon), 109

Demetrius, son of Althaemenes, 120, 160

Demetrius the Somatophylax, 90, 182

Demosthenes, 28, 42
Derdas, 15
Devine, A. M., 46
Diadochoi (see also Successors), 190
Diana, Princess of Wales, 182
Diarium itineris in Moscoviam, 184
Díaz del Castillo, 138
Dicaearchus, 175
Didyma, 96
Dimnus, 89–91
Dinon, 7
Diodorus of Sicily, 8; 47–48 (account of the Granicus battle)
Diodotus of Erythrae, 6
Dionysius of Pontic Heraclea, 138
Dionysus, 148
Dioxenus, 182
Dioxippus, 129–30, 148, 180, 187
Dium, 42
Dnieper River, 92
Domesday Book, 136
Don River, 92
Drangiana, 128, 131, 162
Drangians, 140
Drypetis, 137
Dudo of Saint-Quentin, 174

Eastern Bloc, 37
Ecbatana, 81, 83, 91, 95, 142, 144, 149
Edith (Matilda), wife of Henry I, 188
Edgar (atheling), 136
Edward the Confessor, 188
Edwin (earl), 136
Egypt, 8, 39, 45, 66, 70–72, 74, 91, 97, 114, 180, 190
Egyptian harbor (of Tyre), 67
Egyptians, 34, 39, 71, 72, 180
Eirene, wife of Eunostus, 181
eisangeleus, 184
Ekron, 179
Elagabalus, 148
Elam, 81
Elateia, 17
Emma, Queen, 188

Epaminondas (Theban general), 10
Ephemerides, 6
Ephesus, 40, 43
Ephialtes, Athenian exile, 57, 135
Ephialtes, Greek traitor at Thermopylae, 82
Epigonoi, 140, 143
Epimenes, son of Arsaeus, 111, 185
Epirotes, 13
Epirus, 21, 22, 23
Eretrians, 2
Erigyius, 78, 92, 94
Euacae, 140
Euctemon, 82
Eumenes of Cardia, 6, 130, 178, 190
Eunostus of Soli, 181
eunuch(s), 38, 69, 84, 98, 137, 177
Euphrates, 52, 74
Euripides, 14, 176
Europa, daughter of Philip II, 175
Europe, 1, 24, 32, 40, 83, 88, 92, 147
European Scythians, 182
Eurydice, 15, 22
Eurylochus, 111
Eurymedon, 3
Exiles' Decree, 145–47, 189

Fabius (Q. Fabius Maximus), viii
Fawcett, Bill, 80
feudalism, 173
finances, 41
financial, 3, 34, 45, 57, 85, 137, 174
fleet, 7, 39, 43, 45, 57, 65–69, 71, 98, 122, 124, 127–29, 131–34, 162–63, 187, 190
Fredricksmeyer, E. A., ix
Fuller, Major-General J. F. C., 121

Gandhara, 112, 113, 122, 185
Ganges, 120, 121
Gath, 179
Gaugamela, 64, 75, 80–81, 86, 142–43, 159, 175, 180, 182, 185
Gaza, 68, 70–72, 120, 175, 179
gazophylakes, 87
Gedrosia, 131, 133, 163, 187

Genghis Khan, 150, 183 (Temujin)
Getae, 28, 97, 124
Glaucias, 29
Glaucus, 57
Glycera, 189
Gobares, 183
Goldsworthy, Adrian, 27
Gordian knot, viii, 54
Gordium, 53, 54
Gordius, father of Midas, 54
Gorgias, 116, 119, 160–62, 185–86
Gorgias of Leontini, 37
Granicus, 25, 45, 47, 49–52, 56, 86, 100, 143,
    159, 177–78
Great Game, 94
Great King, 3, 24, 31, 34, 36, 50, 52, 55–57, 61,
    64–65, 75, 82, 84–85, 86, 88, 95, 101,
    106–07
Great Persian War, 42
Great Satraps' Revolt, 56
Greek allies, 50, 84, 87, 143
Greek freedom, 10, 29, 145, 147
Greek hoplites, 26, 40
Greek unity, 37
Gryneum, 43
Gygaea, 15

Habreas, 175
Hadrian, 10
Haemus, 28
Haliacmon River, 13, 29
Halicarnassus, 51, 56–57, 175
Halys River, 74
hamippoi, 26
Hammurabi, Code of, 189
Hannibal, 188
Haranpur, 116
Hari Rud, 182
Harlan, Josiah, 132, 182–83
Harold Godwinson, 188
Harpalus, father of Calas, 54,
Harpalus (treasurer), 135, 144–45, 188–89
Hastings, battle of (AD 1066), 136
Hazara, 126

hazarapatish (chiliarch), 184
Hecatompylus, 84
Hegelochus, 67, 73, 178, 190
hegemon, 2, 146, 148
Helios, 122
Hellanicus, 175
Hellenicity, 176
Hellenistic kingdoms, 110, 141
Hellespont, 1, 17, 25, 40–42, 45, 49
Hellespontine Phrygia, 34, 43, 45, 54, 56
Helmand, 92
Henry I, King of England, 188
Hephaestion, 42, 69, 101, 104, 109, 114–15,
    127–28, 133, 137, 140, 142, 148–49, 160, 179
Hera, 175
Heracles, 14, 66, 68, 124, 127, 129, 148
Heracon, 135
Herat, 88, 182
Hermolaus, 7, 107–11, 184
Herodotus, 42, 96, 106, 173
Heromenes, son of Aëropus (regicide), 24,
    53, 73
hetairoi, 15, 51, 52, 54, 89–91, 102, 104, 109,
    128, 137–39, 143
hetairos, 89, 115
Hindu Kush, 92, 97, 113, 182
hippakontistai, 88
hipparch, 54, 101
hipparchy, 25, 119, 140
Hippostratus, brother of
    Cleopatra-Eurydice, 16
Hippostratus, father of Hegelochus, 73
hippotoxotai, 160
Hitler, ix, 22, 187–88
Hittite origin of Gordian myth, 178
Holt, Frank, 102
Holy Land, 133, 188
Homer, 8, 14, 28, 42, 173, 177
Horatii, 94
Horns of Hattin (AD 1187), 67
Hydaspes, 26, 98, 115, 116, 122, 123, 124, 126,
    127, 160–61
Hydraotes, 186–87
hyparchoi, 99

hyparchos, 113
hypaspist, 26, 129
hypaspists, 23, 26, 27, 42, 46, 61, 68, 70, 71, 75, 78, 89, 128, 143, 159–60
Hyperboreans, 173
Hyphasis (Beas), viii, 26, 120–24, 126, 131–32, 143, 186–87
Hyrcania, 149
Hyrcanians, 177–78

Iaxartes (Syr-darya), 92, 94, 97–100, 104, 124
ilai, 25
Ilam (Mt.), 185
ile, 25
ile basilike, 25
Iliad, 8, 177
Ilium (= Troy), 42
Illyrians, 15, 21, 22, 23, 28, 138, 158
Inarus, 71
Indus Delta, 1, 128, 131
Indus River, 7, 42, 112–16, 122, 124, 126–28, 130, 134
infantry, 17, 25–26, 29, 46, 48, 60–61, 71, 75, 78, 116, 119, 120, 127–28, 131–32, 140, 144, 158–63, 178, 183, 185
inscriptions, 5–6
Iolaus, 182
Ionia, 32, 34–36, 73, 145
Iphigenia in Aulis, 14
Iraqi invasion (Gulf War), 181
Isidore of Seville, 110
Islamabad, 115
Ismenias (Theban), 184
Isocrates, 37–39
Issus, 28, 39, 50, 55, 57–58, 60, 64, 68–69, 70, 72–73, 75, 80, 85–86, 143–44, 159
Isthmian games, 37
Itinerarium Alexandri, (*Itinerary of Alexander*), 8, 10

Jalalpur, 116
javelin-men, 27, 88
Jhelum (*see also* Hydaspes), 115, 126, 186
John, King of England, 185

Jupiter (Zeus), 108
Justin, 8–9, 11, 21, 114

Kabul, 92
Kandahar, 92, 130
Kardakes, 61, 159
Karshi, 184
Karzai, 181
Katgala Pass, 114
Khawak Pass, 94, 182
Koh-i-nor, 1;84
King's Peace, 36
Koine Eirene, 3
komos, 83
Korb, Johann Georg, 184
kowtowing, 106
Kunar, 114
Kuru Çay, 60
Kuwait City, 181
Kuwaitis, 82, 181

Lagus, 8, 83, 114
Lake Urmia, 80
Lamian War, 141, 189
Langarus, 28
Larichus, 52
Larissa, 15
Last Days and Testament of Alexander, 174
Latin East, 67, 188
Lawrence, T. E., 132
le Brun, Charles, 81
League of Corinth, 2, 20, 23, 26, 39, 51, 146
Lefort, 103
legitimacy, 21, 72, 87
Leonnatus, son of Anteas, 106, 133, 152, 163, 184
Leonnatus, son of Antipater of Aegae, 184
Leuctra, 36, 38, 181
liberation, 43
Limnaeus, 187
lochoi, 25
Lonsdale, David, 121, 124
Lower Macedonia, 13
Lucius Flavius Arrianus Xenophon, 10

Lycia, 179
Lycomendes of Rhodes, 178
Lydia, 51
Lydian, 2
Lysander, Spartan navarrch, 35
Lysimachus, 51
Lysippus (his equestrian statues), 51

MacArthur, 80
Mac Donnel, Count, 184
Macedon, 14, 20, 28, 37, 50, 53, 57, 66, 147
Macedonia, 1, 13–14, 17, 20–22, 29, 39, 42,
    45–46, 52–53, 57, 70, 73, 137, 140, 145–46,
    151, 183, 189
Macedonian cavalry, 17, 46
Macedonian garrison, 29, 112
Macedonian phalanx, 16, 26
Macedonians, 14–15, 22–23, 25–27, 36,
    39–40, 46, 52–53, 58, 61, 67, 71–72, 74–75,
    78, 81, 92, 94–96, 98, 100–02, 105,
    107–09, 111–12, 114–15, 129–31, 133, 138,
    140–41, 143, 158–63, 180
Machatas, 15, 127
Madates, 81
Makran, 131
malaria, 151
Mallians, 42, 126, 128, 130, 175, 187
Mallus, 58, 178–79
Maracanda (Samarcand), 97, 98, 99, 100,
    103, 104
Marathon, 2, 36, 181
Marathus, 73
Mardonius, 73
Margiana, 87
Margites, 28, 42
Marsyas of Philippi, 178
Massaga, 114
Massagetae, 64, 75, 98–99, 104–05
Massie, Robert K., 104
Matilda (see Edith)
Mazaces, 72
Mazaeus, 74, 78, 80–81, 180–81
McLynn, Frank, 139
Meda, 16

Media, 81, 148
Medes, 177
Medism, 36, 43
Mediterranean, 4, 13, 65, 67, 71–72, 75, 174,
    179
Medizers, 30, 176
Meleager, 53, 116, 119, 160–62, 185–86
melophoroi, 78
Melqart (= Phoenician Heracles), 66, 68
Memnon, 40, 43, 45, 50, 54, 56–57, 65, 85
Memphis, 71–72
Menander, 136, 185
Menedemus, 98, 102
Menidas, 78, 91, 183
Mentor, 45, 56, 57
mercenaries, 2, 31, 34–35, 43, 45–48, 50,
    55–57, 61, 66, 69–70, 72, 82, 116, 119, 143,
    146, 150, 158–59 177–78, 185, 187
Merv Oasis, 87
Mesopotamia, 55, 58, 80, 182
Methone, 129
Metron, 89
Metz Epitome, 114, 174
Midas, 54
Milesians, 95
Miletus, 51, 56, 65, 179
Minerva Victoria (= Athena NIke), 124
Mithrenes, 51–52
Mithridates, 50
Mithrobuzanes, 178
mole, 67–68, 71
Mongols, 75, 150
monomachia, 125
Montgomery, Field Marshal Bernard, vii
Morcar (earl), 136
Moseiwitsch, Mikitin, 103
Muhammad, 150
Mulla Pass, 132
Multan, 42
Murison, C. L., viii
Muses, 42
Musicanus, 130, 187
Myriandrus, 58, 70, 178
Mytilene, 7, 178

Nabarzanes, chiliarch of Darius III, 53
Nabonidus Chronicle, 173
Nandas, 122
Napoleon, 97, 131, 139, 188
Narses, Byzantine eunuch, 38, 177
Naucratis, 179
Nautaca (mod. Shahrisabz), 94, 104, 184
navarch, 37
Nazis, 176
Near East, 4, 110
Nearchus, 7, 130, 131, 142, 162–63, 173–74
Nectanebo, 71
Neiloxenus son of Satyrus, 92, 113
Nemean games, 37
Neoptolemus, son of Achilles, 176
Neoptolemus, son of Arrhabaeus, 24, 57
Neoptolemus, hypaspist commander, 71, 175
Nereids, 42
Nesean plain, 148
Nestus, 13
New Spain, 137
New World, 183
Nicanor, son of Parmenion, 71,
Nicanor, father of Balacrus, 145
Nicanor of Stageira, 146
Nicanor, fleet commander, 57, 179
Nicanor, member of Dimnus conspiracy, 182
Nicesipolis of Pherae, 15–16
Nicocles, 115
Nicomachus, 89
Niphates, 50
Normans, Norman conquest, 173, 188
North Africa, 9, 150, 189–90
Nubia, 71

Ochus, son of Darius III, 65, 139
Odrysians, 158
Odysseus, 82
Oeta (Mt.), 28
Olmstead, 34
Olympia, 22, 37, 189
Olympian gods, 23, 42
Olympias (mother of Alexander), 15–16,
   20–22, 71, 145, 175, 188

Olympic games, 14, 37
Olympic Games, xi, 146
Olympus, 13
Olynthus, 6, 49
Omphis, 115
Onesicritus, 7, 174
Opis, 139, 140, 142, 144
Ora (Ude-gram), 114
Orcynia, 178
Orderic Vitalis, 173, 188
Oreitae, 133, 163
Oreus, 57
Orontopates, 39
Orxines, 136–37, 188
Otto of Freising, 133
Otumba, battle of (AD 1520), 182
Oxartes, 184
Oxathres, 136, 180
Oxicanus, 130
Oxus (Amu-darya), 92, 94, 99, 104, 183–84
Oxyartes (father of Rhoxane), 105, 183–84
Oxyathres (brother of Darius III), 61

Paeonians, 158
Pages, 23, 185
Palaetyrus (Old Tyre), 66
palimpsests, 6
Panhellenic, 4, 7, 28, 30, 36–39, 42–43, 49,
   52, 55, 80, 82, 84, 86, 96, 110, 130, 177
Panhellenism, 36–37, 143
papyri, 5
Paraetacene, 180
Parapamisadae, 92, 114
Paris (mythical), 177
Parmenion, 7, 24, 27, 39, 43, 45, 47, 49, 53,
   56, 65, 70–71, 74, 78, 80, 83, 88, 90–91,
   101–02, 145, 151, 158, 180–82
Parysatis, daughter of Artaxerxes III, 137, 188
Parysatis, wife of Darius II, 176
Pasargadae, 137
Pasion, 178
Patalene, 127
Patroclus, 42
Patron, 57

Pausanias, *eromenos* of Philip II, 23,
Pausanias of Orestis, 23–24
Pausanias (Spartan), 55
Pausanias, servant of Harpalus, 189
Payas, 60
Peace of Antalcidas, 3, 36
Peace of Callias, 3
pederasty, 23
Peithon son of Agenor, 131, 160, 163, 187
Peithon son of Sosicles, 99
Pelinna, 29
Pella, 14, 56, 137, 190
Pellium, 29
Peloponnese, 53
Peloponnesian League, 3
Peloponnesian War, 3, 34
Pelusium, 70, 72
Penelope, 82
Peneus River, 13, 174
pentakosiarchies, 26
Perdiccas, son of Orontes, 29, 114–15, 129, 138, 140, 148–49, 151, 160, 176
Perdiccas II, 14
Perdiccas III, 15, 24, 53, 73, 90
Persepolis, 80–84, 142, 181
Persia, 3, 20, 31, 32, 34, 35, 36, 37, 39, 40, 55, 57, 66, 72, 82, 83, 85, 87, 124, 137, 139, 152, 174
Persian (or Susian) Gates, 81
Persian army, 27
Persian Court, 3
Persian Empire, 2, 7, 14, 24, 31, 32, 34, 39, 71, 85, 96, 112, 123, 124, 139
Persian garrisons, 24, 43
Persian gold, 35
Persian Gulf, 7, 131, 142
Persian horse, 46, 75, 78
Persian king, 2, 61, 69, 70, 80, 107
Persian Wars, 34, 36
Persians, 2, 25, 27, 28, 34, 35, 40, 46, 47, 48, 55, 57, 58, 73, 75, 80, 84, 96, 106, 107, 113, 139, 140, 143
Persika, 7
Peru, 135, 137, 188

Petenes, 50
Peter the Great (Tsar), 103–04
Peucelaotis, 114, 115, 185
Peucestas, 129, 136, 140
Peucolaus, 182
pezetairoi, 25
pezhetairoi, 25, 26, 46, 61, 70, 75, 78, 159
phalanx, 26, 27, 61, 70, 78, 116, 119
Phanes, 177
Pharaoh, 71, 72
Pharaohs, 71
Pharasmenes, king of Chorasmians, 100, 124
Pharnabazus, father of Artabazus, satrap of Hellespontine Phrygia, 56
Pharnabazus, son of Artabazus, 56–57, 69
Pharnuches, 98
Pharsalus, 78
Phaselis, 53
Pheidon, 109
Pherae, 15
Phila, 15, 138, 145, 189
Philhellene, 14
Philinna, 15–16
Philip II, 2–3, 9, 14–17, 20–26, 28–29, 37–40, 43, 51–53, 55–57, 66, 71, 73, 83, 101, 103, 110, 129, 143–44, 148, 150
Philip III (*see also* Arrhidaeus), 189
Philip of Acarnania, 180
Philip, son of Machatas, 127, 161
Philippeum, 22
Philippic History, 9
Philistines, 179
Philotas (*phrourarchos* of Thebes?), 29
Philotas, son of Carsis, 185
Philotas, son of Parmenion, 80, 88–91, 102, 145, 151, 175, 182, 190
Philoxenus, 136, 145,
Philoxenus of Eretria, 173
Phocians, 16–17
Phocis, 17
Phoenicia, 179
Phoenicians, 34, 66, 68–69
Phoenix, 29
Phrada (mod. Farah), 88, 92

phrourarchoi, 87
phrourarchos, 29, 81, 99
Phrygia, 45, 53, 55, 56
Pillar of Jonah, 58, 60
Pinarus River, 58, 60
Pisidia, 54
Pisidians, 145
Pixodarus, ruler of Caria, 39, 51
Pizarro, Gonzalo, 188
Plataea, 36, 55, 181
Pleuratus, 175
Pleurias, 175
Pliny the Younger, 9
Plutarch, 4, 8–10
poleis, 2, 37, 51
Poltava, 133
Polybius, 7, 60
Polydamas, 91
Polymachus, 137
Polyperchon, 78, 116, 144, 160, 163, 184, 189
Polytimetus River, 98, 99, 102
Pompeius Trogus, 8–9, 11, 21
porpax, 26
Porticanus, 130
Porus, 115–16, 119–22, 124–28, 161–62, 186
Poseidon, 1, 42
postcolonial studies, 173
pothos, 131
Prescott, William H., x, 135
prodromoi, 25
propaganda, 4, 38, 42, 52, 55, 61, 95–96, 109, 121, 189
propagandists, 58, 65, 74
Prophthasia, 92
proskynesis, 7, 52, 102, 106–11 (Alexander's attempt to introduce the practice at court), 184, 189
Proteas, 57
Protesilaus, 42
Prothytes, 29
Ptolemy of Alorus, 15
Ptolemy, son of Lagus (historian), 8–11, 51, 83, 95, 109, 114, 130, 133, 174, 181, 183, 185, 187, 190

Ptolemy, son of Seleucus, 61
Ptolemy, 183
Punjab, 1, 112, 120–22, 126–27, 130, 186
Pythian games, 37
Pythionice, 189
Python (of Byzantium or Catana?), 189

Qattara Depression, 72
Quellenforschung, 10
Quetta, 132

ramp, 71, 115
Rawlinson, Henry, 190
Renault, Mary, ix, 182
Rheomithres, 50
Rhodes, 43, 179
Rhoesaces, 50
Rhoxane, 102, 105, 151, 183–85
Richard II, Duke of Normandy, 174
Rock of Sogdiana, 100
Romadanowsky, 103
Romans, 190
Rome, 11, 72, 152
Royal Journal, 151
Russell, William Howard, 179
Russians, 179

Sacae, 75, 183
Sacred Band, 17, 19
Sacred War, 16, 17
Sagalassus, 54
Sais, 179
Saladin, 67, 179
Salamanca, Juan de, 182
Salamis, 36
Salmous, 134
Sambus, 187
Sangaeus, 115
Sardis, 51
sarissa, 16, 25, 26, 46, 130, 134, 175
sarissophoroi, 25, 175
Satibarzanes, 88, 92, 94, 182
satrap, 3, 31, 39, 43, 45, 51, 53, 70, 72, 81, 86, 92, 100, 101, 104, 122, 126, 127, 131, 139–40, 148

satraps, 34, 40, 45, 53, 55–56, 64, 70, 87, 113, 133–36, 140
Satropates, 182
Satyrus, 15, 175
Sauaces, satrap of Egypt, 39, 70, 72
Saxons, 174, 188 (West Saxons)
Scipio (P. Cornelius Scipio Africanus), 10
Scythians, 75, 92, 94, 97–98, 100, 105, 124, 183
Sea Peoples, 179
Seleucus, son of Antiochus, 139–40, 160, 174
Seleucus, father of Ptolemy, 53, 61
Semiramis, 131
Sestos, 41
Sevastopol, 179
Shein, Alexis, 103–04
Shibar Pass, 182
Sibi, 127
Sicilian disaster, 35
Sidon, 66, 68
Sidonian harbor (of Tyre), 67
Sidonians, 68, 179
Silver Shields (Argyraspides), 140, 175
Simmias, son of Andromenes, 78
Sindh, 122, 127, 187
Sisimithres (see also Chorienes), 104–05, 183–84
Sisines, 53, 178
Sistan, 88, 92
Sitalces, 78, 91, 135
Siwah, 72, 179–80
Skudra (Thracian satrapy), 14
slingers, 27, 140
Smerdis, 86, 182
Sochi, 57–58
Socrates, 14
Sogdiana, 75, 92, 95, 96, 97, 99, 100, 101, 105, 112, 120, 139, 183
Sogdiani (Sogdianians), 96, 160, 183
Sogdianian Rock, 105
Soli, 179
Somatophylakes, 89, 111
Sopolis, 185
Sostratus, son of Amyntas, 185
Soviet Union, 37

Sparta, 3, 14, 17, 23, 34–37
Spartans, 35–37, 41, 51, 66
Spitaces, 161–62
Spitamenes, 95, 98–99, 102, 104–05, 139
Spithridates, 50
Stalin, ix, 22, 187
Stark, Freya, 60
Stasanor, 136
Stateira, daughter of Darius III, 137, 188
Stateira, wife of Artaxerxes II, 182
Stateira, wife of Darius III, 65, 84–85, 101, 180
Stone, Oliver, 81
strategoi, 87, 135
Straton, son of Tennes, 66
Strymon River, 2, 13
stuprum, 21
Successors, of Alexander, 2, 6, 55, 129, 141, 150–51, 174, 177, 189
Sudracae, 115, 126–28, 187
Suetonius, 9
Susa, 36, 50, 81, 83–84, 137, 139–40, 142, 177, 183, 186–87, 189
Susia (Tus), 182
Susiana, 180, 186
Swat, 113
syngeneis, 143
Syrmus, 28
Syria, 180

Tacitus, 9
Taliban, 96
Tamerlane, 184
Tarn, 9
Tarsus, 55, 145
Tauron, 81
taxeis, 25, 75
Taxila, 113, 115–16, 122, 161, 185
Taxiles, 115, 161, 186
taxis, 26, 61
Telegraph Hill, 179
Temenids, 14
Temujin (Genghis Khan), 183
Temur, 184
Ten Thousand, 10, 31–32, 56, 176

Tennes, king of Sidon, 179
Thaïs, 83, 84
Thapsacus, 52, 74
Theaetetus, 82
Thebans, 9, 17, 19, 28, 29, 36, 37, 43, 120, 176
Thebes, 14–15, 17, 23, 25, 29–30, 34, 36, 41, 43, 57, 176
Themistocles, 55
Theopompus, 26, 189
Thermaic Gulf, 13
Thermopylae, 17, 36, 82, 176
Thersites, 8
Thessalian cavalry, 26, 50, 54, 61, 70, 78
Thessalian League, 28
Thessalians, 40, 50, 158
Thessaliscus, 176
Thessalonice (daughter of Philip II), 15
Thessaly, 16, 29, 41
Thibron, 189
Thrace, 16, 53
Thracians, 25, 28, 78, 138, 158
Thucydides, 35
Thymondas, 57
tiara, 87, 101
Tiberius, 9
Tiger Force, 135, 188
Tigris, 7, 74, 75, 142, 143
Timaeus (Limnaeus), 187
Timagenes of Alexandria, 9, 114, 187
Timocrates of Rhodes, 176
Timolaus, 29
Tissaphernes, 31–32, 35, 56
Totonacs, 138
Triballians, 28, 158
Triparadeisus, 176
Tripolis, 70
Tritle, Lawrence, 102
Troy, 42, 129
tyche, 50
typhus, 151

Tyre, 66–69, 71, 74, 175, 179–80
Tyrians, 66–68, 120
Tyriaspes, 136

Urban II, Pope, 181
U.S. Civil War, 6, 179
U.S. Congressional Human Rights committee, 82, 181
Upper Macedonia, 13
Upper Zab (or Upper Zab), 80
Uxians, 81

Vaison-la-Romaine, 9
Vale of Tempe, 13
Vardar, 13
Vasio, 9
Venice, 181
Verschmelzungspolitik, 188
Vietnam, 135

Waksch River, 184
Waltheof, 136
warships, 41, 127
West Nile virus, 151, 190
White Man's Burden, 4
Widukind, 174
Wilcken, Ulrich, 66
William the Conqueror, 136, 188

Xenias, 178
Xenippa, 104, 184
Xenophilus, 81, 186
Xenophon, 10, 31, 32, 34, 37, 52, 64, 110
Xerxes, 2, 34, 36, 42, 55, 73, 83, 96
xyston, 25, 50

Yancey, William, 34

Zagros, 80, 148
Zeleia, 45
Zeus, 21, 42, 72, 148